The future is in your hands Ann

Marie Curie ~
A Nobel Life

Ann Atkins

FLASH HISTORY PRESS

Marie Curie ~ A Nobel Life

By Ann Atkins

Published by: Flash History Press LLC
Address: Paoli, Pennsylvania
Website: www.AnnAtkins.com
Copyright © 2016 by Ann Atkins

ISBN: 978-0-9834784-8-5

Library of Congress Control Number: 2016915613

Editing and page design by One on One Book Productions, West Hills, California

Cover Design by Krohn Design, Bluemont Virginia

Author photo by Morby Photography, Philadelphia, Pennsylvania

DEDICATION

For the beauty and joy of our family ~

Amanda and Terry

Blaine

Cory and Amanda

Your love and support are fuel for my fire

BOOKS BY ANN ATKINS

Biographies

Eleanor Roosevelt ~ Unleashed

Golda Meir ~ True Grit

Marie Curie ~ A Nobel Life

Novels

Crucified (2017)

Reaching beyond 3d stories of 'who, what, and when', Ann Atkins presses to the 4d of 'why' the story is relevant to her audience. Using history, current events or the themes in fairy tales, Ann bridges the essence of any story to **enlighten** and **entertain** her audience and readers.

Her books have reached international shores and her presentations include: the National Press Club, Fox News, International Women's Day in Washington DC, the Free Library of Philadelphia, civic groups and universities. Ann has lived and worked in Korea, England and Germany. Her master's degree from Boston University includes studies at the University of Cambridge.

Paperback and eBook – available through your favorite book dealer, Amazon or from the author at her website: **www.AnnAtkins.com**

Need a speaker for your upcoming event? Contact Ann: **Ann@ AnnAtkins.com**

ACKNOWLEDGMENTS

When Marie Curie, Eleanor Roosevelt and Golda Meir were little girls, no one knew they would someday help change the world to be a better place.

With that in mind, I would like to acknowledge the parents, teachers, friends and family members who give their gracious love to our beautiful next generation. With faith in the human spirit, these adults support each child to live their fullest potential and make the world a better place.

I would also like to acknowledge the people who, at any age, fearlessly continue their personal growth. I continue to meet lovely people like Doris who came up to talk with me after a presentation. She had tears in her eyes and wanted to thank me for these stories that inspired her. Doris is 92 years old. Doris also sent me an email (she's on Facebook too) and she had this tongue in cheek insight, "It doesn't look like I will have the influence of Eleanor, Golda or Marie but every day I try to be a better person and show kindness to the people around me."

"We're all just walking each other home." Rumi

v

TABLE OF CONTENTS

PART ONE

PART TWO

PART THREE

PART ONE

CONTEXT AND COMMENTARY 1

Fire

For thousands of years no one needed to know how to ride the wave of change, because there was barely a ripple. Rivers of innovation were restrained by dams still from the Dark Ages. With the advent of electricity, a tide let loose. The resulting paradigm shift that flooded the world landscape is a story still with effect today.

When fire, the source of light for thousands of years, was usurped by invisible currents, newspapers were all a twitter with articles announcing the new age. A person might think this was the story of the century. It's not. The real story is the subject of change.

With innovations accelerating, a millennial wave grew to be cresting white caps every hundred years. The leading edge of change was increasing in height and frequency breaking faster each year, month and day. Now, we surf the web.

One hundred years ago, people would have had a hard time imagining the swift flow of our lives today. Today, people have a hard time imagining the slow drift of living just one hundred years ago.

Canterbury Cathedral gave job security to stone masons for over 750 years. That's 23 generations. And keep in mind that any preceding cathedral, for over two thousand years, was also built using stones carved with a chisel and hammer. If a great, great, great, great grandfather came back to life, he could get his job back with no retraining. Aside from tools being made from improved metals, picks, forks, spades, axes, scythes, and sickles are the same.

Eons pass knowing only a horse for transportation. Now, a child seeing the first flight in 1903 will witness the progress to jet engines, spaceships and landing on the moon before he dies. The crackle of fire in the kitchen hearth for hundreds of centuries will fall to the ding of a microwave in one generation. Sending a message by carrier pigeon dates back 3,000 years and then radios transpire to house phones and cell phones in less than a century.

> In 1895 a warning of the social impact of change is written by Max Nordau. As he foresees the future: the people will be required to "read a dozen square yards of newspaper daily, ... be constantly called to the telephone ... think simultaneously of five continents of the earth, live half their time in a railroad carriage or in a flying machine." [1] Max is wrong that we will be 'called to the telephone.' Instead, we carry our telephones with us.

Without a war or plague, generations before the 1800s can't remember a change let alone see progress. Masses of people stay insulated in their villages and don't even have last names, unless they are of noble birth. The Dark Ages, from the fall of the Roman Empire to the Renaissance, sees a population in decline, with little or no art. Literature is rarely written and literacy is scorned. The roads, dating back to the Romans, are still the best available and the Catholic Church is proclaiming, "Nulla salus extra ecclesiam." ("Outside the Church there is no salvation.") For over a thousand years the church stands at the door to keep out any reformation of doctrine and this includes ideas for change.

The pursuit of science, questioning and exploring the world around us, will require minds that will be open to change and can stand outside the Pope's reach. The 1600s will bring the start of science societies. Free to explore possibilities of what their research reveals, Germany establishes the National Academy of Germany in 1652. England has "The Royal Society" in 1660. France, soon after, has the "French Academy of Sciences" founded in 1666. These organizations are the gathering place for those in the 'know' and within the halls are the books, journals and research papers of their knowledge.

Yes, these colleagues have brains to pursue new ideas for science, but they can't expand new ideas to society. Members will exclude qualified candidates who are women for more than three hundred years.

The only females allowed in those hallowed halls are carved into stone or dried on a canvas.

Revolutionaries of a new reality never have it easy, let alone if you're a woman. Marie Curie is born into a world with a harsh need to have her conform. She defies this world. She is the first woman in France to have a doctorate in physics, and she makes this accomplishment while she is pregnant. Marie's struggles have only started as she realizes that breakthroughs in science are easier than breakthroughs in society.

Thankfully, Science is blind to gender, and will admit her secrets to whoever is asking. After years of dogged research, Marie fills two gaps in the periodic table, discovers radiation, and reveals the concept of atomic properties. Marie's breakthroughs are the start of a new age for physics.

Society is determined to keep its blind spots. Any breakthrough by Marie is met by the Guards of Status Quo flipping the game to instead break her. Marie will not *break* and she reminds us:

> *"We must have perseverance ... We must believe that we are gifted for something, and that this thing, at whatever cost, must be attained."* Marie Curie

Marie's biography, reaches beyond the realm of her discoveries in science. Her life is a record of surpassing limitations set by a rigid society. For the millions of readers who are visionaries, seekers, and idealists; Marie's story sets your precedent.

1

A CHARLES DICKENS CHILDHOOD

It's the 1870s, on a Saturday afternoon in Warsaw. A father is reading to his children:

> *"It was the best of times, it was the worst of times, it was the age of wisdom, it was the age of foolishness, it was the epoch of belief, it was the epoch of incredulity, it was the season of Light, it was the season of Darkness, it was the spring of hope, it was the winter of despair ..."* A Tale of Two Cities by Charles Dickens published 1859

Charles Dickens doesn't know his story is delighting a little girl in Poland. This precocious child, growing up in a war torn country and bearing tragedy within her family, will live a life of two cities, Warsaw and Paris. If Dickens had used her as a model for his book, his fiction would instead be fact and outshine his tale of two cities because the story of Marie Curie is true.

The home setting for Marie's life is a mother and father devoted to the family, education and their country. The political context for Marie's childhood is Warsaw in the second half of the 1800s, under the thumb of the Russian Czar who denies the Polish people their culture, language and independence. For those who have never experienced living with the daily degradation of tyranny, here is some background.

Poland, once the largest nation in all of Europe, has been divided and conquered for the last 120 years. Not until the end of WWI (1918) will the name 'Poland' appear on a map again. Of the conquering countries (Russia, Prussia, and Austria) ruling over segments of Poland, Russia is the harshest.

Russians quash a Polish revolt in 1830, and the Poles will pay for this, literally and figuratively. The Russian Czar has a citadel built in the middle of Warsaw. Covering eighty-nine acres, the construction requires 76 residential buildings to be demolished, which displaces 15,000 residents. Adding to this public incursion, the cost of the citadel walls and buildings ($139 million) is paid for by the Polish citizens. The number of citadel barracks means 5,500 Russian troops are in the city. Positioned on the walls are 555 pieces of artillery that ensures 360 degree coverage of Warsaw and its citizens.

Entry to the Russian Citadel in Warsaw

In 1863, the Poles attempt a second uprising and once again they are crushed by the Russians. The Russian reprisal this time includes 70,000 Polish citizens imprisoned, 396 executed, 18,672 exiled to Siberia, 1,660 Polish estates confiscated, and a 10% tax as a war indemnity is incurred. As a reminder, the following year, the citadel has five bodies hanging from the ramparts for several days. Killed for their role in the revolt, these

Polish leaders now serve as reminders of the fate for any other heroes who think they can overthrow the Russian regime.

**Polish Scythemen – Farmers taking up their
'weapons' to fight in the rebellion of 1863**

The entrenched torment of the public penetrates the walls of Polish homes, warping the logic of daily decisions. How do you raise children who are smart and gifted, to 'Reach for the Stars' when that reach could have them sent to Siberia? Encouraging your child with today's mantra, "Be So Good They Can't Ignore You" could get them killed.

Marie's family does not escape the trauma permeating their city or the stench filling the air as the hot August sun beats down on the hanging bodies that are decomposing. This setting for Russian revenge is a few blocks from the Freta Street School where Marie's mother is a teacher. In the years to come, Marie and her sisters walk by the Russian Citadel every day on their way to school.

Marie's father is Vladislav Sklodowski. His plans are to attend the Warsaw University as his father had done. The problem for Vladislav is Warsaw University was shut down by the Russians. Maneuvering around that disappointment means Vladislav must travel 750 miles north to attend a Russian university in St. Petersburg. Following graduation, Vladislav's list of languages to read and speak includes: English, French, German, Russian, Greek, Latin, and of course Polish. Vladislav also loves music and literature. He returns to his home in Warsaw as Professor Vladislav Sklodowski.

Vladislav, twenty-eight years old, is employed as a teacher of mathematics and physics. He is making plans to marry Bronislava Boguski.

Bronislava Boguski, who plays piano and sings beautifully, has grown up in a family that believes in educating their daughters. She attends Freta Street School, the only private school for girls in Warsaw. In spite of being monitored by Russian officials, this is the best possible education for a girl in Poland. Bronislava becomes a teacher at Freta Street School. Like Vladislav, she is devoted to education. They are a perfect match.

> Polish last names for women end in 'a' and for men 'i.' Bronislava and her daughters' last name is Sklodowska. Vladislav and the son's last name is Sklodowski.

After their wedding, Bronislava is promoted to headmistress of the school. The position includes a large apartment where she and Vladislav will live. During the next several years Bronislava must balance the dual role of career and mother. In seven years, she bears five children.

Zofia (daughter) is born 1862. Jozef (son) is born 1863. Bronislava (daughter, referred to as Bronya) is born 1864. Helena (daughter, referred to as Hela) born 1866 and Maria (daughter, referred to as Manya) is born 1867. Maria will later write her name as Marie. Until that time in her story, we will know her as Maria or her pet name, Manya.

With both parents being educators, every opportunity at home is a 'teaching' moment that covers weather, nature, science, math, and literature. Polish history, which is forbidden in the Russian schools, is taught at home. The children all know Russian, French and English as well as their native language, Polish.

Bronislava is feeling the toll from running the school, five pregnancies, and she has the additional duties of nursing Vladislav's brother who has come to stay with them. The brother has terminal tuberculosis. Bronislava wistfully says to a friend, "I must confess that I wouldn't mind being Miss Boguski again, now that I see how difficult a woman's life is." [1]

A year after Maria is born; Vladislav has a new job which will mean an increase in pay and an apartment. For Bronislava, with her duties of motherhood, the new home is too far to commute each day to work. She decides to leave her position at the Freta Street School and dedicate her time to teaching Zofia and Jozef at home. To help with family finances, Bronislava has learned how to be a cobbler. She makes and repairs the shoes of her children.

The older siblings are all very bright, but Maria stands out. As a four year old preschooler, Marie is listening to her sister Bronya (three years older) struggling to read a passage in a book. Maria is impatient, picks up the book and reads it aloud, perfectly. The family is astonished. Maria misunderstands her parent's look of surprise and exclaims, "I didn't do it on purpose. It was because it was so easy."[2] (AL 9)

Not only is their little 'Manya' a self-taught reader, her curiosities are not the norm. There is a glass cabinet in the family room where Maria's father keeps scientific instruments. Other children pass by this case and do not give it a moment's notice. Not so for Maria. She remembers being fascinated with the "several shelves laden with surprising and graceful instruments: glass tubes, small scales, specimens of minerals, and even a gold-leaf electroscope."[3]

For Vladislav, these treasures of his trade are a silent display to a dream of research denied to him by Russian rules. The world will never hear the name 'Vladislav Sklodowski' in reference to a brilliant career in physics, but they will hear of his daughter. The government's decree to cut the number of hours to teach science in school won't stop this father from teaching his own children at home

Following the failure of the 1863 uprising, plans of resistance by the Polish people turn from direct revolts to the oblique approach of increasing the intelligentsia class. The ensuing emphasis on education might sound like perfect timing for the teachers Vladislav and Bronislava, but a wrench comes with the Russians. Polish students wanting to continue their education or qualify for jobs, must leave their Polish school and attend government run Russian schools to receive authorized diplomas. In this paradox for Polish families, no Polish history or culture is taught and their language is forbidden. The twist tightens on Polish parents knowing their children are being subjected to Russian propaganda and derisive treatment.

Economic oppression by the Russian government includes replacing head teachers with their own candidates. Vladislav must accept that he will only be an assistant teacher and work under the suspicious eye of a Russian. Vladislav stays with his job in the Russian school in hopes of being a supportive influence for the Polish students and ensure a better education for them. Vladislav's decision to teach in this setting is an example of the harrowed life for Polish adults who must balance how to submit to Russian authorities, stay true to their Polish nationalism, and withstand criticism from fellow Poles who see anyone taking a job with the government as a 'sellout.'

Both families of Vladislav and Bronislava have stood their ground against the Russians. Vladislav's brother, wounded twice in the uprising, has escaped to France. Another brother, teaching law at the Warsaw University, is demoted to the job of a notary in the countryside. Bronislava's brother, captured in the 1863 uprising, is one of the thousands sent in chains to Siberia. Aside from the physical suffering, this family and thousands of others must learn to live with diminished incomes, loneliness, and loss of support from family. Living by "Carpe Diem!" can make life miserable.

The year 1871 ushers in tragedy for the Sklodowski family. Bronislava is losing weight and coughing. Contracted while nursing her brother-in-law, Bronislava has tuberculosis.

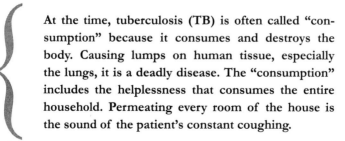

At the time, tuberculosis (TB) is often called "consumption" because it consumes and destroys the body. Causing lumps on human tissue, especially the lungs, it is a deadly disease. The "consumption" includes the helplessness that consumes the entire household. Permeating every room of the house is the sound of the patient's constant coughing.

The family's routine changes. Aside from Bronislava using separate dishes and eating utensils, she also withdraws her physical affection for her children. For this loving family, the loss of intimacy—no kisses, no hugs, no sitting on your mother's lap—is made worse because as custom of their time, no explanation is given to Maria. No one connects for Maria the reason for her mother's restraint is because of her mother's disease. Family evening prayers include, "Restore our mother's health."[4] Maria is only four years old.

Regardless of circumstances, the family thrives together, and Maria can still feel, if not her mother's touch, her mother's devotion. Maria writes later, "Her influence over me was extraordinary, for in me the natural love of the little girl for her mother was united with a passionate admiration."[5]

Bronislava and the oldest daughter, Zofia, leave for Nice, France (1872) hoping the warmer climate will be a cure. Any assumption this is a vacation is an error. Bronislava is homesick for her family, exhausted from the disease, and Vladislav is managing a house with 4 children. Bronislava and Zofia are home one time during their two years away. This photo is taken of all five children. Maria won't see her mother for over a year.

Zofia, Bronya, Maria (Marie), Joseph, Hela, 1872 *Musée Curie (coll. ACJC)*

Maria has started first grade at the Freta Street School, where her mother had been headmistress. By third grade Maria is moved to a Polish school closer to home. The headmistress, with nerves of steel, is Jadwiga Sikorska. Combating Russian control yet showing kindness to her students, Madame Sikorska lives with the constant threat of a one way ticket to Siberia.

Being monitored by Russian officials, Madame Sikorska risks her job and her life as she keeps dual schedules for her students. Everyone from staff to students is involved in a collusion knowing Polish history is listed under "Botany" and Polish literature is actually "German Studies." If an inspector is approaching, a bell is rung and the Polish books are swept to a hiding place. When the inspector walks into the classroom, a Russian book or an embroidery project is on the children's desks.

Madame Sikorska describes the strain of living a parallel life in her diary. It's "a hard life, a double life. We had to do our best to protect and cultivate all that was dear and sacred to us, and at the same time we had to be able to satisfy the authorities in order to be allowed to keep working. I don't think I ever lied to the authorities in the presence of my students, but they were all used to lying anyway, living in a constant state of conspiracy."[6] (MC SQ 44) And Maria plays her part in the conspiracy.

Ranking first in arithmetic, history, literature, German, French, and Russian, it is Maria who is called upon when inspectors visit. The pressure is on Maria, the youngest in the class, to answer correctly, uphold the facade and convincingly betray her beliefs. She knows any misstep could cause violent consequences for her fellow students, Madame Sikorska and Maria's family. The inspector asks, "Name all the Russian Czars since Catherine II?" and "What are the names and titles of the reigning royal family?" For punitive measure he asks, "Who rules over us?" Maria must answer, "His Majesty Alexander II, Czar of all the Russians."[7] When the inspector leaves, Maria is in tears.

> Schools for boys and girls are monitored by Russian officials and their sexist assumptions are to the girls' advantage. The girls' school is under less scrutiny by inspectors since Russians surmise that women, not entering public life or politics, are not a threat.

The Sklodowski family finds relief from the strain of constant surveillance during their vacation time spent with relatives in the country. In these areas of Poland, under the less restrictive control of Austria, the family can speak Polish and sing patriotic songs without fear of being sent to prison. Maria writes, "There we found the free life of the old-fashioned family estates, races in the woods, and joyous participation in the work in the grain fields. "[8]

The reprieve is short lived.

Tension at work is rising for Vladislav. Teaching in a Russian school does not forego the intrusion of Russian inspections. Inspectors review the students homework, not for errors but for any evidence of Polish terms. When one of the students has made this mistake, Professor Sklodowski won't berate the child and instead tells the inspector, "… if that child made a mistake, it was certainly only a slip. … It happens that you, too, write Russian incorrectly at times–and indeed fairly often. I am convinced that you do not do it deliberately, any more than a child does."[9]

Skating on the thin ice of Russian empathy, Vladislav will pay for this small act of defiance. Returning home from the family summer holiday, there is a letter of dismissal waiting. Vladislav is being replaced by a Russian. Aside from the loss of income, they have also lost their living quarters. It's 1873, Maria is six.

To cover this loss of income and his wife's medical expenses, Vladislav opens his home to take in boarders. Over the next ten years the Sklodowski home will have ten to twenty students staying in their apartment with them. Maria sleeps on the couch. She must get up early enough to clear away her bedding and set the breakfast table for everyone. Joseph remembers, "When I think about that time, the impression I have is of some kind of beehive where the noise and commotion never ended. When we (Sklodowski children) returned from school each day, we ate lunch all together–about twenty people–and then we would all sit down to study. Every corner of our apartment was then filled with students–not only those who lived with us, but also those who came just to study."[10] Maria, who will always prefer privacy, writes, "The house was transformed into a noisy barracks and intimacy vanished from family life."[11]

In the fall of that year, Bronislava and Zofia are home again. Maria can run and hug her sister but not her mother. The convalescing trip has not cured Bronislava's tuberculosis and the joy of being together again as a family is only for a short time.

For two years a typhus epidemic ravages Warsaw, killing thousands. Having boarders in their home brings typhus to the family. January (1874) Maria's sisters, Zofia and Bronya are both suffering with symptoms.

{ Typhus is transmitted by lice and rat fleas in dirty clothes and bedding. The symptoms are flu-like and include fever, chills, and headache. A rash develops on the trunk and spreads. If terminal, the patient suffers an end with delirium or in a coma. }

In the Sklodowski household, Bronislava is in one bedroom coughing while Bronya and Zofia are in another room with raging fevers. It's hard to imagine how Bronislava must have suffered not just physically from her illness but emotionally as a mother, unable to care for her daughters in the next room. Bronya, sick for twelve days, recovers. Zofia does not. When she dies the family is in shock. Joseph writes, "I still can't think about her without sorrow. January 31st has been, since her death, the first painful anniversary in my calendar."[12] Maria sees her sister in the coffin, dressed in white.

Hela writes, "Our sister's death literally crushed our mother; she could never accept the loss of her oldest child." Bronislava's grief is coupled with guilt and nagging doubt. Zofia might have survived if she had not been weakened with the travel and care of her mother. Joseph remembers the overwhelming sorrow of his mother, "She had to be almost physically forced to stay home (because she was too ill to go out) on the day of her funeral" [13] Vladislav and the four remaining children walk behind the coffin. Maria is wearing Zofia's black coat.

Desperate to catch the final moments before her daughter is buried, Bronislava moves from window to window to watch as the funeral procession passes by the house.

To help pay for his wife's medical expenses, Vladislav invests his savings in a business venture suggested by his brother-in-law. The prospect fails and Vladislav loses everything. This was the money meant to help his children continue their education at universities. His one hope, the vision of seeing his children have a better life is now lost.

Vladislav must also bear the weight of knowing he is losing his wife. The children know this too. Maria, in her prayers, asks God to take her instead.

The 'soul of the family' is dying. Bronislava calls her family to her bedroom. Upholding her Catholic traditions, she makes the sign of the cross over her children's heads. She tells them, "I love you." There is no last kiss or warm embrace to hold as a memory in the years ahead. Bronislava dies the next day, May 9, 1878. Maria is nine years old.

Vladislav has buried a daughter and now he must bury his wife. He will mourn his beloved wife all his life and never re-marry. Ten years later he writes this poem:

> *An angel, whose celestial light brightened my house*
> *And chased every shadow off my forehead.*
> *When she left, my whole world turned into a cemetery.* [14]

Maria remembers "This catastrophe was the first great sorrow of my life. ... For many years we all felt weighing on us the loss of the one who had been the soul of the house."[15] The grief of losing a sister and her mother, the financial insecurity of her family, their home being overrun with boarders, the double life in both the public and the school is taking its toll on this nine year old child. (Hela remembers that time for Maria, "She would often sit in some corner and cry bitterly. Her tears could not be stopped by anybody."[16])

After her mother's death, Maria is indifferent to any religious beliefs and escapes to her books. Maria calls this time "a lost happiness,"[17] and later writes this apt self description, "I feel everything very violently, with a physical violence." [18]

Maria's fragile state has not gone unnoticed by her teacher.

Madame Sikorska suggests to Vladislav that he keep Maria back a year. Vladislav disagrees. He is aware of his daughter's brilliance and enrolls her in a Russian school, Gymnasium (high school) Number Three. Maria will start in the fall.

Vladislav, in spite of the loss of his helpmate, does not allow the family regimen to crumble. Education continues to be a firm foundation. A walk is an opportunity to talk about science and during evening meals the conversation includes the cultures of other countries. Following dinner there is time to exercise the body as well as the brain. Vladislav teaches his children geography and military history using colored blocks. He risks buying forbidden Polish books of literature. Saturday nights are spent (translating into Polish) reading aloud to the children, *David Copperfield* or *A Tale of Two Cities*. Vladislav pours into his children's spirits a love of learning and an unbeatable passion for life. Helena remembers, "I still remember how enthusiastically we participated in those lessons."[19] Equal standards are held for his daughters and his son. There is no diminishing the dreams of his daughters with talks of ending their education and getting married.

Vladislav is one hundred years ahead of his time.

Maria's beginning days at the gymnasium school are difficult. She remembers, "this period of my early youth, darkened ... by mourning and the sorrow of oppression."[20] A break in the clouds comes with her new friend, Kazia.

Kazia's family has an apartment in the palace of Count Zamoyski. Kazia's mother is a librarian for the count. Maria knocks on the palace door every morning for Kazia to walk with her to school. At the end of the school day, Kazia's mother has lemonade and chocolate ice cream for them. Maria and

Kazia will be lifelong friends.

Having stricter compliance than the elementary school, the Russian rules for the gymnasium are relentless. Student chatter between classes must be in Russian. Maria writes, "The moral atmosphere was altogether unbearable. Constantly held in suspicion and spied upon, children knew that a single conversation in Polish, or an imprudent word, might seriously harm not only themselves but also their families. Amid these hostilities the joy of life is lost, and childhood is weighted with precocious feelings of distrust and indignation weighed upon their childhood. On the other side, this abnormal situation resulted in exciting patriotic feelings of Polish youths to the highest degree."[21]

One "abnormal situation" is the time Maria's group sees that a friend has been crying. When the girls ask what is wrong she replies, "It's my brother. ... He was in a plot. ... He was denounced. ... We haven't known where he was for three days. They're going to hang him tomorrow."[22] Maria, Hela and Bronya and the others, sit with their friend through the night. A normal situation is a sleep-over of giggling girls who gossip into the morning hours. Instead, the girls are crying and praying for a miracle that the brother will be spared. No cries or prayers change what the Russians have ruled.

A daily nemesis in the school is Mademoiselle (Mlle) Mayer, the superintendent of studies, who has resolved to break Maria's "stubborn spirit." Mayer believes the place to start is with Maria's unruly hair. Calling it, "disordered and ridiculous,"[23] Mayer brushes Maria's hair trying to take the curl out and then puts Maria's hair into tight braids. Mayer's intention is curtailed when wisps of Maria's curly hair pop out from the braid. When Maria, taller than her teacher, brings a paper over to where Mayer is standing, she tells Maria, "I forbid you to look at me like that! You mustn't look down on me!" Maria's wit, like her hair, springs out when she responds, "The fact is that I can't do anything else."[24] Mayer says of Maria, "That Sklodowska! It's no use talking to her. It's just like throwing peas against a wall!"[25]

Mlle Mayer has an additional duty, hall monitor. Mayer spends time roaming the halls watching for any rule breakers. When she checks on an empty room she catches Maria and Kazia dancing. Maria writes later that they were dancing for joy, having found out Czar Alexander II had been killed by an assassin's bomb (March 1881). Maria and Kazia continue to be 'partners in crime' for other small acts of rebellion.

Every day on their way to school the girls pass an obelisk that was raised by the Tsar to honor Poles who stayed faithful to the Russians during the uprising. This monument has the inscription, "To the Poles faithful to their Sovereign." For Polish patriots, these 'faithful' Poles are considered traitors. The children's ritual is to spit on the obelisk every time they walk by it. One day the girls realize they have passed the obelisk without spitting. They run back to rectify their oversight.

Maria's sadness has lightened, and she expresses her love of learning in a letter to Kazia. "In spite of everything, I like school. Perhaps you will make fun of me, but nevertheless I must tell you that I like it, and even that I love it. I can realize that now."[26]

In her love of studying Maria is able to maintain a deep concentration. In one instance while she is studying her lessons, Maria puts her thumbs in her ears to block out the noises of her cousins and sisters. The girls are stacking chairs behind

Maria so that when Maria gets up the chairs will crash to the floor and scare her. The crash occurs, and the girls are howling in delight expecting Maria to come unglued. She doesn't. She tells them, "That was stupid," and walks away.

Maria's hunger for knowledge isn't bound to the pages of books. She is in love with nature, trees, gardens, and flowers. Her aspiration for more education coincides with the rise in intellectualism. It is the "Positivist" movement, the hope that Poland will rise again through science, logic and education. Both Bronya and Maria support the ideals of the positivists who demand education for the poor, equal rights for women at work and school, and they want to see the Catholic Church become less powerful. The ultimate goal is changing the political system for Poland and a return to independence.

Maria ends her secondary studies at the gymnasium in 1883. She is awarded a gold medal, best in her class. Maria ranks with Bronya and Joseph who also received this honor, except Maria is finishing first when she is only fifteen, the youngest of her classmates.

Vladislav wants his daughter to finally take a break. He knows Maria is both emotionally and physically exhausted. With his family outside of Warsaw, Vladislav arranges for Marie to have one year away in the countryside.

2

"...build a better world."

Arriving at the country estate of her family, Maria does not burst onto the scene with giddy happiness. The years of family illness, Russian brutality, and financial insecurity have taken their toll. Maria retreats to the guest room with the company of her books.

As the days turn to weeks, Maria gradually puts aside her scholastic seclusion for long walks, playing tag with the other children, sketching in her journal, rolling hoops, riding horses, and fishing. She is reaching toward experiencing a new side of life. Being fifteen, Maria is the delightful mix of one moment being a young woman and the next moment a giggling girl. She writes in her journal, "Sometimes I laugh all by myself and I contemplate my state of total stupidity with genuine satisfaction."[1] Attending late night parties turns the early hours of studying into lazy days of sleeping late. In a letter to Kazia, Maria writes, "I can't believe geometry or algebra ever existed. I have completely forgotten them."[2]

One morning, Maria is returning from a night of music and parties. Her feet are tired and she is carrying her red shoes. Before retiring to bed, she finds the trash basket and there is a 'clunk' as Maria tosses in her shoes. She has worn them out dancing.

> *"All I can say is that maybe never again, never in my whole life, will I have such fun."*[3] Maria's Journal Entry

After a few months Maria visits another family estate in the foothills of the Carpathian Mountains. Here is an aunt who has broken from all constraints and makes it known she doesn't like child care or cooking. Along with these flaunts, she smokes cigarettes. This aunt starts a lace-making school and furniture factory. Maria is absorbing this example of independence along with the continued revelry of being a teenager. Free to dress in traditional Polish costumes and dance their national dances, Maria writes, "We could speak Polish in all freedom and sing songs without going to prison."[4]

One of the guests, Joseph Boguski, is Maria's cousin. Joseph studies chemistry and will be a student of the famous Russian chemist Dmitri Mendeleev. Providing another stunning example of male support, Joseph encourages Maria to study chemistry. She will be meeting him again in a few years, and he will play a key role in Maria's choice to devote her life to research.

> Dmitri Mendeleev created the periodic table in 1865. Although not accepted by the Chemistry Society for another twenty-two years, Mendeleev recognized the pattern for laying out the sequence of elements. This pattern showed the gaps of elements yet to be discovered. Two of these gaps will be filled later by Maria.

Another guest at the family estate is the famous actor, Joseph Kotarbinski. He entertains the girls and the guests with songs, poems, and playing jokes. When Maria and her cousins learn that he is leaving, they make a wreath of flowers and toss it to him as his carriage goes by on the driveway. To their delight, he catches the wreath and puts it on his head as he rides away.

When the year comes to a close for Maria, there is one more short chapter of gayety. An invitation has come from a former student of Maria's mother. The Countess de Fleury invites Maria and her sister Helena to spend the rest of the summer at the Countess's home. The girls are delighted when their train is met by a four-horse carriage and a uniformed coachman. The countess arranges three balls, two garden parties, and several boating trips for the girls. In between events there is hiking, swimming, rowing or playing silly pranks on other guests.

Helena writes of their time at the estate, "The summer passed quickly as a dream, but the memory of it has been lasting. How many times did Manya and I talk about Kepa…and every time we would smile, and even shed a tear of nostalgia. It is good when a person has had at least one such crazy summer in her life."[5]

Maria's spirit is revived and she has a renewed dedication to the ideals of Positivism. It's the fall of 1884.

Maria, sixteen years old, is back in Warsaw with her father. After ten years, he is no longer taking any boarders, although the financial consequence is a smaller apartment. Maria's brother, Joseph, is in medical school at the reopened Warsaw University. However, the doors are only open for men. For women to continue their education, they must incur additional expenses of having to go abroad. Bronya and Maria are considering Paris. First they must raise the money.

To give women the preparation they need for university studies, Polish activists in Warsaw start an academy of higher education for women. The immediate response is enrollment of over two hundred female students. There is also an immediate retort from the Russians. Any teachers caught giving lessons for the academy are sent into exile.

Undeterred, the school goes into stealth mode and more instructors step up to teach. Meeting in various clandestine places, it becomes known as the "Flying University." Enrollment reaches over one thousand women. Maria and Bronya will be two of them.

At these meetings not only is the lesson covered, but information and pamphlets are passed out supporting Polish nationalism. If caught, students and teachers are sent to prison. This resistance is the turn of tactics away from direct revolts and away from those who believe their Catholic faith will save them. Maria is joining this wave of the "intelligentsia."

Attempting to make her ideals a reality, Maria is tutoring children. She writes, "…You cannot hope to build a better world without improving the individuals. To that end each of us must work for his own improvement, and at the same time share a general responsibility for all humanity, our particular duty being to aid those to whom we think we can be most useful."[6] To this end, Maria has an advertisement[7] in the newspaper:

"Lessons in arithmetic, geometry, and French available from young woman with degree. Moderate prices."

Maria's schedule is living up to her quote. She is either studying for her classes at the Flying U or tutoring children. Maria and Bronya want to "be" something. Bronya has her sight set on being a physician and Maria decides she wants to be a scientist. Both sisters hope to raise enough money to continue their education by tutoring children.

Maria walks through Warsaw to the homes of her students. Trying to teach kids who don't care, and parents who are condescending and won't pay is a challenge for her youthful convictions and her income. Maria's next step is applying for a post as a governess. September of 1885 Maria becomes the governess for a well-to-do family. Maria refers to them as the B---"s. She believes the children will be pleasant and motivated to learn.

Reality check.

Maria and Bronya, 1886,
Musée Curie (coll. ACJC)

Maria writes to her cousin, "I shouldn't like my worst enemy to live in such a hell. My relations with [the wife] had become so icy that I could not endure it any longer and told her so. Since she was exactly as enthusiastic about me as I was about her, we understood each other marvelously well. It was one of those rich houses where they speak French when there is company–a chimney-sweep's kind of French–where they don't pay their bills for six months, and fling money out of the window even though they economize pettily on oil for their lamps. They have five servants. They pose as liberals and, in reality; they are sunk in the darkest stupidity. And, although they speak in most sugary tones, slander and scandal rage through their talk–slander which leaves not a rag on anybody. I learned to know the human race a little better by being there. I learned that the characters described in novels really do exist, and that one must not enter into contract with people who have been demoralized by wealth."[8]

After this dreadful experience, the plan Maria contrives to help Bronya is even more remarkable.

Bronya and Maria are separately saving money in order to go to a university. The frustration is, this plan is taking forever. Maria suggests they pool their money and Bronya go to school first while Maria stays behind to work and send support. Once Bronya has her degree and a job, then Bronya can support Maria to attend school.

Maria's promise to Bronya is a five year commitment. Having worked with the B---s Maria knows she could be positioning herself to live her own words, "I shouldn't like my worst enemy to live in such a hell."

Bronya refuses the offer and argues there is no reason she should go before Maria. Maria insists and explains why Bronya should go first, "Because I am seventeen and you are going to be twenty."[9] Within the week Maria has accepted a position to work for the Zorawski family. Hours north of Warsaw, miles from her beloved family, it will be years until she is free of her contract.

January 1, 1886 Maria is off to the country again, except this time it is not to stay in the cocoon of a loving family. Maria remembers, "That going away, remains one of the most vivid memories of my youth. My heart was heavy as I climbed into the railway car. It was to carry me several hours, away from those I loved. And after the railway journey, I must drive (horse and sleigh) for five hours longer. What experience was awaiting me? So I questioned as I sat close to the car window looking out across the wide plains. Once I arrived to my destination, if I wanted to turn and run away, how could I ever be able to retrace that last five-hour stretch and regain the railway?"[10]

Maria arrives at the home of the Zorawski family. The estate includes forty horses, sixty cows, a flock of servants, and

the family income is from a refinery where sugar is extracted from crops of sugar beets. The lady of the house, Mme
Zorawski is kind. After a hot cup of tea, Maria is shown a large
bedroom, which she will have to herself. Maria begins to think
this governess position might work out.

The Zorawskis (Maria refers to them in correspondence
as the Z's) include: M. Zorawski as Maria describes, "Old-fashioned, but full of good sense, likable and reasonable."[11] The
wife, Mme Zorawski, had been a former governess and married
well. Maria describes, "When you know how to deal with her,
she is nice." Maria adds, "I think she likes me well enough."[12]
They have a daughter who is nineteen (one year older than Maria) and three younger children under ten. The younger children
are spoiled and Maria is expected to somehow make them mind.
Of the three sons who are away, two are in boarding school. The
eldest, Casimir, is studying mathematics at Warsaw University.

Maria is finding her balance in the role of governess. It is a
position of straddling the fence. Maria does not belong to the
realm of the family nor the servants. She writes, "In a general
way I observe, in my talk, the decorum suitable to my position."[13]
When she is not busy with governess duties, she uses her free
time to study. Maria writes to tell her father that she is studying
physics, sociology (in French) and anatomy and physiology (in
Russian). Her father sends math problems for her to solve.

With no teacher to influence her, Maria relies on her capac-
ity to think "outside the box." These years of studying alone
are the foundation to her future years of independent research.
Maria writes, "At nine in the evening, I take my books and
go to work, if something unexpected does not prevent it....I
have even acquired the habit of getting up at six so that I work
more....When I feel myself quite unable to read with profit,
I work problems of algebra or trigonometry, which allow no

lapses of attention and gets me back into the right road."[14]

Maria continues to revel in being outdoors and spends time with the children making snow houses and ice-skating. She enjoys learning details about the farm from Mr. Z. Maria writes to her cousin, "If you could only see how exemplary my behavior is! I go to church every Sunday and every holy day, without ever claiming I have a headache or a cold in order to stay home. I almost never talk about higher education for women. In general, I maintain a discretion in my speech that is suitable to my position."[15] Considering her years of training to uphold an outward appearance for the Russians, she plays the role expected of her as the family governess.

The Z's enjoy the compliant Maria and during the 'honeymoon stage' she is treated as a surrogate daughter. The Z's include Maria in their outings to parties and social events. For Maria, she is not flattered with the attention and she is unable to keep up with the standard of dress. More importantly, the additional social schedule is interfering with her study schedule. Maria writes, "They were already speaking of me unfavorably because as I didn't know anybody, I refused to go to the ball."[16]

The prior frivolities Maria enjoyed when she was fifteen, she has outgrown. Marie writes, "whereas the young people of this area are not really at all interesting: the girls are geese who don't open their mouths except to be as provocative as possible. They all dance perfectly. They're actually not bad, some of them are even intelligent, but their education has not developed their minds, and the festivals around here, which are insane and incessant, have ended up making them scatter-brained. As for the young men, almost none of them are very nice or in the least intelligent…."[17] Maria never will be one to relish small talk and meeting superficial people. She concludes,

"The Zorawski family is very cultivated by comparison."[18]

One area in which the Z's prove 'cultivated' will be giving Maria permission to teach the illiterate peasant children how to read and write Polish. Under the Russians, the village children are taught only in the Russian language. Since the peasants and their children don't know Russian, the policy result is a near 100% illiteracy in the rural areas. This ignorance of the masses is to the Russian advantage, and it is considered a crime to teach the peasants in Polish. If caught or exposed by one of the children or parents, the punishment is prison or exile to Siberia. When Maria asks the Z's for their permission, she reminds them, "Think it over carefully. You know that if we are denounced we shall be sent to Siberia."[19] Bronka, the daughter agrees to help. What starts as ten students turns to eighteen. A two hour class sometimes lasts for five hours. The children's parents stay to listen.

> *"We can't hope to build a better world without improving individual people."* Marie Curie

Maria's vision of living the positivist philosophy is being played out. Aside from giving classes, Maria risks being caught when she creates a library for the employees at a garment workshop. Helping to educate the adults is a tiny version of the Flying University. Maria remembers, "The means by which we took action were paltry and the results could not be very great: however, I still believe that the ideas that guided us then are the only ideas that can bring about real social progress. We can't hope to build a better world without improving individual people"[20] Maria, writes to her cousin, "Great joys and great consolations come to me from these little children."[21] Maria believes that there are intellectual gifts and potential among all the classes of people.

Inside any peasant could be a writer, a painter, a musician, or a scientist who has not had the opportunity to be educated.

In the meantime, Maria contends with her young charges who are not so happy with their opportunity to be educated. She writes to a friend in the spring of the first year, "Today we had another scene because she (the younger daughter) did not want to get up at the usual hour. In the end I was obliged to take her calmly by the hand and pull her out of bed. I was boiling inside. You can't imagine what such little things do to me: such a piece of nonsense can make me ill for several hours. But I had to get the better of her."[22]

In December, Casimir, the oldest son is home for the holidays. Meeting Maria, who can hold a conversation with him about mathematics, speaks/reads/writes in three languages, loves nature and plays no games of coquetry, he is entranced. Casimir and Maria fall in love. When he comes home for the summer holidays the two go on walks and horseback rides. They make plans to marry.

Several factors play into the young couple's belief that Casimir's parents will approve. Up to now everyone has been fond of Maria. Mr. Z. has gone for walks with her explaining the farm and manufacturing. Mme Z. had been a governess herself, and she has been 'mothering' to Maria, giving her birthday gifts and flowers. The Z's know Maria's family name is well-respected in Warsaw. Maria's father, brother and sisters have met the Z's when they came to visit Maria.

Casimir tells his parents of his plans to marry Maria. The Z's promptly reply, 'no'. They remind Casimir that Maria is a mere governess and sons from well-to-do families don't marry 'the help.' The Z's point out there will be other women who are available, and they will have dowries. M and Mme add the additional justification that Casimir will lose his social status. If all this isn't enough the final threat is–they will disinherit him. (Apparently Mme Z has conveniently forgotten she was also once a governess.) The Zs tell their son he will never marry someone who works in "other people's house."[23]

Casimir returns to the university having conceded to his parents. Maria, on the other hand, must stay at the house to fulfill her contract. Every day she spends time with people who do not think she is good enough for their son. Maria must hide her hurt and keep up appearances with the Zs. She also needs to reassure her father.

Maria is careful to never add to the burden of guilt Vladislav still carries having lost the money meant for education. Maria writes him, "Above all, and beyond all, my beloved father must stop despairing about not being able to help us. It is inconceivable that my father could do more for us than he has done. We have a good education, a solid cultural background, character which is hardly the worst....Therefore my father shouldn't be discouraged: we'll make out all right, without doubt. As for me, I will be eternally grateful to my dear father for what he has done for me, because he has done so much."[24]

Nor does Maria want to distract Bronya who is studying at the Sorbonne. Only to her brother, Joseph, Maria writes letters that show signs of despair and wanting to escape. Although none of her letters refer directly to her break with Casimir, she writes, "For now that I have lost the hope of ever becoming anybody, all my ambition has been transferred to Bronya and you. You two, at least, must direct your lives according to your gifts. These gifts, which, without any doubt do exist in our family, must not disappear..... The more regret I have for myself the more hope I have for you."[25]

Casimir is home again for Christmas. He tries again to reason with his parents. They repeat 'no.'

During this time Maria writes to Joseph about her sister Helena enduring similar circumstances. "I can imagine how Hela's self-respect must have suffered. Truly it gives one a good opinion of men! If they don't want to marry poor young girls, let them go to the devil! Nobody is asking them for anything. But why do they offend by troubling the peace of an innocent creature?…Even I keep a sort of hope that I shall not disappear completely into nothingness." Later in the letter she adds, "I have fallen into black melancholy."[26] Maria's vibrant energy is fading away.

Another year passes and her turmoil goes deeper when she must see Casimir home again for the holidays. Maria is forlorn when writing to her cousin, "I will get along as best I can, and when I can do no more, will say farewell to this base world. Some pretend that I am obliged to pass through the kind of fever called love. This absolutely does not enter into my plans. If I ever had any others they have gone up in smoke. Have buried them, locked them up, sealed and forgotten them."[27]

Marie's writing might seem melodramatic, except when one considers the tragedies in her still young life. Remembering she has endured situations of injustice beyond her control, Maria's reaction to "…get along as best I can…" and her perspective of "…this base world" has merit.

"Oh! To get away for a few days from this chilly, chilling atmosphere, from these criticisms, from the perpetual watch I have to keep over my own words, the expression on my face, my actions: I need this change as much as a cool bath on a hot day."[28] Maria's journal entry

The calendar is pronouncing spring. What should be the season of hope for Maria is only more struggling. She writes her friend, "If you only knew how I sigh and long to go to Warsaw for only a few days. To say nothing of my clothes which are worn out and need care–but my soul too is worn out."[29] The years of supporting Bronya are taking their toll. She writes, "I have literally not a ruble–not one."[30] Maria doesn't even have money for a stamp.

Of the many lessons Maria will carry into her future she remembers this decision during her governess years, "I was as much interested in literature and sociology as in science. However, during those years of isolated work, trying little by little to find my real preferences, I finally turned towards mathematics and physics, and resolutely undertook a serious preparation for future work."[31]

Hours of studying in books doesn't substitute for the practical work Marie needs to be learning in a laboratory. Like a pianist trying to progress with no keyboard, Maria writes to Joseph "What can I do as I have no place to make experiments or to do practical work?"[32]

Maria still has one more year to stay.

In the fall, a letter from Kazia announces her engagement. Maria responds, "You tell me you have just lived through the happiest week of your life, and I during these holidays, have been through such weeks as you will never know. The thing that softens the memory of them is that I have come through with my head high....I often hide my deep lack of gaiety under laughter, something I learned to do when I found out that creatures who feel as keenly as I do, and are unable to change this characteristic of their nature, have to dissimulate it at least as much as possible."[33]

It is a sign of a solid friendship that Maria can be honest with Kazia and not have to put up a front for her. We also see Maria's internal resolve to "come through with my head high…" and self-control to feign "as much as possible" in order to bide her time. Maria ends the letter with this, "Nevertheless, I shall be as gay and free as ever when I come to you.… Will your mother give us lemonade and chocolate ices as she used to do?"[34]

During her final winter with the Z's, Maria writes to another friend, "While you are living at the center of the movement, my existence strangely resembles that of one of those slugs which haunt the dirty water of our river. Luckily I hope to get out of this lethargy soon." Maria continues to reflect, "I have changed a great deal, physically and spiritually during my stay at Szczuki. This is not surprising. I was barely eighteen when I came here, and what have I not been through! There have been moments which I shall certainly count among the most cruel of my life…I feel everything very violently, with a physical violence, and then I give myself a shaking the vigor of my nature conquers, and it seems to me that I am coming out of a nightmare.…First principle: never to let one's self be beaten down by persons or by events. I count the hours and days that separate me from the holidays and my departure to my own people. There is also the need of new impressions, of change, of movement and life, which seizes me sometimes with such force that I want to fling myself into the greatest follies, if only to keep my life from being eternally the same. Fortunately, I have so much work to do that these attacks seize me pretty rarely. It is my last year here; and I must therefore work all the harder, so that the children's examinations will go well."[35]

Seeing the end in sight, Maria writes to Kazia, "My head is so full of plans that it seems aflame."[36]

"First principle: never to let one's self be beaten down by persons or events." Marie Curie

During this final year, Maria's father is appointed director of a reform school outside Warsaw. Working in a school for young criminals, is a difficult job but it pays well and he can give this money to help Bronya and Maria. Bronya writes to tell Maria to stop sending money and save it for her own trip. Bronya next writes to her father telling him to stop sending her the monthly allowance and instead give it to Maria. The mutual support among the family never wavers.

In the spring of 1889, Maria leaves the Z's and returns to Warsaw and takes another governess position to continue to raise money for her own education. By July 14th, she is working at the home of a wealthy family in Warsaw, M. and Mme. Fuchs. She goes with the family to a summer resort. The F's enjoy Maria and make a pleasant year for her. Maria does not have to tolerate disdain or the prior awkwardness during any holiday visits of Casimir.

When the F's return to their estate in Warsaw, they ask Maria to attend all of their social events, and parties. When Mme F. hosts a salon, she asks Maria to join and introduces Marie as the "exquisite Mlle Sklodowska."

During this year, Maria is attending the Flying University where classes have outgrown the living rooms of instructors. A Danish visitor to Poland writes of the students, "They are women, who even in narrow and straitened circumstances preserve the grand self-esteem which runs in their blood."[37] Maria illustrates his observation.

One of the secret places for the Flying U to meet is the Museum of Industry and Agriculture. The science laboratory is run by Maria's cousin, Joseph Boguski, who had encouraged her years ago. This is Maria's first opportunity to work in a laboratory, and she describes the frustrations of adapting to this new setting. Maria writes, "At times I would be in deepest despair because of accidents and failures resulting from my inexperience. But on the whole…this first trial confirmed in me the taste for experimental research in the fields of physics and chemistry." Maria remembers, "to my great joy [to be] able, for the first time in my life, to find access to a laboratory…."[38] Maria is in love–with research.

Maria is staying the year in Warsaw, to study, spend time with her father, and save enough money to continue her formal education. It would seem obvious the next step is to follow her sister to the Sorbonne in Paris. And yet, her way is not yet clear.

In March, Bronya is finishing her exams. She writes to Maria about her plans to be married. Bronya adds, "And now you, my little Manya you must make something of your life sometime. If you can get together a few hundred rubles this year you can come to Paris next year and live with us where you will find board and lodging…."[39]

The expected response is an immediate "Yes!" But the last seven years have taken a toll on Bronya's 'little Manya.' Maria writes back, "Dear Bronya, I have been stupid, I am stupid and I shall remain stupid all the days of my life, or rather, to translate into the current style: I have never been, am not now and shall never be lucky. I dreamed of Paris as a redemption, but the hope of going there left me a long time ago. And now that the possibility is offered to me, I do not know what to do…I am afraid to speak of it to Father. I believe our plan of living together next year is close to his heart, and he clings to it; I want to give him a little happiness in his old age. And on the other hand my heart breaks when I think of ruining my abilities which must have been worth something."[40]

Maria is settling for the role of supporting others rather than risk reaching for her own dreams. Continuing in the letter to Bronya, Maria writes, "There is also the fact that I promised Hela to find her a post in Warsaw and I feel it is my duty to watch over her."[41] She asks Bronya with help for a loan for Joseph to study in Warsaw. "With this help Joseph can become useful to society, whereas if he leaves for the provinces he is lost. I bore you with Hela, Joseph, and Father, and with my own wretched future. My heart is so black, so sad, that I feel how wrong I am to speak of all this to you and to poison your happiness, for you are the only one of us all who has had what they call luck. Forgive me, but, you see, so many things hurt me that it is hard for me to finish this letter gaily. I embrace you tenderly. The next time I shall write more cheerfully and at greater length–but today I am exceptionally unhappy in this world. Think of me with tenderness–perhaps I shall be able to feel it even here."[42] The doubts and conflicts are deeper than the future of her career. Maria is still hoping to marry Casimir Zorawski, and they are making plans to meet.

That summer Maria tells her father she is going to a resort in the Carpathian Mountains. Father writes to Bronya, "[Maria] has a secret about her future, of which she is to speak to me at length…To tell you the truth, I can well imagine what it has to do with and I don't myself know whether I should be glad or sorry. If my foresight is accurate, the same disappointments coming from the same persons who have already caused them to her, are awaiting Manya. And yet if it is a question of building a life according to her own feeling, and of making two people happy, that is worth the trouble of facing them."[43]

This gracious letter giving his daughter leeway to find her own course…difficult for a parent in any generation, let alone the social norms of the late 1800s. He worries only that his daughter will be hurt. And when Vladislav writes in the letter about Maria's possible choice to go to Paris his grace continues, "…it would be very painful for me to separate from her, but this consideration is obviously secondary."[44]

During Maria's visit to the Carpathians, Casimir perseveres with the same explanation that his parents won't change their opinion and he can't see how to go against them. It begs the question, if nothing has changed, why does Casimir want to meet Maria. Does he have an option—a request for her to be his mistress? That is not unusual and all the more reason Maria's father could have reason to worry his 'Manya' will make a regretted decision.

Maria makes her decision. She has had enough. This back and forth has been going on for almost four years. Maria tells Casimir, "If you can't see a way to clear up our situation it is not for me to teach it to you."[45] There is no record that Maria ever sees Casimir again.

> Casimir Zorawski continues his studies in mathematics and becomes a full professor at the University of Warsaw. He marries a well known pianist and they have three children. Urban legend of Warsaw has it: "Warsaw citizens still remember that as an old man, professor of mathematics at Warsaw Polytechnic, he used to sit quietly and contemplatively in front of one of the statues of Maria Sklodowska. "[46]

Maria has straightened out her own situation and is ready to move forward. Within days Maria writes to her sister, "Now Bronya, I ask you for a definite answer. Decide if you can really take me in at your house for I can come now. I have enough to pay all my expenses. If, therefore, without depriving yourself of a great deal, you could give me my food, write to me and say so. It would be a great happiness, as that would restore me spiritually after the cruel trials I have been through this summer, which will have an influence on my whole life, but on the other hand I do not wish to impose myself on you."[47]

It's been eight years. Maria is ready to launch.

Bronya responds immediately, "Come."

As Maria is saying her goodbyes, she goes to visit her former headmistress, Jadwiga Sikorska who is using her home for Flying University classes. As Marie's former teacher, she feels the joy, pride and sense of fulfillment to know her little Manya is on her way to the Sorbonne.

Marie, Vladislav (father) Sklodowski, Hela and Bronya, 1890,
Musée Curie (coll. ACJC)

The hardest goodbye is to her father. She promises, "I shall not be away long….Two years, three years at the longest…."[48]

3

"Marie Sklodowska."

**Sorbonne University, (University of Paris)
established circa 1150, (www.archives.upenn.edu)**

"It is in Paris that we find the most celebrated and most excellent of schools: it is called the Sorbonne." Martin Luther 1483-1546

Maria's answer barely reaches Paris and Bronya is on her way to Poland. Bronya is coming home to help her sister make preparations and ensure Maria doesn't change her mind.

Maria will be traveling by train in a fourth class car, which means no heat and no seats. Passengers must bring their own blankets and a stool to sit on for the forty hour ride. Bronya helps Maria pack food and drinks to last the trip rather than buy food at train stops. A mattress and linens are sent ahead by freight rail which is less costly than purchasing these items in Paris. Bronya also knows Maria will need her warm winter clothes. She explains to Maria that she will be using the horse-drawn omnibuses to and from the Sorbonne. The cheapest seats are on the top, open to the weather.

The family goes to the train station to see Maria off. What emotions does Vladislav have this day? A father, who has sacrificed his life to raise his children, can breathe a sigh of relief to see his youngest finally able to reach for the higher goals that come with education. He is proud of his little "Manya," and he will miss her very much.

It's the first day of November, 1891. Maria makes the train trip alone. Bronya is staying behind to visit longer with their father. Forty hours of November chill, sitting on a stool, no place to lie down, and when the train stops there is only a quick chance to get out and stretch. Maria eats the food she has packed, and she must make sure she keeps her travel documents secure. The border police for Russian and Prussian segments of Poland, are known to make trouble for young women traveling alone. Maria crosses safely into Germany and continues into France.

Stepping onto the station platform in Paris, Maria is entering a new world.

In fiction, the writer could use this opportunity to increase the conflict by portraying Maria as the naive innocent on a new adventure against the cold cruel world. This portrayal would be an injustice to Maria. Curious? Yes. Single-minded? Yes. Self assured? Yes. There is no evidence to support a portrayal of Maria as a 'babe in the woods.'

Turning twenty-five in a few days, this is the first time Maria has been outside of her Russian-ruled country of Poland. Walking along the streets of Paris, she is surprised to hear people speaking several languages with no one in fear of being arrested. Visiting a bookstore she sees books on the shelves that in her country are banned. The realization of living in a free country is sometimes startling and sometimes subtle. Maria is also free in her heart. After waiting four years in hopes Casimir would make a stand for her, Maria is making a stand for herself.

As Maria walks across the courtyard of the Sorbonne, dressed in her clothes from Poland, she is connecting the past to her future. What she does not bring with her is her name. On the class registration card she writes, "Marie Sklodowska." (For the remainder of the story her choice of using 'Marie' will be used.) In the revived belief of her own self is the energy that will cut her loose for a life beyond her highest hopes. Marie will unleash a new era for science.

On the university notice board she reads:

FRENCH REPUBLIC
Faculty of Sciences-First Quarter
Courses Will Begin At the Sorbonne
on November 3, 1891

Marie's determination to make something of her life is immediately tested when she realizes her French is too faulty and her course preparation in chemistry and physics is inadequate. Cutting into her limited resources, Marie engages tutors to bring her skills up to par with her fellow students who have spent seven years preparing. And lastly, she must find her way past the doors of a paternal society that writes the rules of admission. No tutor or amount of money will fix this. The emotional maneuvering for women is an additional drain of energy, which is not a consideration for male students.

{ Not until the 1950s is there a law in France that re-quires schools to offer the same university prepara-tion classes for girls as it does for boys. }

Bronya and her husband, Casimir Dluski (not Casimir, Marie's ex boyfriend) live in a working class area of Paris. Casimir fled occupied Poland because of his socialist stance, and it is not safe for him to return. Both Bronya and Casimir are medical doctors. The difference being, Casimir can see both male and female patients; although, female patients remain dressed during an examination. Bronya can see only women patients, and since she is a woman, Bronya can examine her patients in the appropriate manner. The couple uses their apartment during the day for a medical office and examining room. Two nights a week Casimir sees patients free of charge.

If it's not patients coming and going from the apartment, it is visitors. Citizens of Poland, either students, or expelled political activists are a continual stream in and out of the Dluski's apartment. Enjoying a place to gather for Polish food, friend-ship, homespun entertainment and political conversations, two of these guests will later become presidents of Poland.

One guest is a pianist struggling to make a career. Marie remembers one night Casimir insisting she stop studying and come with him to hear the man play at a concert. Marie pro-tests, but Casimir insists, "No buts! It's the Polish pianist I told you about. There are very few seats taken, and we've absolutely got to help the poor boy out by filling the hall. I've already re-cruited a whole crowd, and we'll applaud until our hands crack, so it'll seem to be a success anyhow....And if you only knew how well he plays!"[2] The pianist is Ignacy Paderewski. The day will come when, anywhere in the world, his concerts will be sold out. (Paderewski will also be prime minister and foreign minister of Poland after World War I.)

Casimir relishes a hubbub of activity. Marie does not. While Bronya is still visiting with her family, Casimir is under the impression Marie will play hostess to his guests. He realizes he is wrong. In his good nature, Casimir writes to Marie's father, "Dear and Honored Sir: Everything is going very well with us. Mademoiselle Marie is working seriously; she passes nearly all her time at the Sorbonne and we meet only at the evening meal. She is a very independent young person, and in spite of the formal power of attorney by which you have placed her under my protection, she not only shows me no respect or obedience but does not care about my authority and my seriousness. I hope to reduce her to reason but up to now my pedagogical talent has not proved efficacious. In spite of all this, we understand each other very well and live in the most perfect agreement. I await Bronya's arrival with impatience. My young lady does not seem to be in a hurry to get home where her presence would nevertheless be very useful and where she is much in demand. I may add that Mlle Marie is perfectly well and looks it."[3]

Marie, in the meantime, is writing to her brother about Casimir, "...my little brother-in-law...disturbing me endlessly... endure having me do anything but engage in agreeable chatter with him...I had to declare war on him on this subject."[4] Banter, but making a point. Marie is insisting her studies come first. Her father is insisting too.

Marie and her father have a steady correspondence. She is keeping him informed of her progress, requesting packages of particular Polish items, and telling him about the fun she is having in her new life. After writing him about her part in an insignificant political play, a spoof, Vladislav writes back,

"Your last letter saddened me. I deplore your taking such active part in the organization of this theatrical representation. Even though it be a thing done in all innocence, it attracts attention to its organizers, and you certainly know that there are persons in Paris who inspect your behavior with the greatest care, who take note of the names of those who are in the forefront..."[5] From the years of living under Russian rule, having seen family and friends for lesser offenses be sent to Siberia, and knowing Bronya's husband is known as a "troublemaker," Vladislav's fear is not unfounded. Marie heeds his advice, although, more for reasons of commitment to her studies.

Marie is frustrated with the interruptions to her studying and her commute to classes takes up two hours every day. By the end of her first month in Paris, Marie finds an apartment for herself close to the school.

'Apartment' is a stretch of the word. Marie rents a garret room, which is the cheapest rental because it is a room in an attic, six floors up. Summer heat makes the room an oven. Winter cold makes the room a freezer. With no side windows, natural light is only through the skylight. Water is available on the third floor, along with the bathroom. For furniture, Marie has her bed, a kitchen chair, washbasin, oil lamp, a pitcher (to fetch water at the lower floor), and a small heater that uses alcohol to heat food or water. Completing her kitchenware accoutrements are two plates, a knife, fork, spoon, cup, pan and a kettle. When Bronya and Casimir come to visit, she has three glasses for tea and the trunk serves for extra seating. Marie's simple life includes not caring for fashion and she learns to mend her clothes. Marie's neighbors are poor artists, male students, or prostitutes.

Marie writes in her *Autobiographical Notes*, "The room I lived in was...very cold in winter, for it was insufficiently heated by a small stove which often lacked coal. During a particularly rigorous winter, it was not unusual for the water to freeze in the basin in the night; to be able to sleep I was obliged to pile all my clothes on the bedcovers. In the same room I prepared my meals with the aid of an alcohol lamp and a few kitchen utensils. These meals were often reduced to bread with a cup of chocolate, eggs or fruit. I had no help in housekeeping and I myself carried the little coal I used up the six flights." She describes this time as "one of the best memories of my life." and her happiness with the "period of solitary years exclusively devoted to the studies...for which I had waited so long."[6]

The austerity of Marie's life enables her to make every second count, in order to study. Her spirit of autonomy soars and she later writes about this time, that it "gave me a very precious sense of liberty and independence. Unknown in Paris, I was lost in the great city, but the feeling of living there alone, taking care of myself without any aid, did not at all depress me. If sometimes I felt lonesome, my usual state of mind was one of calm and great moral satisfaction."[7]

Marie can walk to the Sorbonne in a matter of minutes.

"Nothing in life is to be feared; it is only to be understood."
Marie Curie

Student poverty hasn't changed much except today Marie might have been eating Ramen Soup instead of a boiled egg. What is remarkable for Marie's time is the fact she is living alone. An historian (Jules Michelet) of the late 1800s records the public opinion, "The worst fate for a woman was to live alone...she could hardly go out in the evening; she would be taken for a prostitute. There are thousands of places where only men go, and if some business should take the woman there, one would be astonished. For example, if she were late, far from home, and became hungry, she would not dare enter a restaurant....She would make a spectacle of herself."[8] Respectable women appear in public only with a chaperone and would never have a male guest in her apartment. Only one type of woman does that.

Male dominance is not mere public opinion. It is law. If a woman runs away from her husband he can legally track her down and have her returned to him. In 1891 women can't bear witness in a civil suit, nor can they spend their own earnings without their husband's permission. A divorce for a woman means giving up all rights to property, income, and child custody. There is no law preventing abuse of women or children. A wife can be charged with adultery and taken to court for her crime. For a husband, if he is charged, it is not even a misdemeanor, and he is dismissed with a wink. An ingenious twist in public pressure on women is the unspoken burden on women to not be 'rude' and spoil this chauvinist 'emperor's parade' by declaring the emperor has no clothes, and Marie is in the heart of where a 'parade' could pop up any time.

Living in the rowdy Latin Quarter, Marie is at ground zero of the local hangout for students who are on a low budget, looking for a good time. While Marie is living here, there is a riot (1893) that requires thirty thousand troops to disband it. The mob is demonstrating **against** the recent crackdown on public nudity during the Parisian annual ball. An American visitor observing the Latin Quarter writes, "Does it not seem strange, that both St. Severin and the Sorbonne...appear to take no notice of the notorious fact that the apartments, whose windows look in upon them, are occupied by filles galantes (loose woman), who live in the most open manner possible with the students, and flourish elbow to elbow with the Church and the University?"[9]

In an example of 'pick your battles', when Marie or her daughter Eve writes of Marie's life, that the emphasis is on Marie's crusade as a student and scientist. Marie will always make a stand for the rights of equal education for women and she will defend her role in science discoveries. Marie does not confront the double standards of society nor does she discuss her own stories of harassment and intimidation. One instance is recorded by other historians: On the streets of Paris, when some male students are becoming too aggressive toward Marie, Marie's friend and fellow student, Mlle Jadwiga Dydynska, defends Marie with her umbrella.

{ Salon: A gathering organized and hosted by a particularly inspiring person with the purpose of sharing knowledge through entertaining conversation. The salon provided a venue where women could express their opinions. At the end of the late 1800s the popularity of the mixed gender salon is slowly fading and the conversation is moving to all-male clubs.}

Women, who had once added to and learned from the discussions as guests or hosts of a salon, are now out of the loop as all-male clubs are on the rise. If a woman tries to join a club, she risks public rebuke. Octave Mirbeau (French journalist, literary/art critic) wrote at the time: "Woman is not a brain, she is a sex, and that is much better. She has only one role in this world, to make love, that is, to perpetuate the women, rare exceptions, have been able to give, either in art or literature, the illusion that they are creative, but they are either abnormal or simply reflections of men. I prefer what are called prostitutes because they at least are in harmony with the Universe."[10]

The male preference of the woman's role is being taught at the Sorbonne. In a lecture on the psychology of women by Henri Marion, he states, "the more advanced a society's civilization, the more pronounced the division of labor between men and women becomes....In the large cities of the great nations of the West where civilization is at its highest, gender differentiation is at a maximum."[11] Marie, being in the most 'advanced' civilization, is inconsistent with Henri Marion's 'gender differentiation.'

Hearing this perspective on women from the hallowed halls of the Sorbonne, it is no surprise the French noun *etudiante* describes two types of women. An *etudiante* is either a female university student or a mistress of male university student. A writer of the times, Henri d'Almeras, explains that etudiantes are not there to study but to distract the male students from studying. Almeras explains, "What distinguishes the serious female student, almost always a foreigner, is that almost no one takes her seriously. If she is treated with a certain courtesy, she should consider herself lucky. The jokes that are made about her are not always in the best of taste....These female students work with great patience, as though they were doing embroidery. Their study makes them ugly. They usually look like schoolteachers and wear glasses. In the examinations, they recite with admirable exactitude what they've learned. They don't always understand."[12] The inference is not subtle. Women students are not taken seriously. A female student, an etudiante, should stick to her role of responding to the sexual needs of the male students. Marie will not fall in with this description.

Marie records, "All my mind, was centered on my studies. I divided my time between courses, experimental work and study in the library. In the evening I worked in my room, sometimes very late into the night. All that I saw and learned that was new delighted me. It was like a new world opened to me, the world of science, which I was at last permitted to know at all liberty."[13] Marie disregards everything but her attendance for lectures or her studies in her room. In a letter to her brother Marie writes, "I am working a thousand times harder than at the beginning of my stay..."[14]

A drawing of Marie during her student days, 1892, *Musée Curie (coll. ACJC)*

Marie is one of 210 women in the midst of 9,000 male students to the Sorbonne. Within the Faculty of Sciences her female colleagues are an even smaller portion. She is one of 23 women among 1,825 students.

Chances of Marie gathering a list of admirers are great except for her singular commitment to her studies. In the next three years, no male suitors will garner Marie's attention. One French man writes her a letter with the hopes that when Marie is done with her studies, he will be a consideration. A Polish student is so upset when Marie doesn't respond to his attentions that he swallows laudanum. Marie responds, "The young man has no sense of priorities."[15]

Marie is an anomaly. Not only is she a woman attending a university, studying in a man's field, and living independently, she is establishing her identity. And that identity is not in the realm of looking for a marriage, fulfillment as a mother, or the thrill of adultery. Exasperated men ask–"Good Grief? What does she want then?"

Marie wants to be a research scientist.

"I take the sun, and I throw it."[16] Prof. Paul Appell (mathematician), Sorbonne University

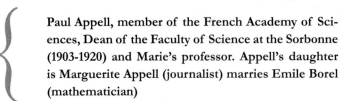

Paul Appell, member of the French Academy of Sciences, Dean of the Faculty of Science at the Sorbonne (1903-1920) and Marie's professor. Appell's daughter is Marguerite Appell (journalist) marries Emile Borel (mathematician)

The timing for Marie to be a science student is perfect for several reasons. 1. The emphasis on science at the Sorbonne is attracting the best scientists of Europe for their faculty. (This attention came after France lost the Franco-Prussian War (1870).) The French government realizes they need to invest money in laboratories so their research will be cutting edge, and increase their chances of winning the next war. 2. The tide of opinion to keep the church out of science is rising. 3. The field of chemistry is abuzz with competition to discover the remaining elements on the periodic table. At this time, there are only seventy nine known elements.

An emphasis on laboratory research being the cornerstone

to the student's education is exactly what Marie wants. She doesn't mind that a science student has to understand everything that is known to science–the mathematics, the laws of physics and chemistry, how to work in a laboratory, use the instruments and know techniques of measurement. At the end of her first year, Marie stays the summer in Paris for additional classes in mathematics, physics and for tutoring to improve her French.

Marie is so engrossed in nourishing her brain that she neglects nourishing her body and has a fainting spell in the library. Casimir is notified and rushes to Marie's attic room. After examining her and seeing nothing in the room for her to eat, he insists Marie come and stay again with him and Bronya until she recuperates. Marie spends time getting well, although not at the expense of missing classes.

Marie has been studying at the Sorbonne for eighteen months. Her father continues to give support, even if he isn't included in Marie's latest plans. He writes to Bronya, "…Your last letter mentions for the first time that Manya intends to take her examinations for the master's.…Write me exactly when these examinations will take place, at what date Manya can hope to pass them, what are the fees for them and how much the diploma will cost. I must think of all this in advance so as to be able to send some money to Manya, and on this my personal plans depend."[17] He makes no recrimination of Marie for not keeping him informed and there is no guilt trip asking when Marie is planning on coming back to Warsaw.

At the end of the term, Marie and another woman are the only two female students left pursuing a degree in science. Marie is worried. "The nearer the examinations come the more I am afraid of not being ready."[18] The exams are in July (1893). The test results will be known in a few days. There is nothing to do but wait. The names are announced in the Sorbonne amphitheater in order of merit.

Amphitheater, Sorbonne

The day the students gather in the amphitheater, Marie does not have to wait long to know the results of her exams. Marking the first time a woman, a foreigner, has graduated top in her class, the first name announced is "Marie Sklodowska."

Going home to Poland, Marie will enjoy rest and time with her family for the summer.

What a sight to see, the reunion of Marie with her father. His little 'Manya' who had earned the gold medal for being first in her class at the gymnasium, now she is first in her class with a degree in physics from the Sorbonne University. And like most proud families–they feed her. Aghast at how thin she has become, by the end of the summer, Marie is taking back with her a few extra pounds.

Also home for the summer holiday is Marie's fellow female

Sorbonne student, Jadwiga Dydynska (the umbrella fighter). Jadwiga is advocating for Marie to receive the Alexandrovitch Scholarship, designated for Polish students studying abroad. Marie is awarded the scholarship which includes money to cover the next year's expenses. (Marie later repays the award money to be used for another needy student.) She returns to Paris to work toward her second degree in mathematics.

Taking the train back to the Sorbonne–it's the fall of 1893. What a difference a mere two years has made. Marie is returning as a graduate student, with a scholarship from Poland. Marie's professor, Gabriel Lippmann, is also arranging for a position for her with the Society of the Encouragement of National Industry. They are going to pay Marie to chart the magnetic properties of various steels. (With the advent of electricity, magnetism has increased industrial value.) Marie is thrilled with this opportunity. The equipment Marie will be using is bulky and there are a large number of metal samples she will need to test. The immediate problem is laboratory space.

This problem will be resolved by the most amazing man she will ever meet.

PART TWO

CONTEXT & COMMENTARY 2

Violent, Vibrant, Vulgar —
Paris Turns to the 1900s

A narchists in Paris make their protests known with eleven bombs exploding from 1892-1894.[1]

AND

"Ne'er has Paris, struck me so forcibly as the capital of a land of madness, inhabited by lunatics."[2] 1895, Edmond de Goncourt

Art is exploding in Paris. Rodin is creating sculptures. Debussy is composing music. Zola, Proust and Stein have their pens to paper busy writing. Painters, transcending tradition, include: Monet, Matisse, Renoir, Toulouse, Cezanne, and Picasso, to name just a few.

Extravagance is the order of the day. Reveling in a glaring spot-light, the extreme wealthy are blind to the suffering around them.

> *"Elegant dress serves its purpose of elegance not only in that it is expensive, but also because it is the insignia of leisure... The substantial reason for our tenacious attachment to the skirt is just this: it is expensive and it hampers the wearer at every turn and incapacitates her for all useful exertion. The like is true of feminine custom of wearing the hair excessively long."* 1898 Thorstein Veblen[3]

Over the top weddings feed the newspaper society columns. The list of gifts for one wedding: bags of diamonds, rubies and sapphires, a Louis XVI table, and a solid gold vase[4]

While wedding guests are gorging at festivities, the French government declares that an eleven hour working day is reasonable with only a one hour break. (In all fairness, it should be said that the following year the daily work day is decreased to ten and a half hours.) For a full day's work men earn 5.7 F, while women, for the same job, earn 1.5 F. Inflated prices gobble down their meager income and a woman uses her wages for the day to buy 1 kilo (2.2 pounds) of sugar that costs 1.15 F. This is assuming the woman has any say in what to do with her pay. By law, women are legally obliged to hand over their wages to their husbands.[5]

Deaths, divorces and drama in the coming years make great material for the new invention of moving pictures. The pace of life picks up when the Paris Metro opens and within a year the metro carries seventeen million passengers. Fifty million visitors for the 1900 Paris World's Fair can 'see and be seen' on the latest sensation, a moving sidewalk.

Here are a few more highlights that set the stage of Marie's world:

1900 – The Summer Olympics in Paris have the first appearance of women in modern game's history.

1901 – Queen Victoria is out. She dies after sixty-three years as the Queen of Great Britain.

1901 – Toulouse is out. Aside from his famous posters, he creates a cocktail mix of cognac and absinthe. His joke of naming the drink "the Earthquake" finally triggers a seismic shift that it kills him. He dies, 36 years old, from the complications of alcoholism and syphilis.

Toulouse Poster

1902 – Rhodes scholarships are established but only for men. Women will wait until 1976.

1902 – The eulogy for Zola is read. His wife, Alexandrine, will be the one to inform Zola's mistress, Jeanne, of Zola's death. Zola had crossed the line of discretion by going for walks in the public parks of Paris with Jeanne, and when Zola was in exile in England, Jeanne joined him. Alexandrine makes peace with Jeanne and her two children (by Zola). Alexandrine provides Jeanne financial support and legally adopts the two children. Giving them the surname Emile-Zola, Alexandrine ensures the children are heirs to the Zola estate.[6]

1904 – Claude Debussy can compose music and play the piano, but his string of women, married or not, makes his personal life a shambles. For one summer (1904) he disappears and only his publisher knows his whereabouts. When Debussy returns, he moves out from his wife who attempts suicide by shooting herself in the stomach. She survives, but Debussy still continues with getting a divorce.[7]

1903 – Car races are in the streets of Paris. For one race over 200,000 people show up to see the horseless carriages.

1899 Race Car, Paris

1905 – A deep sigh of relief comes from women who are now free of wearing a corset. However, it will still be several more years that women are sent to an asylum or prison for demanding their right to vote. Women who fast in prison, as a means of protest, are tied down and force fed. France finally concedes the right to vote for women in 1944.

1905 – Poet Rainer Maria Rilke is staying with Rodin and doing administrative work for him. Rodin's long time housekeeper/partner/mistress is Rose. Rose carries on running the house and studio while Rodin carries on having affairs with his latest models. Rodin finally marries Rose in 1917, the year before he dies.

1910 – French glory starts hitting bumps in the road. Paris is flooded in 1910.

Paris flood, 1910

1911 – The Mona Lisa is missing for a full day before someone realizes it. When a guard is questioned he replies, "Oh, the photographers have it," The Louvre goes in lockdown. After searching the forty-nine acres of museum, all they find is Mona Lisa's frame hidden under a staircase.

60 DETECTIVES SEEK STOLEN 'MONA LISA'

But No Clue Has Yet Been Discovered to Whereabouts of Lionardo's Masterpiece.

FRENCH PUBLIC INDIGNANT

New York Times **headline**

1912 – Aside from the embarrassment of losing the Mona Lisa, France is particularly miffed that they come in fifth place for gold medals in the 1912 Olympics. It isn't that awful to lose to the United States or Sweden, but coming in behind Germany really gets their goat.

1913 – The *Mona Lisa* is returned and the thief, Vincenzo Perrugia. After he serves his time in jail, he opens a paint store in Paris.[8]

Mug shot of the Man who stole the Mona Lisa, Vincenzo Perrugia

1914 – In the next four years, none of this drama will matter. World War I is starting and the total casualty count of military and civilian people is 38 million.

First, Marie needs to meet Pierre.

4

"...a being unique in his freedom."

*"It is necessary to make a dream of life,
and to make of a dream a reality."* Pierre Curie

Pierre Curie, with his dreamer's spirit, is born to an unconventional family on May 15, 1859.

Pierre's grandfather turned from traditional medicine to a new system of caring for patients, homeopathy. Not only did the grandfather dare to work with natural elements (plant and animal) to help a patient heal, he risked his reputation by working in the field that was considered 'women's science.'

The next generation, Pierre's father, Dr. Eugene Curie is also a medical doctor with selfless disregard for society rules. Dr. Curie cares for the wounded rebels during the French Revolution of 1848 and survives the gunfire of government troops that shatters his jaw. His medical practice with the wealthy suffers when he continues giving his services to the lower class and accepts a position as medical inspector with an organization for the protection of children. During a cholera epidemic, Dr. Curie visits contaminated areas that other doctors had abandoned.

Dr. Curie's wife is the daughter of a wealthy cloth manufacturer. The family fortune is lost due to the revolution of 1848. The Curies have two sons, Jacques and Pierre who follow the pattern set in this benevolent family.

When Pierre is twelve, the Parisians rise up again, and the Curie's apartment becomes an emergency clinic for the wounded near the barricades. Pierre and Jacques leave the safety of their home to search the neighborhoods for wounded. Unflinching from the grisly sights, they bring back to their apartment those needing their father's medical care.

When the family moves to Sceaux, a village outside of Paris, Pierre and Jacques enjoy swimming in the river and hikes through the countryside. Dr. and Mme Curie recognize Pierre has a different style of learning, and they choose to home school their son. Marie later writes of Pierre, "His dreamer's spirit would not submit itself to the ordering of the intellectual effort imposed by the school."[1] When Pierre is fourteen the Curies hire a tutor for Pierre in math and geometry. Within two years, Pierre matriculates to the Sorbonne. At eighteen Pierre has a degree in physics.

Pierre doesn't immediately pursue his doctorate since his family is in need of financial assistance. He takes a position as a physics lab assistant at the Sorbonne and as an assistant in the mineralogy department. Pierre agrees to spend ten years working in the public education system in place of military service.[2]

With a gentle character combined with his intellectual observations, Pierre, twenty years old, writes in his diary, "Oh, what a good time I have passed there in that gracious solitude, so far from the thousand little worrying things that torment me in Paris. No, I do not regret my nights passed in the woods, and my solitary days. If I had the time I would let myself recount all my musings. I would also describe my delicious valley, filled with the perfume of aromatic plants. ...Often in the evening I would start out and ascend again this valley, and I would return with twenty ideas in my head."[3]

His joy in solitary days and deep thoughts also leads him to write his introspections and doubts. Pierre writes, "What shall I become? Very rarely have I (complete) command of myself; ordinarily a part of me sleeps. My poor spirit, are you then so weak that you cannot control my body? Oh, my thoughts, you count indeed for very little! It seems to me that my mind gets clumsier every day. Before, I flung myself into scientific or other [diversion]: today they don't hold my interest. And I have so many, many things to do! And Pride, Ambition–couldn't they at least propel me, or will they let me live like this? I should have the greatest confidence in the power of my imagination to pull myself out of this rut, but I greatly fear that my imagination is dead."[4]

In the midst of his youth and brilliance, Pierre is struggling with the question all people, renowned or unknown, in any generation, must ask themselves. "Who am I?" Pierre writes, "To drink, to sleep, to caress, to kiss, to love, that is to say to partake of the sweetest things in life and at the same time not succumb to them. It is necessary while doing all that to keep the anti-natural thoughts, to which I'm devoted, dominant and active on their impossible path in my poor head; one must make life into a dream and make the dream into a reality."[5]

Pierre wants to make the traditional social expectations (what he calls 'the sweetest things in life') of having a home and a wife, not his reality but a dream. In place of this, what he is deeming "anti-natural thoughts" (a life of research and science) to make this dream, into a reality. He is answering his "Who am I?" question.

These journal entries, when Pierre is twenty, coincide with a tragedy for Pierre that he never fully explains. Fifteen years later he tells Marie, "When I was twenty I had a dreadful misfortune. I lost, in terrible circumstance, a childhood friend whom I loved. I haven't the courage to tell you all about it. I was very guilty. I had and will always have a great remorse about it. I went through days and nights with a fixed idea, and experienced a sort of delight in torturing myself. Then I vowed to lead a priest's existence. I promised myself to be interested only in things after that and never again to think of either myself or of mankind. Since the tragedy I have often asked if this renunciation of life was not simply a trick I used against myself to acquire the right to forget."[6]

A parallel to Marie's earlier years, Pierre and Marie turn from an event of sadness to science.

Pierre and Jacques succeed in making for themselves a world of research. Their time of romping in the woods and exploring nature is bringing results. Having observed earth's examples of symmetry, flowers, snowflakes or the human body, the symmetry in crystals captures their attention. Over the next few years they publish nine papers on the study of crystals.

The brothers know that certain kinds of crystals, placed in a fire, will attract (like a magnet) wood and ash to their surfaces. At the same time, the famous physicist, Lord Kelvin has shown that when certain crystals are heated they generate electricity. This has become a popular phenomenon called pyroelectricity (electricity from fire). The brothers study to see if pyroelectricity applies to all crystals. Their lab results conclude, no. Their next interest is to prove that pressure on some crystals has the same effect as heat. Using tools as simple as a jeweler's saw, tinfoil, hardened rubber and a vise, they prove—yes, some crystals under pressure produce electricity.

At this stage, the problem the brothers encounter is not

having an instrument to measure the small amounts of electricity being produced under pressure. This leads to Pierre building an instrument he calls an **electrometer** which measures tiny amounts of electric charge. Marie explains, "Their experiment led the two young physicists to a great success: the discovery of the hitherto unknown phenomenon piezoelectricity ...Several well-known scientists of other nations have made further investigations along this new road opened by Jacques and Pierre Curie." [7]

The partnership between the brothers shifts when Jacques marries and takes a position at a university in southern France. They continue their research when Jacques returns during vacations. The papers they write on this subject are the foundation for today's electronics industry to explore more uses for piezoelectricity, such as ultrasound, mobile telephones, television tubes and quartz crystal watches.[8] For military use it is the beginnings of the development of sonar, detecting enemy submarines, torpedoes, mines and icebergs. In WWII the U.S. government will use approximately fifty million quartz crystals for various military purposes. Pierre develops a scientific scale he names the "Curie Scale" and discovers what becomes named "Curie's Law."

At this same time, Pierre has a new position at the School of Industrial Physics and Chemistry in Paris. He is an instructor and he is in charge of a laboratory. Although teaching is a step up from lab assistant, the move is considered a 'step down' from working at the Sorbonne. Pierre doesn't care. He refuses to play the necessary game of politics in order to garner higher appointments. His students benefit from Pierre's self-effacing style and willingness to share whatever knowledge he has. Recalling Pierre's journal entry to make his dream a reality–Pierre is living his dream.

> Lord Kelvin: Mathematical physicist and engineer. His research brings the science of physics into the modern era. He is knighted for his work on the trans-atlantic telegraph project, improving the mariner's compass to be more reliable, and he establishes the correct value of absolute zero. The unit of 'Kelvin' is in his honor.

In the next few years Lord Kelvin, takes note of Pierre's work on the effect of heat on crystals. Kelvin comes to Paris and visits Pierre. (This is comparable to Bill Gates showing up to visit an up and coming computer programmer.) Later, when Kelvin is testing for his own results and he needs to measure the electricity produced, he asks Pierre to send him an elec-trometer. Kelvin writes a thank you note to Pierre adding, "I have written a note to the Philosophical Magazine, making it clear that your work preceded mine."[9]

The summer of Lord Kelvin's visit to Pierre is the summer Marie places first in physics and then goes home to Poland. Marie will be returning to the Sorbonne in October to start classes for her second degree in mathematics. It is this year that Marie's professor, Gabriel Lippmann, has arranged for the Society of the Encouragement of National Industry to pay Marie to study and chart the magnetic properties of various steels. This is the point where Marie is in need of lab space to do her work.

Marie and Pierre, their commitment to a solo life of re-search, will shift to a duet. They didn't see it coming.

The Sklodowska and Curie fathers have parallel themes. Both love the study of science and yet they forego the path of research to have positions with sufficient pay to support their families. Both are nonconformists in the realm of religion and do not belong to the Catholic Church. And while Dr. Curie studied the inoculation for tuberculosis, Professor Sklodowski understood the impact of this disease on a personal level. Both families share the trait of closeness between siblings and with their parents. Their compassion is not confined to the circle of their family. Daring to stand up to government oppression, they have lived through revolutions and continue to stay outspoken.

"I have lived under a regime of oppression. You have not. You don't understand your own good fortune in living in a free country…" Marie Curie

Aside from the similarities of families, Pierre and Marie share the heartbreak that comes with losing a loved one. Both come out of the experience with a monk like commitment to continue their life of science, swearing off the possibility of ever again being in love.

Marie's favorite picture of Pierre, *Musée Curie (coll. ACJC)*

There are two Polish visitors to Paris, Professor Kowalski and his wife. The wife knows Marie. They met when Marie was a governess for the Zs. Professor Kowalski, aware of Marie's search for lab space, knows a scientist who might be able to help. The Kowalskis invite Marie to a small gathering, a chance to meet this scientist. Whether a matchmaker plot or the interest of pure science, we will never know.

Marie writes, "When I came in, Pierre Curie was standing in the window recess near a door leading to the balcony. He seemed very young to me, although he was then aged thirty-five. I was struck by the expression of his clear gaze and by a slight appearance of carelessness in his lofty stature. His rather slow, reflective words, his simplicity, and his smile, at once grave and young inspired confidence. A conversation began between us and became friendly; its object was some questions of science upon which I was happy to ask his opinion."[10] Marie goes on to add, "There was a surprising affinity between his conception of things and mine, despite the fact that we came from different countries, and this was no doubt attributable in part to a certain similarity in the moral attitudes of the families in which each of us grew up."[11]

Pierre had written in his journal years earlier, "Women of genius are rare."[12] He realizes he has met a "woman of genius." He reconsiders his previous point of view and writes, "I am far away these days from the principles I lived by ten years ago."[13]

Marie and Pierre meet again at the French Society of Physics and again at Pierre's laboratory. He has arranged space for Marie to do her work. Marie writes, "He was as much and much more than all I had dreamed at the time of our union. …He lived on a plane so rare and so elevated that he sometimes seemed to me a being unique in his freedom from all vanity and from the little-nesses that one discovers in oneself and in other …"[14]

Marie thumbs her nose at convention when she asks Pierre to visit her garret room. This suggestion is unheard of for a proper woman in 1894.

Pierre brings Marie a gift. Chocolates? No. Flowers? No. Pierre brings Marie a copy of an article he has written, "On Symmetry in Physical Phenomena, Symmetry in an Electrical Field and in a Magnetic Field." He has inscribed on the inside of the booklet, "To Mlle Sklodowska with respect and friendship of the author P. Curie."[15] Marie writes of the visit, "Pierre Curie came to see me and showed a simple and sincere sympathy with my student life."[16]

On another visit Pierre brings Marie a book by Emile Zola, *Lourdes*. Emile Zola, a famous French author, risks his career and prison when he challenges the prejudices and corrupt decisions of the French government during the Dreyfus Affair (1894-1906). Zola's open letter in a Paris newspaper, "J'accuse," is not only the turning point for justice for Captain Alfred Dreyfus (a falsely accused French captain who is a Jew), but an example of the intelligentsia being able to sway public opinion. Pierre has heard students parading down the streets screaming "Death to the Jews!" Normally quiet in his political opinions, Pierre is horrified that an innocent man has been falsely imprisoned. For the two Positivists, Marie and Pierre, Zola's action is 'Exhibit A' for the affirmative results of their beliefs.

Over the next few months, Marie and Pierre meet for dinner and go on walks. They discuss social justice, religion, and their curiosity of mysticism. All conversations lead back to science and for them this means research. Their style of research is a 'disinterest' (Marie uses this word repeatedly in several writings) in the monetary value of any scientific work in public industry. Pierre and Marie believe research should be free to push the boundaries of discovery without an economic motive.

Pierre, with his single minded concentration, could be the caricature of the 'absent minded professor.' Once, too engrossed in the lab work with students, he realizes it is after hours and the building is locked up. Pierre and his students leave the school by climbing out the window and down the gutter pipes. With Marie, Pierre is so captivated in conversation he misses the last train to Sceaux. He walks home.

Pierre is not absent minded about Marie's work as a student. At the end of the term, he is adding up her scores on the mathematics exam to see if she will place first, second or third in her class. Marie's name is not announced first this time. For her degree in mathematics from the Sorbonne, Marie's name is announced second.

With exams over, Marie is returning to Poland. Any attachment to Pierre does not deter her plan. Pierre is distressed at the idea that Marie will not be a part of his life and he writes to her, "But you're coming back in October? Promise me that you will come back! If you stay in Poland you can't possibly continue your studies. You have no right to abandon science now. ..."[17] And yet, Marie feels she has no right to abandon her family and her country. Marie believes it is her duty to be a part of the intellectual movement that will hopefully free Poland.

Letters are exchanged through the summer of 1894. Pierre will not relinquish his hope for a life with Marie. In August he writes to her, "Nothing could have given me greater pleasure than to get news of you. The prospect of remaining two months without hearing about you had been extremely disagreeable to me..."[18] He continues, "We have promised each other–haven't we, to be at least great friends. If you will only not change your mind! For there are no promises that are binding; such things cannot be ordered at will. It would be a fine thing just the same, in which I hardly dare believe, to pass our lives near each other, hypnotized by our dreams; your patriotic dream, our humanitarian dream; and our scientific dream. Of all those dreams that last is, I believe, the only legitimate one. I mean by this that we are powerless to change the social order and even if we were not …we should never be sure of not doing more harm than good …by retarding some inevitable evolution. From the scientific point of view, on the contrary, we may hope to do something; the ground is solider here, and any discovery that we may make, however small, will remain acquired knowledge. But if you leave France in a year, it would be an altogether too platonic a friendship, that of two creatures who would never see each other again. Wouldn't it be better for you to stay with me? I know that this question angers you, and that you don't want to speak of it again—and then, too, I feel so thoroughly unworthy of you from every point of view. … Believe me, your very devoted, Pierre Curie."[19]

Pierre wants assurance that Marie will return to Paris and Marie is hesitant to make any commitment. When she is visiting Prof. Kowalski and his wife in Switzerland, Marie invites Pierre to come and visit. Rattled with the unexplored emotions of love, Pierre declines for fear of looking too pushy. He regrets his decision and writes, "I was on the point of leaving. But then I was attacked by a sort of shame at pursuing you like this against your will; and finally, what decided me to stay, was the near-certainty that my presence would be disagreeable to your father and would spoil his pleasure in your company. Now that it is too late, I am sorry I did not go. …"[20]

Pierre continues his debate using Marie's future work as leverage. In September 7, he writes, "As you may imagine, your letter worries me. I strongly advise you to come back to Paris in October. It would be a great grief to me if you did not come back this year; but it is not out of a friend's selfishness that I tell you to come back. Only, I believe that you would work better here and can do a more solid and useful job."[21]

When Marie sends a photo of herself, Pierre has some relief and assurance that Marie will return. Pierre refers to this photo of Marie as "the good little student" and keeps the picture in his wallet the rest of his life.

Marie, "The good little student", 1892, *Musée Curie (coll. ACJC)*

Pierre writes to her, "Your picture pleases me enormously. How kind of you to send it to me! I thank you with all my heart. And finally, you are coming back to Paris; that gives me great pleasure. I want very much for us to become at least inseparable friends. Don't you agree?"[22]

Marie is still hesitant to seal her fate with Pierre. She knows that once she is married, a wife's world becomes raising children and running the household. This is not Marie. Marie wants a world of discovery and research not diapers and recipes.

Returning in October, Marie rents a room beside Bronya's medical office. Pierre suggests they share an apartment that he has found. It is divided into two separate units. Marie declines and explains to Pierre that she is planning on returning to Poland at the end of the school year. She encourages Pierre to finish his doctoral thesis.

During earlier conversations with Pierre, Marie has proclaimed, "Later on I shall be a teacher in Poland; I shall try to be useful. Poles have no right to abandon their country."[23] Concerned Marie will follow through with her devotion to Poland, Pierre offers an ultimate sacrifice. Rather than expect Marie to stay in France, he will leave behind his science career and go to Poland. He will find a job teaching French. Will she marry him? Marie still holds back.

This offer to leave France and relinquish his research is even more generous considering Pierre's mother is terminally ill with cancer. One evening Pierre sends Marie a note saying, "I'm not coming to see you tonight. My father has rounds to make and I will stay at Sceaux until tomorrow afternoon so that Mama won't be alone. I sense that you must be having less and less esteem for me while at the same time my affection for you grows each day."[24]

The next step in convincing Marie is he invites her and Bronya to his parents' house. Marie has no need to worry this will be a repeat of Zorawski's disdain. Pierre refers to his parents as "exquisite"[25] and they adore Marie. Pierre's mother says to Bronya, "There isn't a soul on earth to equal my Pierre. Don't let your sister hesitate. She will be happier with him than with anybody."[26]

Marie does hesitate. She is sifting through her emotions, her commitments to her family and to Poland. Since her past experience of being rebuffed by the Z family, she has come a long way. Pierre had written previously to her, "You have no right to abandon science."[27] This is true. She doesn't want to abandon science by becoming married and playing the role of 'wife.' And despite the other reasons of Marie's family and duty to country, what gets Marie up in the morning is Science.

Marie waits another ten months. During this time Pierre

finishes his doctoral thesis in March 1895. Marie and Dr. Curie are in the audience when Pierre presents his dissertation. Marie writes of her admiration for Pierre, "I remember the simplicity and clarity of the exposition, the esteem indicated by the attitude of the professors, and the conversation between them and the candidate, it seemed to me, that day sheltered the exaltation of human thought."[28]

Marie is slowly shifting her reservations of leaving Poland and reversing her resolve to never again be 'involved.' She writes about her change of heart, "After my return from my vacation, our friendship grew more and more precious to us; each realized that he or she could find no better life companion."[29] Marie finally answers Pierre, "Yes."

Writing letters to her family, Marie tells them of her engagement to Pierre. To Kazia, Marie writes about Pierre, "…Fate has caused us to be deeply attached to each other, so that we can't bear the idea of separating."[30]

The Sklodowski family, with a long history of rallying around to give love and support, is very happy for their little Manya. Joseph writes Marie, "As you are now M. Curie's fiancée, I offer you first of all my sincerest good wishes, and may you find with him all the happiness and joy you deserve in my eyes and in the eyes of all who know your excellent heart and character. …I would infinitely rather see you in Paris, happy and contented, than back again in our country, broken by sacrifice of a whole life and victim of a too-subtle conception of your duty. …A thousand kisses, dear Manya; …Tell him that I welcome him as a future member of our family."[31] As if that weren't enough he continues. Joseph addresses Marie's fears of abandoning her family and her country by adding, "And no just person can reproach you for it. Knowing you, I am convinced you will remain Polish with all your soul, and also that you will never cease to be part of our family in your heart. And we, too, will never cease to love you and consider you ours. …"[32]

As the wedding date nears, any loneliness by Marie for her mother's presence is filled by Bronya's mother-in-law, Mlle Dluski who offers to have a wedding dress made for Marie. Marie, who will always be austere, accepts the offer with this condition, "I have no dress except the one I wear every day. If you are going to be kind enough to give me one, please let it be practical and dark so that I can put it on afterwards to go to the laboratory."[33]

Pierre and Marie wedding picture, 1895, *Musée Curie (coll. ACJC)*

Marie's father and sister Hela arrive from Poland. Bronya and Casimir attend along with some university friends. Marie and Pierre exchange their wedding vows in a small civil ceremony on July 26, 1895. Dr. and Mlle Curie have the reception in their rose garden. The father of the bride tells the father of the groom, "You will have a daughter worthy of affection in Marie. Since she came into the world she has never caused me pain."[34]

Not holding to any tradition for the wedding, it is no surprise that their honeymoon is also unconventional. Marie and Pierre have purchased bicycles and plan on biking along the coast of Brittany and the mountains of Auvergne. Marie will always remember their honeymoon as their "wedding tramp."[35]

Marie and Pierre, leaving for their honeymoon, 1895, Musée Curie (coll. ACJC)

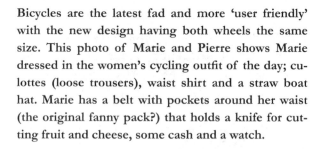

Bicycles are the latest fad and more 'user friendly' with the new design having both wheels the same size. This photo of Marie and Pierre shows Marie dressed in the women's cycling outfit of the day; culottes (loose trousers), waist shirt and a straw boat hat. Marie has a belt with pockets around her waist (the original fanny pack?) that holds a knife for cutting fruit and cheese, some cash and a watch.

As Marie and Pierre cycle along the back roads through villages their conversation sways from crystals to the foliage in the countryside. Marie writes, "We loved the melancholy coasts of Brittany …and the reaches of heather and gorse …which seemed like claws or teeth burying themselves in the water which forever rages at them."[36] Passing by the older generation onlookers, the provincial villagers are shocked with Marie not wearing full length skirts. They might have been muttering, "Kids nowadays …what is this world coming to?"

During their weeks away the newlywed couple stays with Bronya and Casimir who are renting a house for a summer vacation. Included in this warm family gathering is Mme Dluska, Hela, and Bronya's daughter Helen. Vladislav, having navigated his family through so many stormy years, is also with them.

5

"We are sure..."

With no concerns for maintaining appearances, Marie and Pierre have a simple fourth floor apartment in Paris. Their furniture includes; one table, two chairs, an oil lamp and a bed. The modesty of their home keeps Marie's housekeeping chores to a minimum. The only accoutrements are a flower vase and books, particularly their physics books. Their 'low maintenance' lifestyle involves evenings spent seated at the table, studying, enjoying the fragrance from the flowers on the table, and a view of trees out the window.

On weekends, they ride their bikes to visit Pierre's parents. Marie's research measuring magnetic properties and Pierre's exploration of crystals is not interrupted. Dr. Curie has a room equipped for them to continue their work.

Pierre is still teaching at the School of Physics and even with his promotion to Chair of Physics, his salary is comparable to a factory worker. The illustrious Sorbonne is loathe to ever hire Pierre. This same academic stuffiness denies him acceptance to the French Academy of Science. Not having membership, Pierre does not have access to their library which includes current scientific papers. Nor can he attend lectures or their social gatherings where the discourse with members would provide useful. (This barrier to information is akin to a researcher not having access to the Internet today.)

Pierre's grueling schedule as a teacher includes preparing one hundred and twenty lessons per school year on top of overseeing his students' experiments. His income is supplemented with consultant fees from a company that is using his equipment. Some of his tasks are made easier by kind people, such as the laboratory chief at the school, Petit, who is devoted to Pierre. Marie will write, "This good man, whose name was Petit, felt a real affection and solicitude for us, and many things were made easier because of his good will and the interest he took in our success."[1]

Unusual for the time, Marie feels a sense of responsibility to help with finances. She writes, "I want to get my degree, and then I will look for work." [2] Marie enrolls in a certification course to become a physics teacher. She will still make time for her research and attend classes on crystals in order to better understand Pierre's work. Marie and Pierre postpone a trip to Poland the following year in order for Marie to complete her certification exam. Marie graduates first in her class.

Following Marie's teaching exams, Pierre and Marie take another bike tour of the coast and countryside. With both having a knack of being absorbed and inattentive to time, there is no 'check and balance' between the two of them. One afternoon, they realize they have stayed out too late and they can't find their way back in the dark. Marie and Pierre have a lovely memory of the night they slept in a field, with the cows.

Marie's schedule is taken up with her research and writing. In the spring, 1897, she finishes her studies on the magnetic properties of steel. Writing an article about her research, Marie is recognized for her work when the article is published in a scientific journal. She continues her research and has permission to work in an area of Pierre's lab as long as she can cover her expenses. The balance of time for Marie's daily life is about to become more strained.

Adding to the daily itinerary are bouts of morning sickness. Marie is pregnant with their first child and she writes to Kazia, "For more than two months I have had continual dizziness, all day long from morning to night. I tire myself out and get steadily weaker, and although I do not look ill, I feel unable to work and am in a very bad state of spirits. My condition irks me particularly because my mother-in-law is now seriously ill [with incurable breast cancer]."[3] To her brother Joseph, Marie writes more of her concern, "I am afraid, above all, that the disease will reach its end at the same time as my pregnancy. If this should happen my poor Pierre will have some very hard weeks to go through."[4]

The baby is due in September. Vladislav comes to France for the summer to be with Marie. He is renting a house on the coast. Marie and her friend Jadwiga Dydynska, the umbrella fighter, are spending some time at the shore with Marie's father.

For Pierre and Marie it is their first time apart since their marriage. Their correspondence is full of touching sentiments.

Pierre writes, "…I miss you very much–my soul has run off with you."[5]

Marie writes, "I am very sad without you. Come quickly. I wait for you from morning to night and I don't see you coming."[6]

Pierre writes, "I think of my darling who fills my life, and I would like to have new mental powers. It seems to me that if I concentrate my mind exclusively on you, as I have just done, I ought to be able to see you, to follow what you are doing, and also to make you feel that I belong to you completely at this moment–but I can't manage to get a picture."[7]

Not only is their love of each other entwined but also their love of learning. Marie writes Pierre, "I work as much as I can but Poincare's book is harder than I thought. I have to talk to you about it and we have to look at it again together and see what has given me so much trouble."[8]

And their letters swing back to the practical family matters. Pierre writes to Marie about his progress tracking down special baby clothes and supplies. It is entertaining to see diapers are a topic of new parents in any era. While today it is the expense of disposable diapers, for Marie and Pierre they discuss a diaper pattern. There is something beautifully sincere reading about two brilliant scientists who can measure miniscule levels of electricity while they are genuinely wondering what the right measurements of a diaper should be for their baby.

Marie must balance her roles in life: work, wife, woman, and now mother is added to the list. Marie (work) is still studying. Marie (wife) and Pierre want to go on a bike ride. Marie (mother) is eight months pregnant. Marie (woman) wants to show society and herself she is free to ride a bike, pregnant, in public.

While they are still at the summer house, Marie and Pierre are out for a ride on their bikes. Marie goes into labor and is rushed back to Paris. September 12, 1897, Pierre and Marie have their first child, a daughter. Her name is Irene. Dr. Curie, Irene's grandfather, is the one to help bring Irene into the world. Irene, forever close to her grandfather, will only have a grandmother for two more weeks.

Marie is up during the nights, and comes home at lunchtime and dinner to nurse Irene, whom she calls, "my little queen."[9] Irene is not gaining enough weight and Marie is exhausted and worried. A visit to the doctor shows there is a lesion on Marie's left lung. With this early sign of tuberculosis, the doctor suggests Marie visit a sanatorium for several months. It's hard to imagine how Marie must have felt, remembering her mother with this diagnosis, going off to a sanatorium, missing her children, and she had died. Marie chooses to ignore the doctor's suggestion.

One concession Marie makes is to hire a wet nurse for Irene. Marie writes to her father, "in spite of the sorrow it causes me and in spite of the expense—I wouldn't for anything in the world to hurt my child's development."[10]

During these months, Dr. Curie comes to live with them. Marie can relax knowing Irene is in the constant care of her grandfather. The routine becomes Marie feeding and dressing Irene in the mornings, and in the evenings she bathes, feeds and puts Irene to bed. In the evenings, Marie makes notes in a journal of the date Irene first rolls over, holds an object in her hand and when Irene starts calling her 'Me.'" (for ma or mom) Any other free time Marie is sewing clothes for Irene. It's Marie's opinion that ready-made clothes are too expensive and fancy.

> Dr. Curie is not an additional burden at the house. He cares for Irene and helps with household duties, freeing Marie to continue her research. Dr. Curie is a striking example of a man stepping away from the traditional male role in 1897.

The general opinion of society would agree that Marie should **not** push having a professional life any further. In fact, Marie would have heard a sigh of relief from society if these had been her sentiments: "I have done enough. I am the first woman to have not one but two degrees from the famous Sorbonne. I have a wonderful husband and child. I will work as his assistant in the lab, teach at the girl's school and just be happy."

These are not Marie's words. She wants more. Marie wants to earn a doctorate...in physics.

Marie's decision of what to study for her doctorate is first broken down between two choices. If Marie leans toward advancing earlier discoveries, she will spend the bulk of her time reading scientific papers. If she pursues new discoveries, Marie can start immediately with research. Never a better example of "Follow Your Heart"–Marie ops for the path of research, pursuing new discoveries.

> Note to Readers: Scientific descriptions written in this book are for the purpose of portraying the tenacity of Marie's character and brilliance. While the descriptions are accurate, they are minimal and not meant as a 'go to' science reference.

Before we see where Marie's decision leads, a few details for the context of science during this era will help readers comprehend the magnitude of Marie's work.

An 'invisible light' has been discovered three years earlier by Wilhelm Roentgen (Germany, 1895). Using the term 'X' (X stands for unknown), these light rays will be called 'X-rays' and the name sticks. X-rays are shocking the science world. The X-ray beams can penetrate tin, paper, rubber, even wood. Only lead is capable of not having an X-ray pass through it. Roentgen is passing around an X-ray photo of his wife's hand and everyone can see the ring on her finger.

> It would be interesting to know how Mr. R. asked Mrs. R. to put her hand in front of these mysterious rays. "Honey, could you come here a minute? I need your help. Could you just...."

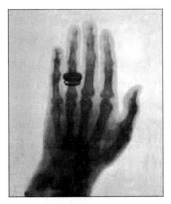

First X-ray,
Mrs. Roentgen's hand,
1896, *Musée Curie*
(coll. ACJC)

The picture of Mrs. Roentgen's hand goes viral and becomes the most famous photograph in the world. German Kaiser Wilhelm II presents Roentgen with the "Order of the Crown." X-rays, with a ballyhoo of possibilities, become part of the pop culture. X-rays are the subject of cartoons and there are jokes of husbands spying on their wives through locked doors. X-ray opera glasses are sold with the purpose of being able to see through costumes to the naked bodies of the actors. X-ray proof suits are available for businessmen in London who are worried someone will use X-ray glasses on them. New Jersey is considering a ban on X-rays to prevent "lewd" possibilities.

Within the next year, fifty books and a thousand papers on X-rays hit the press. A magazine in England claims, "You can see other people's bones with the naked eye. On the revolting indecency of this there is no need to dwell."[11] Misinformation runs rampant. The Purity League in the United States proposes a law that theater goers be banned from using X-rays in their opera glasses. X-ray proof corsets, better known as 'modesty gowns'; are being sold in clothing stores.

{ This influence on pop culture continues into the 1930s. Superman's X-ray vision can't see through lead and the mysterious substance kryptonite has power that can be neutralized only when sealed in a lead box. }

Industry quickly puts X-rays to work. Two weeks from the discovery, X-rays are used in the United States to locate a bullet in a patient's leg.[12] Just in time for Marie, the X-ray discovery is a wakeup call to the world of physics that had put the subject afloat on the backwaters of science.

Another piece of groundwork and person to know before we get back to Marie–

Henri Becquerel, described as arrogant and entitled, is a fourth generation scientist. His family has money which enables Becquerel to have a fully equipped laboratory and the pleasure of changing his starched shirt twice a day. His character is opposite from the Curies, but their paths will cross.

Becquerel's father had studied phosphorescence (light emitted by a substance without combustion or perceptible heat) and he invented the phosphoroscope. Becquerel has decided to see if there is a link between X-rays and phosphorescence. Becquerel, in a series of experiments, discovers another type of penetrating ray when he is using uranium salts. The rays from the uranium salts he refers to as "Becquerel rays." Becquerel has also discovered that rays from uranium cause the surrounding air to conduct electricity. This 'electricity' is actually ionizing the air. (This is what causes a Geiger Counter to click). He publishes six papers on the subject.

Becquerel does not try to explain the source of these new rays. He has bumped into the edge of his understanding. Thinking nothing more can come of it, he drops the subject.

What Becquerel drops, Marie picks up.

Marie decides her doctoral studies will be to further explore Becquerel's recent experiments with X-rays and to better understand the source of the rays coming from uranium. Marie hopes, "to determine the intensity of the radiation, by measuring the conductivity of the air exposed to the action of the rays."[13] Marie will also see if other elements give off these same rays too, which is similar to her previous work studying different elements to see which ones are magnetic. What begins with the goal of "measuring" will turn the world of physics upside down.

Marie starts work December 16, 1897. We know this because it is the date she writes in her research journal. It is touching to see that the journal is one given to her by Pierre. The first few pages of the journal are his notes.

To measure the strength of the rays, Marie needs equipment capable of measuring weak electrical currents with great precision. Where will she find that? It is the electrometer that Pierre and Jacques had built. Pierre takes time from his own research on crystals and works for fifteen days to modify the electrometer for Marie to use. He makes sure Marie also has a piezoelectric quartz. Marie needs this because it "measures in absolute terms small quantities of electricity as well as electric currents of low intensity."[14]

Marie spends three weeks learning and perfecting how to use the piezoelectric scale. Henri Becquerel had tried to use this equipment, and he had given up. The scale is so sensitive a fingerprint can change the reading. The steps for working the equipment are a precise synchronization of the scientist's movement: the body must sit perfectly still and the eyes stare straight ahead at a glass plate. While doing this, the right hand places weights on the scale of the equipment and the left hand holds a stopwatch to keep track.

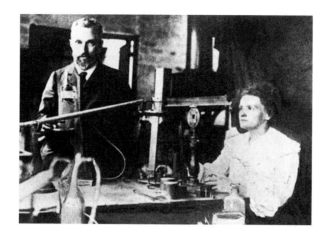

Pierre and Marie using the piezoelectric scale, 1898,
Musée Curie (coll. ACJC)

{ Years later, Marie's granddaughter, French nuclear physicist, Helene Langevin-Joliot is asked to give a demonstration on how to use the piezoelectric scale. She responds, "Impossible! No one at the Institute has the sleight-of-hand or the concentration to do it. In fact, I know of no one alive who has this skill."[15] }

Marie's supplies include wire, glue, wood, crystals, tin, and glass. If Marie needs more glass beakers, she makes them herself. Marie will also need to use the new invention, vacuum tubes. Marie and Pierre make their own vacuum chambers with a hand pump to extract the air.

Pierre helps Marie have space to conduct her research. He convinces his boss to let Marie use a storage area that is full of old equipment and piles of lumber. Marie is happy to have a place to work. The room has no heat and in February she writes in her notebook, "6.25 degrees Celsius" (44 degrees Fahrenheit). In her journal entry she adds six exclamation points. [16] Marie doesn't care about the temperature for the sake of her comfort. What she cares about is that the cold will affect her equipment and the measurements.

Marie is borrowing mineral samples from colleagues and from the collection in the Museum of Natural History. She tests each element to see if any rays are emitted and she measures the rays. Her next step is what indicates her brilliant mind. Marie retests the elements that emit rays to see if the energy is different while the element is in the liquid or solid states or by being exposed to light or heat. The fact that these tests show there is no change in the rays emitted or the energy level of the rays, even when the conditions change, leads to Marie's shattering discovery. Marie states that the ability of some elements to give off the rays is a characteristic of the atom itself—an atomic property.

Although Marie becomes most famous in the general public for her discovery of radium, what sets the world of physics agog is her declaring that atoms have properties. No one in the science world has considered this possibility. The impact of this finding, an atom having a characteristic, is the 'shot heard round the world' in the science domain. Atoms were previously seen as being a simple solid ball. Marie is questioning a 2,000 year old scientific belief.

Everyone believes the makeup of an atom is exactly what the word 'atom' indicates, indivisible. Ernest Rutherford (father of nuclear physics, 1908 Nobel Prize in chemistry) said, "I was brought up to look at the atoms as a nice hard fellow, red or grey in color according to taste."[17] As far back as 460-370 B.C., Democritus had stated the atom was the smallest part of matter and could not be broken down further. In 98 B.C. a poet described an atom, "the only eternal and immutable entities of which our physical world is made."[18] And James Clerk Maxwell (mathematical physicist, 1831-1879) writes, "Though ancient systems may be dissolved and new systems evolved out of their ruins, the molecules [atoms] out of which these systems are built...[are] the foundation stones of the material universe and remain unbroken and unworn. They continue to this day, as they were created."[19]

Aside from the belief the atom is the least common denominator, there is the law of the universe stating that energy cannot be created or destroyed. Matter is believed to be inert. This is brought into question by Marie's work studying these rays with their unknown energy source. It's as if a light bulb is sitting on a table by itself and giving off light. So, it appears, these radioactive substances are radiating with no understandable energy source. (At that time the gradual deterioration of the element, its half life, is not known.)

What the best scientists in the world have believed is being challenged by a woman. Ugh.

Coinciding with Marie discovering atoms having properties, Marie discovers that thorium also has the trait of emitting rays. And this quality, the ability of an element to emit rays, needs a name. Marie calls this characteristic "radioactivity."

Pierre, still teaching at the Ecolé de Physique, has no laboratory and conducts his research in a corridor of the school. When the chemistry-physics chair is available at the Sorbonne, Pierre, being the most qualified candidate, applies for the post. This position would not only double his salary, more importantly; Pierre would have access to a lab. The Sorbonne, stubborn with stuffy standards and the unspoken priority of pandering to the self-importance of their boys club, selects a lesser qualified candidate. Keeping Pierre free of this new position will be to the Curies' advantage, but at the time, the game of backdoor politics is disheartening to Pierre.

Marie's recent discoveries are creating more questions about radioactive elements; therefore, she stops work on all other inactive minerals and concentrates on the radioactive ones. After testing and concluding that only uranium and thorium are radioactive, Marie is testing a uranium ore known as pitchblende. There is about to be another shake up to science.

Knowing how much uranium is in the sample of pitchblende, Marie should know how much radioactivity will be measured. The level of radioactivity that registers literally doesn't 'add up.' The level far exceeds what can be accounted for with uranium. Marie measures and measures again. The results keep showing an additional level of unexplained radioactivity.

Marie knows that chemists have analyzed pitchblende and they have accounted for 99% of the minerals found in it. Marie realizes there must be a new radioactive element in pitchblende (in the unaccounted 1%) that is making the increase in the reading. She also knows this new element must be extremely radioactive since it is giving off such a high level of radioactivity for such a miniscule amount of pitchblende.

At this time, when other scientists are busy in the race to discover the elements that will fill in the gaps of the periodic table, Marie has come upon a new element in the midst of her researching radioactivity. Frederick Soddy (who worked with Ernest Rutherford and later explained that radioactivity is due to the transmutation of elements) writes of the Curies, "Pierre Curie's greatest discovery was Marie Sklodowska. Her greatest discovery was…radioactivity."[20] Marie's new method of discovering elements–by measuring their radioactivity–is what leads to more discoveries about atoms and their structure.

Marie writes, "These minerals would have had nothing astonishing about it, if it had been in proportion to the quantities of uranium or thorium contained in them. But it was not so. Some of these minerals revealed an activity three or four times greater than that of uranium. I verified this surprising fact carefully, and could not doubt its truth."[21] Marie writes to Bronya, "The radiation from the pitchblende that I couldn't explain comes from a new chemical element. The element is there and I've got to find it. We are sure!"[22]

Marie uses the word "We" because Pierre has joined her. With the Sorbonne snub and the recent revelations by Marie, she writes, "He abandoned his work on crystals to join me in the search for this unknown substance."[23] With this decision, Pierre risks his reputation and losing the edge he has as the lead expert in crystals. For the next eight years, their work melds in collaboration. The entries in their notebooks always read "We found" or "We observed"[24]

By March 1898, Marie establishes that several minerals give off more energetic rays than pure uranium. The Curies develop a method of chemical research that separates out other elements from ores such as pitchblende. Each element is measured to see if there is any 'abnormal' level of radioactivity. In this process with pitchblende they realize there is not just one new element but two. Marie's colleagues tell her she has made a mistake in the experiments and suggest to her to be more careful. The Curies are sure there is no mistake.

How to find this new element? The genius of Marie is her idea of finding the unknown substance by looking for the rays to be different than the rays of substances that are known. Marie writes, "As we did not know at the beginning, any of the chemical properties of the unknown substance, but only that it emits rays, it was by these rays that we had to search."[25]

Marie writes a paper in April that will establish the method of discovering new elements by measuring their radioactivity.

The paper is presented to the Academy of Sciences by Gabriel Lippmann, Marie's former professor and mentor. (Marie and Pierre are not members and only members can present papers.) Entitled "Ray Emitted by Compounds of Uranium and of Thorium," the paper is printed within ten days and is circulating throughout the scientific community of the world. The paper reads: "...It was necessary at this point to find a new term to define this new property of matter manifested by the elements of uranium and thorium. I proposed the word radioactivity."[26] This is the beginning of the new field of atomic science.

Three game changers in this paper are Marie stating that radioactivity can be measured, to use this measure as a means to discover new elements, and that radioactivity is an atomic property. When Marie is lecturing, she acknowledges that radioactivity might be a unique chemical reaction that defies the principles of the atom being indestructible. She suggests that "this hypothesis strikes just as serious a blow at accepted ideas in physics as the hypothesis of transformation of elements does at the principles of chemistry, and one can see that the question is not easy to resolve." [27]

Marie has subtracted out every element except bismuth, and when she starts eliminating that, the sample is one hundred and fifty times more active than uranium. While working in the lab, Pierre is heating a solution of bismuth sulphide and the glass test tube cracks. Luckily Pierre doesn't cuss and throw away the damaged tube. Instead he notices the thin layer of black powder left on the tube and he measures the radioactivity of the powder. It measures three hundred thirty times more active than uranium. As they continue to extract any remaining bismuth from the powder it leads to stronger results. (Like making a reduction sauce, as you boil away more liquid the flavor is stronger.) This is their discovery of the new element. Marie names the new element Polonium, after her home country Poland.

Marie and Pierre have prepared a joint paper to be presented to the Academy of Sciences. This time it is presented by Henri Becquerel. The title is, "On a New Radioactive Substance Contained in Pitchblende."[28] The paper announces the existence of the new element, "We propose to call it *polonium* from the name of the country of origin of one of us." Marie has not lost her edge of humor. She knows that her research will be published and read in Russia, Germany and Austria. These occupiers of her country will be reminded there is still the dream that Poland will someday reclaim its independence.

Marie sends a copy of her papers to her cousin in Warsaw. Joseph Boguski, who had first opened the doors of a laboratory for Marie, sees his encouragement to Marie was not in vain.

The difficulty for the Curies is in identifying and quantifying the energy of a radioactive element. Marie calls it "the chemistry of the invisible."[29] Taking a creative leap, Marie doesn't rely on the usual means of verifying a new element, which is weighing the sample to find its atomic weight. Marie's samples are too small, a thousandth part of a milligram. Marie must use a different means of proving the existence of a new element, seeing a new spectral pattern.

What is known is that when heat is applied to an element, the result is a spectral pattern. This pattern, like a fingerprint for an element, is different for each element. Seeing a new pattern will be the means of identifying a new element. By measuring the rays that the sample emits, Marie is able to 'weighs' it.

An expert in identifying spectral patterns is Eugene Demarcay. The Curies have brought to him several samples in hopes of identifying a new spectral pattern. These samples had not been pure enough, so no new pattern has shown. Finally Marie brings another sample and through his spectroscope, Demarcay sees a pattern he has never seen before. This is the proof Marie needs.

The previous paper presented in June at the academy was a preliminary step, like announcing an engagement. Having the evidence of the spectral lines makes it definite. July 18, 1898, Marie can officially name the new element "**Polonium**."[30]

By December of this same year, another new element is identified. Marie names this **Radium**. It is the most powerful radioactive substance ever discovered.

This same July, the Academy of Sciences is impressed with Marie's prior work on magnetic properties of steel and now on radioactivity. The Academy awards Marie the Gegner Prize with 3,800 francs ($1,267 equivalency in 2015). The award is for, "the precision of the procedural methods of Madame Curie."[31]

Recognition of a woman's achievement only goes so far. As a means of continuing their stance to not acknowledge women, the Academy doesn't directly notify Marie. Instead, they tell Pierre and ask him to inform her. Becquerel also speaks only to Pierre, "I congratulate you very sincerely and beg of you to present my respectful compliments to your wife."[32]

Recent discoveries have moved Marie and Pierre forward; however, a setback for Marie is Bronya and Casimir's return to Russian-controlled Poland to start a new sanatorium for tuberculosis patients. Marie, bereft at this loss, writes to Bronya, "You can't imagine the hole you have left here. When I lost you two, I lost everything I care about in Paris besides my husband and my child. Now I feel as though Paris doesn't exist outside of our house and the school where we work."[33]

Marie goes on to ask Bronya for advice. She writes, "Ask Mother Dluska if the green plant you left here should be watered and how many times a day. Does it need a lot of warmth and sunlight?" And then she fills Bronya in on the latest news of Irene. "Irene is turning into a big kid. She is very difficult to feed, and except for tapioca pudding she will eat almost nothing regularly, not even eggs. Write me what sorts of foods children of that age should be eating."[34]

Marie and Pierre visit Bronya and Casimir. This occasion becomes a family reunion that includes Vladislav and all Marie's siblings. (Joseph, a medical doctor with his wife and children, Bronya and Casimir with their two children, Hela a teacher and her husband, a prosperous business man in photography). Pierre tells Marie, in Polish, "This country is very beautiful. I understand now why you love it."[35]

It will be the last time they are all together with their father.

For Pierre there is more professional disappointment that year. Pierre's work on crystallography, piezoelectricity, symmetry, and magnetism are well known, add to this his work with Marie, discovering radium and polonium. One would think this garners the attention of the Sorbonne. When a chair in physical chemistry becomes available the winter of 1898, Pierre is the obvious choice. He might be obvious, but he is not the choice. (Opinion for why Pierre is not selected is his well known acknowledgement/support for Marie. This is not playing by the boys' club rules. Keeping Pierre out is a means of keeping any acknowledgement of Marie at a distance.)

Aside from needing to isolate the new elements, the other question is–what is the source of this energy? The Curies record that the radium gives out heat in large enough amounts that it can be measured by their simple laboratory techniques. Marie, after a series of experiments writes, "No change occurs in this material which radiates the energy."[36]

This undetermined energy source is breaking the basic law of physics. The law of conservation of energy states that energy can neither be created nor destroyed. So, if heat energy cannot be created, where is it coming from? Marie proposes either the radioactive substances are borrowing the energy from an external source and then releasing it, or that the radium is the source of the energy itself.

> The Curies had initially believed that something outside the element is causing the energy. Rutherford believes the answer is within the atom itself. Rutherford will be right. The radium and polonium are gradually breaking down, "decaying" and that process is the change that causes the atom to give off rays. Hence the law of conservation of energy can stay intact.

As the enigma of radioactivity is being unraveled, another question is, "Why are some elements radioactive and others are not?" Marie's answer will eclipse her discovery of polonium and radium. Marie continues her train of thought from radioactivity being an atomic trait to realizing this is an atomic process.

December 26, 1898, the Curies are getting one last paper in before the turn to the new year. This paper to the Academy is presented by Becquerel and it will be published in a scientific journal. The Curies make the official announcement of Radium, "a new strongly radioactive substance contained in pitchblende." The results are supported by Demarcay's report that there is a unique color on the spectral line "known to no other substance."

Marie, happy with her life, writes to Bronya, "I have the best husband one could dream of; I could never have imagined finding one like him. He is a true gift from heaven, and the more we live together, the more we love each other."[37]

6

"...this life we have chosen."

"There can be no doubt of the existence of these new elements, but to make chemists admit their existence, it was necessary to isolate them."[1] Marie Curie

In spite of the clear evidence of distinct light rays for both Polonium and Radium, this is not the absolute proof required in the field of chemistry. The elements must have an atomic weight.

If the decision had been up to Pierre, he would have moved on to other things and let someone else find the atomic weight. Irene explains later, "Pierre Curie was attracted above all by the fascinating problems posed...by the...mysterious rays emitted by these new materials....Marie Curie had the stubborn desire to see salts of pure radium, to measure radium's atomic weight."[2]

Marie is not going to rest (literally) until she can fill in the atomic weights for the Periodic Table. They will focus first on radium. Jean Perrin writes twenty-two years later, "It is not an exaggeration to say today that [the isolation of radium] is the cornerstone on which the entire edifice of radioactivity rests."[3]

{ For two reasons the discovery of radium will outshine polonium. Polonium, having such a short life, will prove next to impossible to isolate and it has no immediate value for the industrial world. }

The Curies divide their work. Pierre takes on the physics by exploring the origin and nature of radium's activity. Marie takes on the chemistry. Starting with small quantities of pitchblende ore, Marie realizes this won't suffice. To find the atomic weight, the Curies will need tons of pitchblende. Marie writes, "The result of our experiment proved that there were in reality new radioactive elements in pitchblende but that their proportion did not reach even **a millionth** per cent."[4]

Marie will now embark on the most physically demanding task in the history of scientific research. She will extract one fourth teaspoon of radium salts, from two hundred tons of pitchblende.

Pierre and Marie have been using their money to buy large quantities of pitchblende to continue their research. The quantity they need now exceeds their budget. The Curies are told the Austrian government has been mining pitchblende and extracting the uranium (used for making color in pottery). The remnants, several tons of pitchblende slag, are piled in the woods. Striped of uranium, this pitchblende is worthless.

For the Curies, the slag minus its uranium is exactly what they need. Being worthless to the Austrian government makes it affordable for the Curies. The Austrians are persuaded to give the first ton to the Curies, but they don't cover the transportation. With no financial support from the science society, the Curies use their own money to cover this expense. Later the Curies are able to have the pitchblende delivered due to the financial support from Baron Edmond de Rothschild.

> This is an example of the disadvantage for the Curies not being members of the Society of Science. The 'Society' usually provides funds for such research expenses.

The first sacks of pitchblende arrive in early 1899. Marie writes, "How glad I was when the sacks arrived, with the brown dust mixed with pine needles and when the activity (radioactivity) proved even greater than that of the primitive ore. It was a stroke of luck that the residues had not been thrown far away."[5]

Aside from needing tons of pitchblende, the more difficult problem is finding a place to work. The bureaucrats in charge of the Sorbonne buildings say 'no' to Pierre's request for a room. The School of Physics, where Pierre is teaching, comes through for them. Although, Pierre's new boss has petty grievances against Pierre and what is offered is less than optimal.

The "Shack" for the Curie laboratory, 1898,
Musée Curie (coll. ACJC)

The room is a shack that had been used by the medical students to store and dissect cadavers. They abandoned the shack, declaring the building unfit. The roof has skylights that leak.

The floor is bitumen, a black mixture used for road surfacing and roofing. The minimal furnishings, a preference for the Curie's apartment, are drawbacks for their laboratory. Accessories include: several old plank kitchen tables and a black board. There are no shelves for their equipment and no heater except a cast-iron stove with a rusty pipe. After a German chemist visits the Curies' laboratory he writes, "It was like a stable or a root cellar, and if I hadn't seen the work table with its chemical equipment, I would have thought this was a practical joke."[6]

Marie remembers this time, *"...And yet it was in this miserable old shed that the best and happiest years of our life were spent entirely consecrated to work. I sometimes passed the whole day stirring a mass in ebullition, with an iron rod nearly as big as myself. In the evening I was broken with fatigue. This went on for four years."* [7]

The 'laboratory' is sweltering in the summer and freezing in the winter. The chemical treatments they use include hydrogen sulfide, a toxic gas. Having no exhaust fans in the shack, Marie works outside, in the courtyard. After months of processing the pitchblende, the final stages of solution come down to crystallizing in rows of petri dishes (named after J.R. Petri, bacteriologist). The samples must be protected from dust and the particles of coal from the fire in the stove. On rainy days the samples and the equipment need to be moved away from water dripping from the ceiling.

Marie's only complaints are, "It is true that the discovery of radium was made in precarious conditions: the shed which sheltered it seems clouded in the charms of legend. But its romantic element was not an advantage: it wore out our strength and delayed our accomplishment. With better means, the first five years of our work might have been reduced to two, and their tension lessened."[8]

In front of the shack are 800 bags of pitchblende at 25 pounds each. This isn't romantic. It is hard manual labor.

"The chemical separation and fractional crystallizations that they [the Curies] employed were nothing short of heroic in scale. 'Courageous' is neither too strong nor too romantic a word to use for the woman who designed and led this incredibly difficult quest..."[9] Written eighty -five years later, chemistry professor, Robert L. Wolke

Marie describes this quest for her and Pierre: "The life of a great scientist in his laboratory is not, as many may think, a peaceful idyll. More often it is a bitter battle with things, with one's surroundings, and above all with oneself. A great discovery does not leap completely achieved from the brain of the scientist, as Minerva sprang, all panoplied, from the head of Jupiter; it is the fruit of accumulated preliminary work. Between the days of fecund productivity are inserted days of uncertainty when nothing seems to succeed, and when even matter itself seems hostile; and it is then that one must hold out against discouragement. Thus without ever forsaking his inexhaustible patience, Pierre used sometimes to say to me: "It is nevertheless hard, this life that we have chosen."[10]

Aside from time at the 'laboratory' shack, the Curies prepare weekly lessons for classes, teach, and oversee lab work for students. Regardless, Marie is determined to stay in the lead of their research. Ernest Rutherford, writes his mother, "Right now I'm very busy writing up some notes for publication and doing new experiments. I can't stop. There are always people trying to overtake me. My most formidable adversaries in this field are Becquerel and the Curies in Paris, who have done very important work on radioactive bodies during the past few years."[11] Later when Rutherford sees the shack, in a typical British fashion, he comments, "You know it must be dreadful not to have a laboratory to play around in."[12]

 When industry takes over the process of extracting radium for the results of getting one gram (¼ teaspoon) of radium crystals it takes: 500 tons of ore, 500 tons of chemicals, 1,000 tons of coal, 10,000 tons of purified and distilled water, the labor equivalent of 350 men working full time for a month.[13]

In a simplified explanation here is the process to isolate radium.

Marie's Recipe for radium salts:

Step 1–2 sacks of pitchblende (approx. 50 pounds), pour into a big cauldron, add a strong alkali and boil over a fire. Stir with a 5 foot long iron pole.

Note: Each ton of pitchblende will require fifty tons of rinsing water.

Step 2–keeping the residue that is left after boiling–apply chemicals that continue to reduce the residue clearing it of the other components (the 99% that has been accounted for in the pitchblende).

Place tiny amounts of this solution in rows of petri dishes and allow the liquid to evaporate. This leaves crystals. Redissolve the crystal in a liquid and wait for the liquid to evaporate. Crystals are formed again with a little more of the barium evaporated away and the sample is a little more pure.

Step 3–Test what is radioactive and keep that. What is not radioactive toss out.

Step 4–Repeat steps 1 and 3 hundreds of times until pure radium chloride is obtained.

Marie writes of those few years of pure research: "A great tranquility reigned in our poor, shabby hanger; occasionally, while observing an operation, we would walk up and down talking of our work, present and future. When we were cold, a cup of hot tea, drunk beside the stove, cheered us. We lived in a preoccupation as complete as that of a dream."[14] Marie continues, "We saw only very few persons at the laboratory; among the physicists and chemists there were a few who came from time to time, either to see our experiments or to ask for advice from Pierre Curie, whose competence in several branches of physics was well-known."[15]

After Irene is put to bed, Marie remembers, "We would sometimes come back in the evening after dinner to look in our domain. Our precious products, for which we had no shelter, were set out on table and boards; we could see their faintly luminous silhouettes all around us, and these glowing lights, which seemed to be suspended in the darkness, always thrilled and delighted us all over again."[16] Pierre tells Marie, "I should like it to have a beautiful color."[17] He is not disappointed. While pure radium salts are colorless, the radiation that it gives off is a bluish-mauve tint. In time, there will be enough radiation in the rows of small dishes that the bluish-mauve colors glow in the shack.

Throughout 1899 this singular focus of the Curies is impairing their health. Aside from not eating well or getting enough rest, Pierre and Marie are noticing their fingertips become hard and painful after handling containers of radioactive material. (One hundred years later the Curies' personal items and articles from their laboratory are still radioactive) Their daughter Eve remembers, "The days of work became months and years: Pierre and Marie were not discouraged. The material which resisted them, which defended its secret, fascinated them. United by their tenderness, united by their intellectual passions, they had, in a wooden shack, the anti-natural existence for which they had both been made."[18]

The Curies are also beginning to garner recognition in the public. Doctors are recognizing that radium salts can be used to reduce cancerous tumors. The Curies provide these salts and the treatment becomes known as Curie-therapy.

On Sunday afternoons young research scientists gather at the Curies' home. One of them is Paul Langevin, Pierre's former student. Another is André Debierne. Debierne is hired by the Curies as an assistant. He is a chemist and will later discover another radioactive element, actinium, in the pitchblende residue.[19]

Marie is hired to teach at the Normal School at Sevreś his is an elite preparatory school for women to become teachers in France. With an all male staff, Marie is the first woman to be named to the faculty. The school, not wanting to overcome all sexist standards, allows Marie to teach only the first and second year students.

The start of the school year is difficult. The students, disdainful of having a woman as their teacher, make fun of Marie's Polish accent. They sing a ditty that goes like this—

Wouldn't she be better off,
Cooking for her husband-prof,

Instead of talking in a stream,
To a class that's bored enough to scream.[20]

Marie recognizes many of the twenty-year-old students are not able to follow the level of math she is teaching. Like Marie's early education, the women have not been taught the necessary preparatory classes. The women will learn now with Marie. The students will also work in the laboratory. Most of the students have never touched a piece of equipment, let alone work in a laboratory. Marie doubles the length of her class so her students have time to do more experimental work.

"She held us with her simplicity, her desire to be useful to us,
the sense she had of both our ignorance and our possibilities."[21]
Written by one of Marie's students

By the second year, Marie's students are performing their own experiments and they adore her. One student writes, "But in the case of Madame Curie, we didn't wait for the ringing of the bell. We watched from our windows for the arrival of the professor, and as soon as we saw her little grey dress at the end of the alley of chestnut trees we ran to take our seats in the conference room."[22]

The temperature in the shack reads 100.22 F (37.9 C). Marie is continuing to condense the solutions. July 23rd, Marie writes, "Pure radium in the dish." On the 27th she writes in her notebook the weight of an atom of radium: 174. Then Marie writes, "It's impossible." She knows something in her operations is not accurate and that two years of work and eight tons of pitchblende are gone.[23] There is no record of questioning what the next step is. The next step for Marie is clear. She must start again.

"One never notices what has been done; one can only see what remains to be done." Marie Curie

The lost time and resources will not stop the Curies and neither will their loss of health, tight finances, and dilapidated laboratory. Pierre is having pains in his legs, which the doctors have diagnosed as rheumatism. Marie is losing weight and her skin is pale. Dr. Curie has her tested for tuberculosis. Marie writes of their budget, "We have to be careful, and my husband's salary isn't quite enough to live on, but up to now we have had several unexpected additional sources of income each year, which means we have no deficit."[24] And of the shack Marie writes, "deplorable state.…In our laboratory the situation has become acute and we no longer have any apparatus properly insulated."[25] In other words, everything has been contaminated with radiation.

There is some relief when a chemical company offers to take over the initial processes to refine the radium. André Debierne is put in charge to supervise the factory operations. Marie, no longer stirring solutions in a cauldron over an open fire, can focus on the final meticulous stages of distilling the samples.

Marie and Pierre are busy documenting their work. Between 1900 and 1903 the Curies publish more than thirty papers.[26]

The 1900 World's Fair, held in Paris, is attended by over fifty million visitors who are flabbergasted with the possibilities of electricity and agog with electric lights. They have no idea that concurrent to their World's Fair is the Physics Congress already discussing the next generation of energy–nuclear.

At the Physics Congress, the Curies and their new radioactive elements are the topic de jour. The Curies' paper is entitled, "On Induced Radioactivity and their Gas Activated by

Radium." They describe in their paper, "radioactivity gradually transmits itself through open air from the radiant material to active bodies." The fact they need to explain this emphasizes the point of how much is still unknown about radioactivity.

France continues to disregard the magnitude of research being done by the Curies, and when the dean for the University of Geneva offers Pierre a physics chair, an annual salary, a housing allowance and the directorship of a laboratory, the Curies are interested. Pierre is assured there will be a proper laboratory and the laboratory will have a staff of two assistants, equipment request lists will be fulfilled, and Marie will be given an official position in the laboratory.[27] Marie and Pierre visit Geneva, and Pierre accepts the offer. He will finally have the laboratory of his dreams. However, when they return to France, Pierre changes his mind.

Pierre, who had left his own research of crystals to support Marie's work, realizes that any interruption in their research will be an irreversible setback. An alternative is to go to Geneva, and when Marie finishes her doctorate, she can join him. Pierre will not take this option. He sends a letter of resignation. Marie later explains, "Pierre Curie was very tempted to accept [the Swiss offer] and it was the immediate interest of our research into radium that finally made him refuse it."[28]

The French, worried they will lose the Curies, offer Pierre a teaching position at the School of Physics, Chemistry, and Natural Sciences. True, it is a part of the Sorbonne, but it is not a full staff position and as such only adds to his work load. This puts their finances in a better position but still no laboratory. Having more classes to teach, prepare more lectures and including commute time means more time away from their research.[29]

Support (albeit belated) is also forthcoming from the French Academy of Sciences. They award the Curies twenty thousand francs. The money is used to buy more pitchblende. They still have not isolated polonium or radium to find either atomic weight.

Marie's work, isolating radium metal, was the most difficult process known to science. It has never been repeated.[30]

By 1902, Marie has succeeded in extracting one-tenth of a gram (equivalent to a few grains of sand) of almost pure radium from 200 tons of pitchblende and sandstone[31]. She can finally provide the atomic weight of radium. March 28, 1902, she writes in her black notebook "Ra=225.92, the weight of an atom of radium."[32] Marie, with her assistant Debierne, has done it. Having the atomic weight of radium puts it on the chart. (She will continue her work and by 1905 she has one gram of radium. It will be worth, at that time, $150,000.)

For Pierre, his professional aspirations, to have a proper laboratory, are undone again by political games he refuses to play. A chair in mineralogy is available at the Sorbonne. Pierre, with his prior work in crystalline physics is once more the perfect choice and he is not given the post. He writes to a friend, "I regret, when all is said, having lost time in paying visits for this brilliant result…."[33]

In the same year, 1902, Pierre is encouraged by friends to apply once more for the open seat in The Academy of Science. This too requires precious time away from his work and again the vote goes to a lesser candidate. Pierre doesn't fit. He won't dance to the Academy's tune.

A colleague who does support Pierre is recommending him for the prestigious Legion of Honor award. Marie encourages Pierre to accept the recommendation. Pierre responds, "Inform him that I do not feel the slightest need of being decorated, but I am in the greatest need of a laboratory."[34]

Marie writes about the reckoning of the scientist and their sacrifice to science, "…more often, before they can secure possible working conditions, they have to exhaust their youth and their power in daily anxieties….Neither public powers nor private generosity actually accord to science and to scientists the support and the subsidies indispensable to fully effective work."[35] The toll of Marie's work is affecting her sleep. She is starting to sleepwalk.[36]

In May, Marie receives a message from her family in Warsaw. Her father is deathly ill. Marie takes the train home to Poland but does not arrive in time. Marie is beside herself with grief and insists the coffin be opened so she can see her father one last time. The anguish of losing her dear father keeps sweeping over Marie as she weeps. It is Bronya who must pull Marie away.

Vladislav had dedicated his life to helping his children succeed. The risks he was willing to take were offset with his sense of caution born out of years of living under Russian rule. Six days before he died, Vladislav wrote to Marie, "You are now in possession of pure radium salts. If we consider the amount of work done in obtaining this, it would certainly be the most expensive of chemical elements. What a pity it is that this work has only theoretical interest."[37] Curie-therapy, and its potential for combating cancer, is just developing.

Marie, seeing past the necessity of a pragmatic view by her father later writes, "My father, who in his own youth had wished to do scientific work, was consoled…by the progressive success of my work."[38]

In September, Marie returns to Paris.

At this time, the Curies know that radium causes local burns, but the more serious and systemic effects are unknown. Pierre exposes his arm to radium and lesions appear. Marie has radium in a sealed tube she is carrying around in her pocket. This leaves burns on her skin. They have postulated that by destroying diseased cells, radium could cure certain forms of cancer. Collaborating with physicians, these studies result in radium therapy. Tubes of radon are used by doctors to destroy diseased cells in skin cancer and the epidermis that is destroyed grows back healthy. This leads to the media frenzy of radium cures.

June 1903, Pierre is asked to lecture at London's Royal Institution, founded in 1799. This organization, the British equivalent of the Academy of Science for Paris, is upstaging the Parisians who thus far have denied Pierre entrance or an invitation to speak at their Paris Academy. In England, the Curies meet the scientists Sir William Crookes, Lord Rayleigh, Sir Oliver Lodge, H.E. Lankester, Ray Lankester, Professor William Ayrton, and Lord Kelvin. All of them had doubted that radium was a new element. They cannot doubt radium now and they cannot doubt Marie's part in the discovery. During the lecture, Pierre mentions four times Marie's role in their work. Marie has the pleasure of hearing Pierre's lecture. She is the first woman to be admitted to the sessions of the Royal Institution.

During Pierre's demonstration of the radium, he shows the audience the radium burn scar on his arm. He tells them,

"The action of radium on nervous centers may result in paralysis or death. They seem to act with particular intensity on living tissues in the process of growth."[39] He stresses that radium has possible therapeutic value in treating lupus and cancer. When Pierre shows the audience a small tube that holds a solution of radium the audience can see the glow of the radium. Pierre says, "Look…this is the light of the future."[40]

{
    Pierre spills a miniscule amount and fifty years later the radioactivity in the building is still high enough that the building is decontaminated.[41]
}

Marie and Pierre, honored as guests at several society receptions, keep their priorities and don't trip over themselves to be in step with fashion. Marie is wearing her one formal black dress she has been using for the last ten years. Pierre comments to Marie after one of the extravagant events, "Do you know, during dinner when I didn't know what to think about, I discovered a game: I calculated how many laboratories could be built with the stones that each woman present was wearing around her neck. When the time for the speeches arrived, I had got up to an astronomical number of buildings."[42]

In this era of 'Society,' when guests at receptions have a valet to help them dress, Pierre could have legitimately used some help. He is very ill and having trouble changing into his formal evening attire. For Marie, if she was a woman of society, she would have stayed home. Society ladies don't appear in public when they are with child. Aside from expecting their second baby, Marie finds it discomfiting when the crowds are staring at her as a curiosity, a woman physicist.

One person who understands Marie's unease is the research scientist, Hertha Ayrton, wife of Professor Ayrton. Hertha, like Marie, is from Poland. Marie can share with Hertha the frustration of unwanted gawking and the disdain of being seen as a foreigner. What Marie doesn't share is the additional disregard Hertha must navigate being the daughter of a Jew.

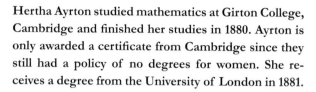

Hertha Ayrton studied mathematics at Girton College, Cambridge and finished her studies in 1880. Ayrton is only awarded a certificate from Cambridge since they still had a policy of no degrees for women. She receives a degree from the University of London in 1881.

Returning from London, six days later, Marie defends her doctoral thesis. Her name is listed as "Madam Sklodowska-Curie."

Bronya comes from Poland to attend the event but first takes Marie to a dressmaker. Marie wants the new dress to be appropriate for working in a laboratory. Not much has changed since her wedding day. What has changed, for the two sisters, is this occasion closes their dreams as young women. After all these years, they both have achieved their goals in education. The morning Marie is to defend her dissertation (June 25, 1903), Pierre and Marie ride their bikes to the Sorbonne.

Twelve years earlier Marie came to Paris as a new student and lagging behind the power curve. Now her work and results are ahead of the power curve in the science community. It is the beginning of the atomic age. She presents her paper, "Researches on Radioactive Substance, by Madame Sklodowska Curie." Marie is the first woman in France to receive a Ph.D. in physics.

In the audience, to hear Marie's presentation, are Pierre, Gabriel Lippmann (Marie's professor and mentor), physicists Jean Perrin and Paul Langevin. Marie's father-in-law also attends along with her students at the women's school. As Marie speaks, she chooses her pronouns purposefully to include Pierre. She states, "**Our** researches upon the new radioactive bodies have given rise to a scientific movement."[43]

When Marie finishes, M. Lippmann, the president, announces, "The University of Paris accords you the title of
doctor of physical science, with the mention 'tres honorable.'
And in the name of the jury, Madame, I wish to express to you
all our congratulation."[44] The auditorium fills with applause
for the first woman to break into this male fortress. Lippman
writes, "The findings represented the greatest scientific contribution ever made in a doctoral thesis."[45] Marie's paper is published in science journals in both England and France.

*"Radium is not to enrich anyone. It is an element; it is for all
people."* Marie Curie

Marie and Pierre have a brief conversation whether the radium information should be free or should they patent it. The
conversation is finished faster than these two sentences can be
typed. They agree the information should be free.

Pierre and Marie could have made millions if they had pat-
ented radium and the process to extract it. (Physicists, traditionally publish the results of their research but not always the
process. The technique/process information is income for the
discoverer.) The income source would have ensured the financial security of their daughters and built the laboratory of their
dreams. Marie explains it "would be contrary to the scientific
spirit…If our discovery has a commercial future that is an accident. Radium is going to be of use in treating disease.…It
seems to me impossible to take advantage of that."[46]

Years later, Marie is asked if she believed they made the right decision. "Yes, I still believe that we have done right."[47] This includes the
Curies giving away samples of their radium, at no cost. Marie wrote,
"Our research on new radioactive substances gave birth to a scientific
movement."[48] The demand for radioactive material is international.

Marie, Pierre, and Irene leave for a vacation in Brittany. Marie and Pierre are on one of their bicycle jaunts, and this puts Marie into premature labor. Marie is rushed to Paris. She gives birth to a baby girl. Born too early, the baby dies in a few hours.

Marie is crushed with grief and guilt. She writes Bronya, "I had grown so accustomed to the idea of the child that I am absolutely desperate and cannot be consoled. Write to me, I beg of you, if you think I should blame this on general fatigue–for I must admit that I have not spared my strength… and I regret this bitterly as I have paid dearly for it. The child– a little girl–was in good condition and was living. And I had wanted it so badly!"[49]

Sorrow, for both Pierre and Marie, continues. News arrives from Bronya that her second child, their five year old son, has died of tubercular meningitis. The familiar cycle of death, snatching members of her family, haunts Marie. She writes to Joseph, "I can no longer look at my little girl without trembling with terror. And Bronya's grief tears me to pieces."[50]

Heartaches and the nature of their work are exacting a price on the Curies. Pierre continues to be very ill and lies awake at night in pain. Marie, anemic and exhausted, has lost ten pounds. When a friend sees them, he is so shocked at their poor health he writes Pierre a ten page letter begging them to take better care of themselves and get some rest.

In November 1903, Pierre and Marie are scheduled to go to London again. This time it is to receive England's highest award; The Davy Medal. Marie is still ill and mourning the loss of their baby. Pierre goes to London by himself to receive the award.

Another award medal will be offered and the invitation does not include Marie. The medal given is gold and portrays the image of two women. The nominating committee believes that is the only way women should be included.

The Nobel Prize Medal for Chemistry and Physics

In 1901 and 1902 the Curies are nominated for the Nobel Prize in physics. It is probable they are not given the award at that time because the same men that keep the door closed to women becoming members of the science societies guard the gates of the Nobel Prize. However by 1903, the phrase, "Be so good they can't ignore you." comes into play. The Curies' work is so famous, they can hardly be ignored and not awarded the Nobel Prize in physics. No matter, the committee is determined to find a way around Marie.

The official letter from the nominating committee is a complete fabrication with the credit for discovering radioactivity being given solely to Pierre. The letter is written by four scientists, three of them have been involved directly with Marie's work. One of the signers is Gabriel Lippmann. This is not only Marie's advisor but a few months earlier it was Lippmann who announced Marie being awarded her doctorate with honors and stating, "The findings represented the greatest scientific contribution ever made in a doctoral thesis."[51]

The prize will also be awarded to Henri Becquerel for his initial work. In an example of 'spin doctors' for physics, the award letter states, the two men "worked together and separately to procure with great difficulty, some decigrams of this precious metal."[52] The committee gives credit to Pierre for isolating polonium and radium and includes Becquerel because it was impossible "for us to separate the names of the two physicists and therefore we do not hesitate to propose that the Nobel Prize be shared between Mr. Becquerel and Mr. Curie."[53]

It could be understandable if the general public maintains a mindset of underestimating Marie. In their ignorance they keep the opinion that Marie is merely an assistant to Pierre and doesn't deserve recognition, but, professional colleagues denying what they know? Willing to twist the truth rather than acknowledge Marie's work, clearly being well-educated does not include courage to speak the truth.

One man, Magnus Mittag-Leffler steps out from the status quo. He is a member of the Nobel Prize Committee. He alerts Pierre of the intention for the award to exclude Marie.

> Magnus Mittag-Leffler is an early advocate for women's equality. He adds his mother's maiden name to his paternal surname and he is key in ensuring Sofia Kovalevskaya (Russian Mathematician) becoming the first full professor of mathematics in Stockholm.

Pierre writes to Mittal-Leffler, "If it is true that one is seriously thinking about me [for the prize], I very much wish to be considered together with Madame Curie with respect to our research on radioactive bodies."[54] Leffler pressures the committee to include Marie. It would be interesting to know what was said at the meeting, but somehow the decision is changed. November 14, 1903 the Curies receive a telegram. They will be sharing the Nobel Prize for physics with Becquerel. Pierre responds their acceptance.

Marie is the first woman to be awarded a Nobel Prize.

More stunning is a woman earning the award in the category of physics, not the more acceptable realm for women of literature or peace. The next time a woman receives a Nobel Prize in science the award once more goes to Marie, in chemistry (1911). There will be no Nobel Prize in science again for a woman until 1935 and it will be for Marie's daughter, Irene.

> Early women Nobel Prize recipients include:
> 1905–Bertha von Suttner–Peace,
> 1909–Selma Lagerlof–Literature,
> 1911–Marie Curie–Chemistry
> 1926–Grazia Deledda–Literature
> 1928–Sigrid Undset–Literature
> 1931–Jane Addams–Peace
> 1935–Irene Joliot-Curie-Chemistry

Since 1935, there have been numerous Nobel Prizes for women in the categories of Peace, Literature or Physiology, but there have been only three more Nobel Prizes awarded to women in physics or chemistry.

December 10, 1903–The Academy of Science of Stockholm makes the official announcement for the Nobel Prize recipients. The Curies are not able to attend due to their teaching commitments and Marie is still too ill to travel. The Nobel Prize requires the recipients to present a lecture. The Curies will not go for another fourteen months, the spring of 1905. Becquerel is there in December to accept his prize and give a lecture. The Curies' gold medal is accepted by the French minister.

Traditionally, the split for the monetary prize, when awarded to three people, is each recipient receives an equal amount. Not so for the Curies. They are counted as one and therefore they are given the same amount as Becquerel.

On December 11, 1903, the day after the public announcement is made, Marie writes her brother, "Dear Joseph, I thank both of you most tenderly for your letters. Don't forget to thank Manyusa (Joseph's daughter) for her little letter, so well written, which gave me great pleasure. I shall answer her as soon as I have a free moment." Marie goes on to discuss the details of the Nobel Prize. She does not mention the original intent of the committee to exclude her. She ends her letter, "I kiss you all tenderly, and implore you not to forget me."[55]

In the biography of Pierre written by Marie or the biography of Marie written by her daughter Eve–neither Marie nor Eve delve into the initial plan for Marie to be excluded from the Nobel Prize. Marie will challenge her right to research, but she will not challenge the unspoken rule for women to stay silent about their enforced inequality.

The monetary award of seventy thousand francs [approx. twenty thousand dollars] is received in January. Pierre can finally leave his teaching job, and they have money to pay for a lab assistant. Marie sends money to her sister Hela. Bronya and Casimir are given money to help build the sanatorium they have started. Some money is used to buy bonds for the City of Warsaw. Marie gives money to a few of her Polish students, lab assistants and the poorer students at her school. Marie's childhood French teacher, who lives in Poland, had always hoped to make a return visit to France. Marie sends her money for the trip. The Curies have a modern bathroom put in their house and one room has new wallpaper. Marie does not leave her teaching position. She feels strongly that her teaching is a means of supporting women.

The Nobel Prize brings some relief to the Curies' finances,

but it comes at the price of their privacy. Marie writes to her brother, "We are inundated with letters and with visits from photographers and journalists. One would like to dig into the ground somewhere to find a little peace."[56] Aside from the intrusion of time, the reports from the press are infuriating.

The media is more interested in making a story of the Curies' marriage than exploring the nature of their discoveries. *The Vanity Fair* of London writes, "He (Pierre) soon discovered he could not do without her....She fanned the sacred fire in him whenever she saw it dying out."[57] Marie is portrayed as a poor immigrant girl, suffering in a cold apartment as she studies late into the night. Pierre is cast as her saving prince. With Marie portrayed as riding on Pierre's coattails, it's no wonder the public will continue to see Marie in the role of support person. It is inconceivable to the populace that Marie could have accomplished this work. Pierre is the genius and Marie the assistant.

"Mrs. Curie is a devoted fellow laborer in her husband's researches and has associated her name with his discoveries."[58] The *New York Herald*, 1903

A reporter, visiting the Curie house for an interview proves his priority is provocation when his story reads, "Mlle Irene ate all alone, so that her mother could win the Nobel Prize."[59]

"But we're not worth an article. We have only existed since yesterday."[60] Pierre's response to a reporter

Pierre writes his friend Gouy, in January, "I wanted to write to you a long time ago; excuse me if I didn't; it is because of the stupid life I am leading just now. You have seen this sudden fad for radium. This has brought us all the advantages of a moment of popularity; we have been pursued by journalists and photographers of every country on earth; they have even gone so far as to reproduce my daughter's conversation with her nurse and to describe the black-and-white cat we have at home….letters and visits from eccentrics…requests for money…there is not a moment of tranquility."[61] Pierre continues, "Finally, the collectors of autographs, snobs, society people and even at times, scientists, have come to see us…. and every evening there has been a voluminous correspondence to send off. With such a state of things, I feel myself invaded by a kind of stupor. And yet all this turmoil will not perhaps have been in vain, if it results in my getting a Chair and a laboratory…."[62] Pierre will soon get the Chair position at the Sorbonne. The laboratory, won't be up and running for another ten years.

Having their laboratory in the shack, the media pounces on this fodder for their story. One article describes, "…in a narrow, dark and deserted street such as those shown in the etchings to illustrate melodramatic old novels…a lamentable enclosure which had endured the worst insults of time,…entered a laboratory of astonishing simplicity: the floor was of rugged beaten earth, the walls of ruined plaster, the ceiling of rather shaky laths, and the light came in weakly through dusty windows….It was cold drops of water that were falling from a tap…."[63] It is easier to provide readers with this dramatic description rather than a description of the Curies' discoveries.

Marie wants the acknowledgement and credit for their discoveries but by no means hungers for celebrity status. When she is asked, "Aren't you Marie Curie?" She answers, "No, you are mistaken."[64] Pierre writes, "Never have we been less at peace. There are days when we have hardly the time to breathe. And to think that we dreamed of living like wild people far from the other human beings!"[65]

When the Curies are out in public they are the focus of cameras, unabashed stares, and pointed fingers. Strangers come to the laboratory or their home and look through the windows. When Marie and Pierre are attending a concert or the theater, the press makes snide comments about their out of date clothes.

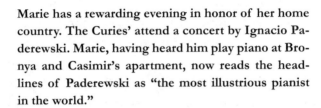

Marie has a rewarding evening in honor of her home country. The Curies' attend a concert by Ignacio Paderewski. Marie, having heard him play piano at Bronya and Casimir's apartment, now reads the headlines of Paderewski as "the most illustrious pianist in the world."

France is pretty close to exemplifying–too little too late. Once the Curies are awarded the Nobel Prize, the president of France visits the laboratory for a photo op. Realizing a decrepit shack is hardly fitting for France's world renowned scientists, a position at the Sorbonne is created for Pierre but not Marie. And for the Academy of Science in Paris, who has rejected Pierre twice, they will finally open their doors to Pierre, but not Marie.

For the school year 1904/05 Pierre is offered a professorship at the Sorbonne, still no laboratory. Pierre replies to the offer saying he will not take the position without a laboratory. The Sorbonne agrees and sets aside funding to build the lab and for staff. (This offer is for only a few rooms and still does not cover the expenses of buying equipment for a laboratory.)[66] The position of chief of laboratory is offered to Marie. It will be the first time she has the official right to be in Pierre's laboratory rather than Pierre asking permission from his superiors.

Marie writes about the frustration of always having to fight for a laboratory, "One cannot help feeling sorrow in realizing that this was a last concession, and that actually one of the first

French scientists never had an adequate laboratory to work in, and this even though his genius had revealed itself as early as his twentieth year....Can we fully imagine the regret of an enthusiastic...worker in a great work, who is retarded in the realization of his dream by the constant lack of means? And can we think without a feeling of profound grief of the waste...of the nation's greatest asset..."[67]

"I have not yet discovered what is the use of the Academy."
Pierre Curie

To become a member of the Academy of Sciences, a person who wants to be a candidate must put forward his name for consideration. A candidate, much like a politician, is expected to go and visit the Academy members and solicit their vote. Pierre writes a friend, "I am not accustomed to this form of activity, demoralizing in the highest degree. I think that nothing is more unhealthy to the spirit than to allow oneself to be occupied with things of this character and to listen to the petty gossip people come to report to you."[68]

Pierre is assured the Academy will vote in his favor. This time, the assurance is correct. Pierre is voted in and writes his friend, "I find myself in the Academy without having desired to be there and without the Academy's desire to have me.... What's the use? In that house they can do nothing simply, without intrigues." Later he writes, "...I went to the institute on Monday, but I must really say I don't know what I was doing there. I have nothing to do with any of the members, and the interest of the meetings is null. I feel very clearly that these circles are not mine."[69]

Pierre's membership at the Academy means a magazine interview for Marie. The article, tilted toward the traditional role for women, asks Marie if she is also expecting a position to the Academy. The article has this response from Marie, "Oh, I'm only a woman, nothing but a woman, I will never have a seat under the Coupole (in the Academy)."[70] When Marie sees the article she is furious at this concocted answer. She writes to the magazine and they acknowledge that the response is a fabrication, but of course, the magazine has already gone out.

In spring of 1904, the Curies continue to struggle with exhaustion. Marie writes to a friend, "The fatigue resulting from an effort which surpassed our strength, and which had been imposed upon us by the unsatisfactory physical conditions of our work was increased by the invasion of publicity. The shattering of our voluntary isolation was a cause of real suffering to us and had all the effects of a disaster."[71]

That same spring, Marie, thirty-six years old, is pregnant. She stops teaching at the Sevres. Drained by all the media attention, and having miscarried in her last pregnancy, she spends more time resting. Bronya comes to help Marie. A baby girl, Eve Denise Curie, is born December 6, 1904.

Eve is a happy baby, full of energy and within weeks, Marie is back to her usual busy schedule. In the mornings she tends to the matters of the house, cares for the children and then is off to teach and her research. Marie maintains her sense of humor. When a stranger admires baby Eve, Marie responds that she doesn't know where the baby came from and that Eve is an orphan. The joke continues as Marie will refer to Eve as "my poor orphan baby."[72]

June 1905, the Curies go to Sweden to give the lecture required of Nobel Prize recipients. Pierre is to give the lecture, not Marie. Whether the Curies' decided to concede this point or not, Pierre makes clear in the presentation that Marie is a full partner in the research, not an 'assistant.' Ten times, Pierre mentions Marie by name in his lecture. Every pronoun is 'our' experiment not 'my'. (When their daughter, Irene and son-in-law jointly receive a Nobel Prize in 1935, both give a presentation. Irene goes first.)

Some scientists are voicing their concerns about radium. One scientist writes, "Radium and radioactivity have transformed the earth into a stock house stuffed with explosives, inconceivably more powerful than any we know of."[73] Pierre also reflects on their concerns. Becoming the most quoted Nobel speech of all time, Pierre states, "They are also a terrible means of destruction in the hands of the great criminals who lead the peoples towards war. I am among those who think, with Nobel, that humanity will obtain more good than evil from the new discoveries."[74]

As Marie is sitting in the front row of the audience, is she missing her father? Twenty-three years earlier Vladislav had seen his daughter receive the gold medal, placing first in class at the gymnasium. Now Marie receives another gold medal, The Nobel Prize for Physics.

Pierre starts his first lecture at the Sorbonne with a tribute to his previous school. Before a large audience he gives credit to the school that had employed him:

"I wish to point out here that we made all our researches at the School of Physics and Chemistry of the City of Paris. In all scientific production the influence of the surroundings in which work is done has a very great importance, and part of the results obtained is due to this influence. For more than twenty years I have been working at the School of Physics. Schutzenberger, the first director of this school, was an eminent man of science. I remember with gratitude that he procured the means of work for me when I was only an assistant; later on, he permitted Mme Curie to come and work with me, an authorization which, at the time, was an innovation far out of the ordinary. The present directors, Mm. Lauth and Gariel, have kept up the same kindliness toward me. The professors of the school and the pupils who have finished their studies constitute a benevolent and productive circle which was very useful to me. It is among the former pupils of the school that we found our collaborators and friends, and I am happy to be able to thank them all here."[75]

Honoring his prior employer and acknowledging their support to not only his research but for Marie as well, is a poke at the Sorbonne. The proverbial–you could have heard a pin drop–seems to apply to the moments after Pierre's introductory words.

As Pierre and Marie settle at the Sorbonne, both are unassuming and willing to help the students. Pierre knows Marie is the better choice for assistance with Math and tells the students to ask to her. Marie writes that Pierre "was always disposed to aid anyone in a difficult situation and even to give of his time which was the greatest sacrifice he could make."[76] An assistant remembers of the Curies, "a more distinguished instance where husband and wife with all their mutual admiration and devotion preserved so completely independence of character, in life as well as in science."[77]

"Science is a wonderful thing if one does not have to earn one's living at it." Albert Einstein[78]

Pierre, having a chair at the Sorbonne, does not enable him to have more free time to work in the laboratory. He writes his friend, "As you have seen, fortune favors us at this moment; but these favors do not come without many worries. We have never been less tranquil than at this moment. There are days when we scarcely have time to breathe..." and "It is now more than a year since I have been able to engage in any research, and I have no moment to myself. Clearly I have not yet discovered a means to defend ourselves against this frittering away of our time which is nevertheless extremely necessary. Intellectually, it is a question of life or death."[79]

7

"A body without a soul..."

"To love someone deeply gives you strength. Being loved by someone deeply gives you courage." D. H. Lawrence

Marie and Pierre garner strength and courage from their love for each other. In the domain of family or physics, their lives compliment and blend together as a duet. They both want to work in the solitude of their laboratory and remain 'indifferent' to the accolades.

"We dreamed of living in a world quite removed from human beings." Pierre Curie[1]

The problem is human beings in the world are consumed with the lure of radiation. Industry is finding more uses, ethical or not, for the Curie's radium. Their 'rock star' status means constant intrusions with no staff to shield them or answer the mail.

Invitations to banquets, box seat tickets for opening shows, honored guests at banquets are all opportunities for the Curies to 'see and be seen.' Their RSVP is usually 'no' and Marie answers 'no' to a request for naming a racehorse 'Marie Curie.' All this is what they don't like and why Marie wrote to her family saying, "Above all, don't forget me!"[2] The Curies prefer quietly working at the laboratory rather than make small talk at an event, especially when small talk leads to gossip. Marie lives by her motto—"We must be interested in things, not in persons."

Although one night, in a wistful moment Pierre sees his beautiful Marie in her gown as they get ready to go out for the evening and he laments, "It's a pity. Evening dress becomes you!"[3]

An invitation they can't refuse is when the French president invites the Curies to a dinner. During the event, the president's wife asks Marie, "Would you like me to introduce you to the king of Greece?" Marie, not realizing who is asking, responds, "I don't see the need."[4] Then Marie realizes it's the president's wife who is asking and responds, "But, of course." Another guest is the ambassador of Austria-Hungary. He represents the government that made it possible for the Curies to have pitchblende. So yes, they must go talk with the ambassador.

There are some highlights in this attention on the Curies. A famous dancer from the United States, Loie Fuller, is known as the 'light fairy.' She writes to the Curies asking how to use radium on her costume. Fuller wants her outfit to glow while she is dancing on stage. The Curies write back and explain that having "butterfly wings of radium" will not work. Loie responds, "I have only one means of thanking you for your having answered me. Let me dance one evening at your house, for the two of you."[5] The Curies agree, but it is more than they bargained for because first the electricians show up to transform the dining room into a stage setting. However, the Curies, touched by Ms. Fuller's genuine kindness and beautiful performance, become close friends.

> Fuller doesn't give up the idea of radium wings. Her assistants experiment with phosphorescent salts. When an explosion blows off their eyebrows and eyelashes, they finally give up. Others pick up the effort and soon nightclub dancers are glowing on stage with costumes covered with radium paint.

Radium is being marketed as a 'cure all.' It's the next generation of a snake oil miracle drug. Companies selling fraudulent products, with false quotes by the Curies, see their sales skyrocket when radium is listed as an ingredient. Claims are made that radium will cure blindness, tuberculosis, and neuralgia. One company claims that radium is added to its fertilizers and it is guaranteed that the farmer's crop will double. When Marie tests the fertilizer, there is no radium.

Health spas offer long soaks in radium mud, rinse with radium water, and a final application of radium crème. Since Viagra hasn't been invented yet, radium is the answer for "sagging men."

The craze will last forty years into the market of toothpaste, tea, health tonic, lipstick, bath salts, and butter. Curie Hair Tonic promises to stop hair loss. Added to an inhaler, radium ensures richer blood. Strap a bag of radium mixture to your waist to heal arthritis. Household products that boast having the power of radium include: heating pads, toys, watches, and clocks. Industry is promising that radium will heat houses and light the streets. There is no regulatory commission to challenge the claims and there is no end to the ideas to make a profit.

The Radium Water Worked Fine Until His Jaw Came Off

* * *

Cancer Researcher Unearths A Bizarre Tale of Medicine And Roaring '20s Society

By Ron Winslow
Staff Reporter of The Wall Street Journal
In 1927, a steel mogul and socialite

Distilled Water and Radium

Dr. Macklis says Mr. Bailey "was a born con man" who had been peddling various miracle cures, especially for impotence, for years. But none achieved the success of Radithor, an over-the-counter tonic he asserted was the result of years of laboratory research, but which was really just distilled water laced with one microcurie each of two isotopes of radium.

He sold more than 400,000 bottles for $1 each—a 400% profit, says Dr. Macklis, adding: "He was the chief impresario in the radioactive patent medicine field."

Mr. Byers was 47 when he fell out of the berth and injured his arm. Over the next several weeks, he complained of muscular

Wall Street Journal article

Into the 1920s there is a drink being sold, Radithor, containing one part radium salts to 60,000 parts zinc sulfide. (This is high considering the energy emitted by pure radium can be diluted up to 600,000 times.) With promises to cure cancer, mental illness, and restore sexual vigor, a wealthy American golf star, Eben Byers, drinks a bottle of Radithor every day for four years. His facial bones disintegrate and he dies of cancer of the jaw.

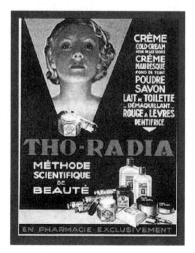

Like the desire to sport the most recent iPhone, men and women attending social gatherings are carrying glass vials of radium bromide in their pockets or purses. Pierre is shocked and writes a paper warning the public of the health risks. His warnings fall on deaf ears.

A doctor, using the name "Alfred Curie" is marketing Crème Tho-Radia. When Marie reads this, she asks a lawyer to write him to stop. Alfred Curie continues.

Until the stories of suffering start to glare, it won't stop.

For the next few years, the public alarm is growing and fifteen deaths are attributed to radium exposure. The shift to more accurate reporting is in spite of the purposeful misinformation and denial from William Bailey, Director of the United States Radium Corporation. Bailey, motivated by corporate greed, invokes Marie's name (without consulting her) as he proclaims, "No one has worked longer or with greater amounts of radium than has Mme Curie. For over twenty-five years she has toiled increasingly in her laboratory and today she is not only alive but reported recently to be in excellent health."[6] It is Bailey's company employing 'dial painters.' The dial painters are the workers who become known as the Radium Girls.

Around 1917, the Radium Girls are female factory workers in New Jersey hired to paint watch dials with a self-luminous paint. Told the paint is harmless, the women are instructed to keep the tip of the brush pointed by licking their paintbrushes. An alarming number of workers start suffering from anemia, bone fractures, and necrosis of the jaw. Five women take the company to court.

The company launches a smear campaign against the women claiming their sickness is due to syphilis. The wheels of justice are slow and wobbly, but the case is eventually won by the women and becomes a cornerstone in the field of health physics and the labor rights movement.

In the meantime, the Curies receive letters requesting information about the technique for extracting and purifying radium. If the Curies had decided to patent their information they would have had a royalty income on all future manufacturing of radium around the world. Years later Marie writes, "No detail was kept secret, and it is due to the information we gave in our publications that the industry of radium has been rapidly developed. Up to the present time this industry hardly uses any methods except those established by us. The treatment of the minerals and the fractional crystallizations are still performed in the same way as I did in my laboratory, even if the material means are increased."[7]

While radium has become the darling of public interest, Marie is watching over her polonium. A German scientist believes polonium is not a new element but instead just a compound. Marie, goes to her lab, renews her research of polonium and writes a paper, in German, to refute the accusations. She explains that the element the German scientist is describing, that he claims to have isolated and discovered, is in fact polonium, what Marie already discovered.[8]

For the summer of 1905, the Curies spend their vacation at the shore. Irene will be eight in September and is flourishing in the nontraditional parenting style of her parents. Irene, more an introvert like her parents, is never required to give a mandatory smile or greeting to adults. Eve, not yet a year old, is already outgoing. During these quiet weeks away with their children, Pierre and Marie enjoy their long walks and equally long talks.

Marie's sister Helena has joined them for the holiday. As Marie and Hela walk the beach they reminisce about their childhood, and that crazy teenage summer visiting relatives and dancing till dawn. The discussion turns to the political unrest that continues in Poland. In January, one demonstration in Warsaw becomes known as Bloody Sunday. More than one hundred and forty thousand peasants and workers, including women and children, marched to the Winter Palace in St. Petersburg to present a petition. The peaceful demonstration ends in disaster when Tsar Nicholas II gives the order to open fire on the crowd. Five thousand innocent civilians are wounded and over one thousand are killed.

Marie worries about her homeland, and she is worrying about Pierre. He has constant pain in his legs. He is unable to walk on the beaches because his balance is so unsteady. Marie tells Helena, "Maybe it is some terrible disease that doctors don't recognize. Maybe Pierre will never be well again."[9]

Returning to Paris, Pierre cuts back on his schedule. There are days he is too weak to dress himself and the pain in his bones keeps him awake at night. When Marie expresses her fear of a life without him, Pierre replies, "It is necessary to continue no matter what."[10]

Spiritualism and séances are in fashion at this time. For women, the séance room gives them a chance at gender equality. The ability to have "otherworld" experiences, see the future, or manifesting spirits is a position of power.

Considering the unknown is revealing itself in forms of new elements and new energy, it is no surprise scientists are searching for answers in the realm of the spiritual. William Crookes, an English chemist and physicist, writes, "Spiritualist phenomena that cannot be explained by any physical law at present known, is a fact of which I am as certain as I am of the most elementary fact of chemistry."[11] Crookes, President of the British Society for Psychical Research, claims to have met a ghost.[12]

Jean Perrin (physicist and Curie's friend) and his wife, Henriette, along with Crookes, George Gouy (physicist), Paul Langevin (physicist), Pierre's brother Jacques all attend numerous séances with the Italian medium Eusapia Paladino. What is a difference from the conventional customers seeking comfort; these visits are comparable to a scientific experiment. Pierre writes to a friend, "I hope we are able to convince you of the reality of the phenomena or at least some of them."[13] He goes on, "The result is that the phenomena really exists. It is not possible for me to doubt it any more. It's unbelievable, but that's the way it is. It is impossible to deny it, after the séances which we have had under conditions of perfect control. Strange, shapeless, fluid members are formed from the medium…separate from her own arms and legs, capable of pushing objects around….What is troubling is that one feels very strongly that by admitting to the existence of some of these phenomena one could, little by little admit the ghosts…How to explain that such transformations of matter can happen so rapidly and without using prodigious quantities of energy."[14]

Pierre is attempting to make sense of this territory of unknown. His curiosity continues, "I wanted to see if the air was ionized [able to conduct electricity] around the medium. But the sound of a small fan which stirred the air was enough to upset her and stop her working. Enough difficulty comes from the fact that she tries to cheat even if she knows how to produce certain phenomena, because this is less tiring for her."[15]

After the last séance Pierre attends, he writes, "There is here in my opinion a whole domain of entirely new facts and physical states in space of which we have no conception."[16]

Eusapia Palladino is later exposed as a fraud. The point remains that these esteemed physicists are willing to consider the scientific possibility in the spirit world. They are unabashed in their search for new knowledge and in their desire to discover unknown sources of energy. The last few years caught scientists by surprise when they realized the discovery of radioactivity came from a source they had written off. Scientists are willing to look under any rock, even spiritual rocks, for the next big revelation.

In January 1906, there is good news for the Curies. Pierre, now a member of the French Academy of Sciences, will be the one to present Marie's latest paper, "On the Diminution of the Radioactivity of Polonium Over Time."[17] (When a person writes this type of paper, is it any wonder the Curies don't enjoy chit chat?)

Family life continues into 1906 with its usual mundane dilemmas. Marie writes to Bronya for advice on parenting and cooking. Marie's journal entries at home are full of notes on skinned knees, fevers, making jellies and domestic duties.

Not so mundane is Pierre's ill health. Pierre is feeling the need to make the most of his time, and he is putting in more hours. This is bothersome to Marie. She is torn with wanting to go to work with Pierre and yet wants to take a small step back and enjoy their young family. They are a couple trying to stay in tune with each other and balance their priorities. It's no different today.

Marie worries about Pierre. She has lost her mother, sister, father, a newborn child, and a nephew. Marie asks him that spring, "Pierre…if one of us disappeared…the other should not survive….We can't exist without each other, can we?" Pierre prophetically responds, "You are wrong. Whatever happens, even if one has to go on like a body without a soul, one must work just the same."[18]

In April, the Curies take a short getaway. Marie is out of sorts that Pierre doesn't leave on the same day with her and the girls. He arrives the next day on the train. Any indication of a spat between Pierre and Marie is the fact that Marie sends Irene to the train station to meet her father.

Peace and tranquility are restored as the family of four goes for a walk through the fields. Irene is chasing butterflies and Eve is toddling through the tall grass. Marie remembers, "Nothing was going to trouble us….We were happy."[19] Pierre reaches over and touches Marie's hair and says, "Life has been sweet with you Marie."[20]

Pierre stays through the weekend, which is Easter Sunday, and leaves on Monday. He takes with him a small bouquet of fresh flowers from their walk. Marie and the girls return to Paris on Wednesday. There are the usual hassles for a mother on the first day back. Marie is busy with the children, laundry, and shopping for food. Pierre is upset with the maid and says her work is sloppy.

The Curies might be world famous physicists, but they are also just a family. This scene could have been any household of working parents with young children. The Curies must stay mindful of their professional responsibility, the needs of their children and yet both of them are in poor health.

Events the next day are going to shake the world. On the side of the United States, citizens of San Francisco suffer the upheaval of an earthquake which leaves behind a broken city. On the side of Europe, the world of science experiences a seismic shift and Marie's heart is broken.

Pierre asks Marie to go with him, but Marie wants to stay with the girls. When Pierre is on his way out he calls up to Marie and asks if she will come later in the afternoon. Marie calls back that she has too much to do. Their friend, Joseph Koval-ski, (the Polish physicist that had introduced them) is coming over for dinner that night. In exasperation, Marie adds to her response, "Don't torment me!"[21]

After his work at the university, Pierre goes to a luncheon and discussion. Pierre, as a means of resolving his irritations with the Academy of Science, has helped form a new group, the "Association of Professors of the Science Faculties." Pierre is vice president and the group's purpose is to challenge the current system that promotes teachers based on seniority rather than ability, to annul rules that deny girls a science edu-cation and to change the dangerous working conditions for lab assistants. These are radical ideas for 1906.

The meeting on this day includes Jean Perrin, Paul Lan-gevin and their dinner guest for that evening, Joseph Kowalski. Pierre, so delighted with the meeting, wants to continue the conversation after the lunch is over. He invites everyone to his house for dinner that evening. When he leaves the meeting, it is raining out and he puts up his umbrella. He needs to stop by a print shop to proof an article he has written.

Is he preoccupied? Is he deep in some train of thought? No one will know. What we know is he steps into the street. He is knocked over by a horse pulling a loaded cart. The horses don't trample him and for a moment it seems Pierre might escape. It's the wheel of the wagon. It crushes his head. Pierre dies instantly.

The wagon driver stops. He is sobbing. A crowd starts to gather at the scene. Cabs are hailed to bring the body to the police station, but they refuse because it is so bloody. Checking the wallet to know the victim's identity, the name Pierre Curie buzzes through the onlookers. Realizing this loss to their country, people start blaming the wagon driver. Someone goes to inform Paul Appell, the dean of the department at the Sorbonne.

Pierre Curie Accident, 1906

Pierre's body is finally taken to the police station. A doctor arrives. Nothing can be done for Pierre except to ease the tremendous blow about to strike his wife. The doctor wraps a bandage around the top of Pierre's crushed skull. He cleans Pierre's face. André Debierne arrives at the police station. Debierne is the one to bring Pierre's body home.

Ahead of Debierne arriving, Paul Appell and Jean Perrin are on their way to the Curie's home. They are in shock with this divergence from reality. Just a few hours earlier Perrin was talking with a happy Pierre who was inviting everyone for dinner.

Dr. Curie answers the door to see these two men he has known for years. Dr. Curie realizes immediately that something is horribly wrong. Appell and Perrin ask to see Marie. Dr. Curie doesn't answer their request. Instead he says, "My son is dead." Appell and Perrin explain what has happened. Dr. Curie is crying and says, "What was he dreaming of this time?"[22]

Marie, out finishing errands, comes home with the girls. Paul Appell tells Marie what has happened. Marie cannot fathom Appell's words. The world becomes surreal with this sudden devastating news. She responds, "Pierre is dead? Dead? Absolutely dead?"[23]

Marie leaves the room and goes out to sit in the garden. Thousands of raindrops are pouring down from the sky. Nature, that Pierre had loved, turns her spring rain into tears of mourning. Marie sits on the garden bench, waiting for Pierre's body to be brought home.

The police inspector arrives with Pierre's belongings for Marie. Marie looks at Pierre's keys, wallet, and watch. His belongings look normal, like nothing has ever happened. Debierne arrives with the ambulance and tremors shake Marie as Pierre's body is placed in a room downstairs. Marie goes in the room and shuts the door behind her.

"I shall not attempt to describe the grief of the family left by Pierre Curie." Marie Curie[24]

Not only to describe the grief is painful but it is private and by now we understand the Curies' need for privacy. Marie does record, "In the study room to which he was never to return, the water buttercups he had brought from the country were still fresh."[25] That is the insight, the shock of sudden grief or calamity, your world has just shattered, and wrenched emotions come with seeing these flowers. On one level the flowers, free of this tragedy, are the sweet memory of their recent time together. On another level, considering the enormous shock that Marie has just felt, how did this not hit the flowers too? How has the vase not crashed to the floor as Pierre's body passed by? How do the flowers not wilt from the quaking grief coming from behind the door?

A message is sent across the yard to the Perrin's house where Irene is playing. Marie, shielding her daughter from this gruesome catastrophe, asks if Irene can stay the next few days. Marie sends a telegram to Bronya. Does Marie struggle to find the words to a reality so new and awful? The telegram says, "Pierre dead result accident."[26]

Jacques arrives the next morning. Marie and Jacques, too stunned for words, can only cry.

Any privacy is short lived. Over the next few days, the doorbell is a continual interruption as it announces each visitor. The president of the republic, the president of the council, and senior members of the Sorbonne are arriving at the Curies' home. These are condolences from the very people who had cared so little about Pierre and now they are invading Marie's privacy.

If the doorbell isn't announcing a guest, it is declaring the arrival of another telegram. Aside from the obligatory notes, many are sincere expressions of grief and sorrow from royalty, scientists, and everyday people. Pierre's laboratory assistant writes later, "…his immense kindness extended even to his humblest servants, who adored him: I have never seen sincerer or more harrowing tears than those shed by his laboratory attendants at the news of his sudden decease."[27] Lippmann writes to Marie, "It seems to me that I have lost a brother: I did not know by what bonds I was attached to your husband, and I know it today. I suffer also for you, Madame."[28]

And Marie is suffering. She writes in her journal, ""Pierre, my Pierre, you are there, calm as a poor wounded man sleeping with his head wrapped up....Your lips, which I used to call greedy, are pale and colorless. Your little beard is touched with gray. Your hair is hardly visible because the wound starts there, and above your forehead, to the right, is the bone that has been broken. Oh! How you were hurt, how you bled, your clothes were soaked in blood. What a terrible shock your head suffered, your poor head that I stroked so often, taking it in my two hands....I would kiss your eyelids, which you would close so that I could touch them, bending your head down to me with a familiar gesture...."[29]

Making plans for the funeral, the French government wants to suddenly honor their favorite son not with the laboratory he was promised for years but with a state funeral. Marie, knowing Pierre's desire to minimize the fuss, declines. She will not have Pierre's funeral a public event. The burial will be at the Sceaux cemetery where Pierre's mother is buried. It will take place Saturday, three days after Pierre's death. There will be no grand funeral, no ceremony, and no speeches. Guests will be family and friends, only.

"Your coffin was closed and I couldn't see you anymore. I couldn't let them cover it with the awful black cloth. I covered it with flowers and sat down next to it."[30] Marie

Marie writes, "...They came to get you, an unhappy group, I looked at them, I didn't talk to them. We took you back to Sceaux and we watched you go down into the large, deep hole.

Then there was a frightful parade of people. They wanted to take us away. We resisted, Jacques and I, we wanted to watch till the very end. They filled up the grave, they put sheaves of flowers on it, it was all over. Pierre was sleeping his last sleep under the earth. It was the end of everything, everything, everything."[31]

Paul Langevin, gives a eulogy of his friend, and teacher "my finest memories of my school years are those of moments passed there standing before the blackboard where he took pleasure in talking with us, in awakening in us fruitful ideas, and in discussion of research which formed our taste for the things of science."[32]

On April 22, the day Pierre is buried, *Le Journal* has this: "On the arm of her father-in-law, Mme Curie followed her husband's coffin to a grave that had been dug at the base of the cemetery wall in the shadow of the chestnut trees. There she remained motionless for a moment, with a fixed and hard look on her face; but when a spray of flowers was brought up to the grave, she took it suddenly and began pulling out the flowers one by one and scattering them over the coffin. She did this slowly and deliberately and seemed to have completely forgotten the other people gathered there, who were deeply impressed and did not make a sound. The master of ceremonies, however, felt obliged to warn Mme Curie that she would have to receive the condolences of the people present. Then, without saying a word, she let the bouquet fall to the ground and rejoined her father-in-law."[33]

At a time when Marie, grieving her husband, friend, and intimate work partner should be able to forget "the other people gathered" there is pressure to meet the public expectations. Previously, Pierre and Marie would withstand this pressure together. Now, Marie will face the challenge alone.

Eve writes these insights, "It is commonplace to say that a sudden catastrophe may transform a human being forever. Nevertheless, the decisive influence of these minutes upon the character of my mother, upon her destiny and that of her children, cannot be passed over in silence. Marie Curie did not change from a happy young wife to an inconsolable widow. The metamorphosis was less simple and more serious. The interior tumult that lacerated Marie, the nameless horror of her wandering ideas, were too virulent to be expressed in complaints or in confidences. From the moment when those three words, "Pierre is dead," reached her consciousness, a cape of solitude and secrecy fell upon her shoulders forever. Mme Curie, on that day in April, became not only a widow, but at the same time a pitiful and incurably lonely woman."[34]

Marie is now "the famous widow."[35] Headlines from the *New York Times* blare, "Prof. Curie Killed in Paris Street." Marie's age, thirty-eight, and the fact that Pierre is dead, might be the only accuracy in the media. The torrent of misinformation due to blind spots or purposeful slant begins–"Success Followed Early Hardship- Curie Was Greatly Aided by Mme. Curie." "In his researches he was aided by Marie Sklodowska, a Pole, who was born at Warsaw, in 1868." and the article claims Pierre leaves behind–one daughter.[36]

Marie writes about the funeral day, "…We put you into the coffin Saturday morning, and I held your head up for this move. We kissed your cold face for the last time. Then a few periwinkles from the garden on the coffin and the little picture of me that you called "the good little student" and that you loved. It is the picture that must go with you into the grave, the picture of her who had the happiness of pleasing you enough so that you did not hesitate to offer to share your life with her, even when you had seen her only a few times. You often told me that this was the only occasion in your life when you acted without hesitation, with the absolute conviction that you were doing well. My Pierre, I think you were not wrong. We were made to live together, and our union had to be."[37]

Marie later reflects on the effect on Irene of losing Pierre. "The loss of her father will weigh on her existence, and we will never know how much harm this will have done to her. Because I dreamed, my Pierre, and I often told you so, that this daughter, who promised to resemble you in her serious, calm thoughtfulness, would become your workmate as soon as possible. And that she would owe the best of herself to you. Who will give her what you could have?"[38] And for Eve, too young to remember her father, Marie remembers the last night with Pierre. She writes, "Eve was ill. I made you take your shoes off to avoid noise. At night Eve woke and I had to rock her in my arms. Then I put her down between us…you kissed her several times. She went to sleep soon after…."[39] Suffering the loss of having a partner to discuss hopes and dreams for their children, Marie writes, "We were talking about education which interested us so much…It was to give children a great love of nature, of life and the curiosity to explore them. You thought like me and felt that we shared a rare and admirable mutual understanding."[40]

Marie is not prepared for how to handle the news with Irene. The day after the funeral Marie goes to see Irene at the Perrin's house. She tells Irene that her father has died. Irene, who is eight years old, is quiet and leaves the room. Marie says to Mrs. Perrin, "She's too young, she doesn't understand."[41]

When Marie leaves, Irene is found crying and wants to go home. When Irene goes home she sees her mother sobbing. A few days later, Marie writes of Irene, "Now she doesn't seem to be thinking about it anymore."[42] Marie, in a state of shock, is not able to take in any more anguish than her own and misjudges her eldest daughter. Where Marie is emotionally absent, filling any gaps for Irene and Eve are Aunt Bronya, Grandfather Curie, Uncle Jacques and Uncle Joseph. With a life story of support for each other, this is one more chapter.

Marie remains far away in her grief, wrestling with the turmoil of loss. Her brain waves are unable to cross the fault line that has gaped open. Mourning is difficult for a person to maneuver in private life, but, worse for a public figure.

"Everyone is talking. And all I can see is Pierre, Pierre on his deathbed."[43] journal entry by Marie

Marie writes in her journal, "My Pierre, I can't stop thinking about you, my head is bursting and my mind is confused. I can't understand that from now on I have to live without seeing you, without smiling at my life's sweet friend."[44] And a few days later she writes, "My Pierre, I get up after having slept quite well, relatively calm. Hardly a quarter of an hour later and here I am again wanting to howl like a wild animal."[45]

And what is the torment that raises her grief to a howl? Remorse. She writes, "In the morning you went out in a hurry...You left, and asked me from downstairs if I was going to the laboratory. I answered that I had no idea and begged you not to torment me. And this is how you left. And the last sentence I spoke to you was not a sentence of love and tenderness. And I only saw you again dead."[46] Marie's last words to Pierre, haunts her.

The Curie tombstone at the cemetery now bears his name. Marie goes to visit. She writes, "Yesterday, at the cemetery, I did not succeed in understanding the words, "Pierre Curie" engraved on the stone. The beauty of the countryside hurt me, and I put my veil down so as to see everything through my crepe." "I want to tell you, I want to tell you, I want to tell you."[47]

As the days go by she reveals, "I sometimes have the absurd idea that you are going to come back. Didn't I have it yesterday, when hearing the sound of the front door closing, the absurd idea that it was you?"[48] For the Curies, being spiritualists, her wondering is more than wishful thinking. She writes, "I put my head against [the coffin]…I spoke to you. I told you that I loved you and that I had always loved you with all my heart.… It seemed to me that from this cold contact of my forehead with the casket something came to me, something like a calm and an intuition that I would yet find the courage to live. Was this an illusion or was this an accumulation of energy coming from you and condensing in the closed casket which came to me as an act of charity on your part?"[49]

Wavering with the will to move forward, Marie is suffering. Every aspect of her life is crushed and must be restructured. Eve describes the multiple points of connection between her parents, all the things Marie is missing. Eve writes, "Ideas big and little, questions, remarks and advice were thrown back and forth at every hour of the day between Pierre and Marie. Compliments too, and friendly reproaches. Between these two equals, who admired each other passionately but could never envy, there was a worker's comradeship, light and exquisite, which was perhaps the most delicate expression of their profound love."[50]

Marie can only grieve. "I endure life, but…never again will I be able to enjoy it.…I will never be able to laugh genuinely until the end of my days. I no longer am able to devote any time to social life. All our friends in common will tell you that I never see them any more except for business, for questions concerning work or education of the children. No one visits me, and I don't see anyone and I haven't been able to avoid offending some people in my circle and my laboratory who don't find me sufficiently friendly.…I have completely lost the habit of conversations without a set goal."[51]

But what is not lost is her North Star sense of scientific integrity. Dr. Curie and others suggest to Marie that she make the radium she has produced her personal property. Worth a million francs, they point out this would assure her daughters' financial future. Even in this chapter of darkness and insecurity, Marie stands by her previous decision to donate the radium to the laboratory.[52] Marie will also uphold the decision of her and Pierre's to keep public their techniques.

Trying to find solace, Marie goes to their laboratory. The question of how to continue confronts her. She writes, "…I want to talk to you in the silence of this laboratory, where I did not think I could live without you. I tried to make a measurement for a graph on which each of us had made some points, but…I felt the impossibility of going on…The laboratory had an infinite sadness and seemed a desert. It seems at one moment that I feel nothing and that I can work and then the anguish returns."[53]

The simple act of walking down the street is filled with torment. "In the street I walk as though hypnotized, without care about anything. I will not kill myself…[but] among all these carriages, isn't there one which will make me share the fate of my beloved?"[54]

Making public Marie's journal entries might appear a violation of her privacy except there are records of Marie's requests to destroy some of her writing. What has been made public has been sifted through by her daughter Eve. For the journal entries, now in print, it is plausible these writings are Marie's way of saying what she wants known. Marie knows her life will be recorded with or without her input and she is all too aware of the media warping stories about the Curies. If they start to twist the story of her and Pierre, Marie wants her words as a record. What Marie wants known is the complete devotion Pierre and Marie had for each other.

The family must adjust around the great yawning gaps of having no father, husband, friend and son. Dr. Curie asks Marie if she would rather he move in with his son Jacques. Marie replies, "If you went away it would hurt me. But you should choose what you prefer." Dr. Curie replies, "What I prefer, Marie, is to stay with you always."[55]

And how to make your way back, the slow crawl out of the deep pit. Marie writes, "Yesterday for the first time since the terrible day, something funny Irene said made me laugh, but I was hurting while I was laughing. Do you remember how you reproached yourself for laughing…after your mother's death?…I try to start living again. I think it is an illusion…I realize, however, if I am to have the least chance of success in my work, I must not think any more of my misery by working.…But the very idea of it revolts me. It seems to me after having lost Pierre I will never be able to laugh from the heart till the end of my days."[56]

A burden for the family after the death of an income earner is the question, 'What about finances?' Pierre's friends suggest having a public collection. Marie says 'no.'

What about the Sorbonne? What will they do with the vacancy of Pierre's position? Will they allow Marie to still be chief of the school's laboratory?

The obvious choice is for the Sorbonne to offer Pierre's position to Marie. Her qualifications are equal to Pierre's, except one. Marie is not a man. The Sorbonne hedges and offers Marie a pension like they allotted to Louis Pasteur's widow. If the committee is hoping Marie will accept their offer and slip quietly into the shadows, they are disappointed. Marie declines the offer and informs the Sorbonne she will work and earn her own living.

The faculty knows Marie is the only person qualified to replace Pierre, yet they can't fathom a woman teaching at the Sorbonne, let alone hold the position of a chair. In this self-inflicted quandary, the Faculty of Sciences makes an offer. They suggest Marie become the director of the laboratory (still needing to be built) and that Pierre's chair stay empty. Marie would be expected to do Pierre's job without officially having the title. Finding this loophole allows the Sorbonne to still uphold their policy that no women are on their teaching staff.

At this point, Marie's colleagues pressure the Sorbonne to offer Marie the position Pierre held. Jacques Curie and Georges Gouy tell the dean of faculty that Marie is the only French physicist able to continue the work. Still in a dither, the Sorbonne makes the offer of assistant professor. Marie takes the position. Marie, teaching the only classes on radioactivity in the world, is not promoted to full professor until 1908.[57]

A newspaper headline declares, "A Great Victory for Feminism."[58] The article points to the obvious, "For if a woman is allowed to teach upper-level courses to students of both sexes, what does that say about so-called male superiority? I tell you, the time is very near when women will become human beings."[59]

Marie records no entries in her journal of rancor and bitterness. There is sadness to the circumstance but not spite. Marie writes in her journal, "I also want to tell you that they nominated me for your chair and some imbeciles congratulated me…I cannot conceive of anything which would give me real personal happiness, except perhaps scientific work, and not even that, because if successful, I would be distressed that you didn't know about it. This laboratory gives me an illusion of keeping the remains of your life…I found a little picture of you near the scales, with such a lovely smiling expression that I can't look at it without sobbing, since I will never again see that sweet smile."[60]

Pierre had already given Marie the encouragement to go on when he had told her earlier, "Whatever happens, even if one has to go on like a body without a soul, one must work just the same."[61] Marie follows Pierre's direction and becomes the first woman to teach at the Sorbonne. She is the first woman to hold a full science professorship at a university that has had a 'glass ceiling' in place for 750 years. Her first lecture will be in November, 1906.

PART THREE

CONTEXT AND COMMENTARY 3

The Liberation of Man ~ Breaking the Patriarchal Contract

It's not about 'Women's Lib.' It's about the liberation of men and women to be free from the Patriarchal Contract that pressures society to uphold a mantra that keeps both men and women in a preordained role. Upholding the contract leaves no one free to explore their full potential. Women catering to object roles such as 'eye candy' and men struggling to be 'machismo' are trapped in a performance.

The Patriarchal Contract is inherently a life of living on the surface.

While we continue the journey of Marie, here are just a few quotes and stories showing the context for Marie's struggle to live authentically as a scientist.

1873 – "Higher education for women produces monstrous brains and puny bodies; abnormally active cerebration and abnormally weak digestion; flowing thought and constipated bowel."

E.H. Clarke, *Sex in Education: A Fair Chance for Girls*, 1873

SEX IN EDUCATION;

OR,

A FAIR CHANCE FOR GIRLS.

BY

EDWARD H. CLARKE, M.D.,
MEMBER OF THE MASSACHUSETTS MEDICAL SOCIETY; FELLOW OF
THE AMERICAN ACADEMY OF ARTS AND SCIENCES;
LATE PROFESSOR OF MATERIA MEDICA
IN HARVARD COLLEGE,
ETC., ETC.

BOSTON:
HOUGHTON, MIFFLIN AND COMPANY.
The Riverside Press, Cambridge.
1884.

1889 – The names of seventy-two Grand Prix recipients are etched in stone on the Eiffel Tower. (Eiffel does this as a means of quelling the protests against the tower.) Not included is the recipient Marie Sophie Germain. This is particularly galling since Germain's work explores the elasticity of metal which helped to make the construction of the Eiffel Tower possible.

The Grand Prix names are engraved on all four sides of the tower, in the squares just below the platform above the arch.

1902 – Simmons College offers a 1-year domestic science program referred to as the "diamond ring" course.

1903 – Not allowed to check into a hotel by themselves, women start the Colony Club as a place in New York City to gather or rent a room for the night.

Coach leaving the Colony Club in 1911

1903 – *The Settlement Cookbook*, by Lizzie Black includes the tagline, "The way to a man's heart." The tagline continues at least into the 50s as seen on this cover.

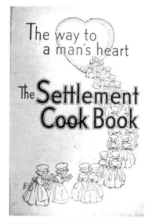

The Settlement Cookbook
1950s edition

1900s–Propaganda against suffragettes

1905 – Former president **Grover Cleveland** writes this in an article for *Ladies' Home Journal*, April 1905, "Sensible and responsible women do not want to vote…The relative positions to be assumed by men and women in the working out of our civilization were assigned long ago by a higher intelligence than ours."

Cleveland's letter, dated June 26, 1905, informing *Ladies Home Journal* that he is sending the article

Musée Curie (coll. ACJC)

1910 – Vanity Fair Cover of Marie and Pierre. What's wrong with this picture?

1929 – "Light a Lucky and you'll never miss sweets that make you fat." Lucky Strikes cigarettes advertisement

1950s – Rules for a stewardess: must be 5-foot-2 or more, weigh less than 130 pounds, not married, no children, retire by age 32.

Most women average just 18 months on the job. The organization, Stewardesses for Women's Rights, is organized in the 1970s and it forces airlines to change their policies. The mandatory retirement age is dropped by the 1980s along with the marriage restriction. Weight restrictions don't end until the 1990s.

Airline Stewardesses 1950s

1967 – Women are not allowed to run in the Boston Marathon. It's too far to run for a "fragile woman."

Kathy Switzer, Boston Marathon 1967

Picture 1: #261, Kathy Switzer is the first woman (numbered) to run in the Boston Marathon. Race official, Jock Semple, is seen in photo 1 trying to knock Switzer out of the race. Semple shouts "Get the hell out of my race and give me those numbers."

Picture 2: #390, Tom Miller, Switzer's boyfriend, is knocking Semple away.

It won't be until 1972 that women are officially recognized to participate in the Boston Marathon.

1974 – March 4th, fifty women's groups picket the *New York Times* for their refusal to use the designation "Ms." The *Times* doesn't concede until the mid 1980s.

Several men in Marie's life refuse to live by the Patriarchal Contract; Pierre, Vladislav, Dr. Curie, Debierne, Jean Perrin, Petit, Emile Borel, Gabriel Lippmann, Jacques Curie, her brother Joseph, and her cousin Joseph. Without their courage to stand up to the traditions of the day, it is doubtful we would have the advancements to science and society by Marie Curie. So let us move on with Marie's story.

Marie is already a member of the Swedish, Dutch, Czech, and Polish Academies, the American Philosophical Society and the Imperial Academy in St. Petersburg. A few French citizens think it's a little embarrassing that Marie is not yet a member of the French Academy of Sciences.

A feminist of the time, Marguerite Durand writes, "The principle of masculine supremacy is going to crumble because nothing justifies it in a time when the power of brains is happily more important than that of muscles."[1] Durand relates of the feminist perspective, "It isn't admiration that it claims, it's equity."

The rebuttal to Durand is not from a man but from a woman. The journalist Madame Regnier answers, "One must not try…to make of woman the equal of the man! The more we differ from him, the more we are ourselves….The "equal of the man" these words alone are terrible! They destroy all that which makes for grace, charm, beauty, fantasy; they abolish all privileges; they ban our tyranny, they give us rights, these famous rights which forbid us to have caprices….Mesdames (Marie), you must not become part of the Academies." Regnier adds, "The most illustrious women of past times, who still shine, have been the lovers. The most surprising glory is to love and to be loved and it is by love alone that some women can hope to be numbered one day among the immortals."[2]

> Madame Regnier would have liked the role of women in John Wayne movies.

Marie has no desire to be 'numbered one day among the immortals (male noun)'. Marie will be counted as an *Immortelle*.

8

"When one considers the progress..."

It would be nice to finish chapter seven as an end to Marie's grief. As a writer, I don't want to risk boring you with more references to this period in her life. However, if we are to travel this journey of knowing Marie, then we must know the following months continue with near despair. Let us not be akin to the master of ceremonies at Pierre's funeral, who hurried Marie to end her time of mourning.

In the months following Pierre's death, Bronya is with Marie. One evening in June, Marie asks Bronya to come into her room. Marie is kneeling beside the fire in the fireplace and has a bundle on the floor beside her. As Marie opens the package, Bronya sees the clothes Pierre was wearing the day of the accident. Marie unfolds his shirt revealing the stains of dried mud and blood. Chips of bone and bits of brain are gruesome and haunting remnants of Pierre. Marie is cutting the clothes into pieces and throwing the scraps into the fire.

This is one more step of Marie saying goodbye. She is crying and explains to Bronya, "I could not have endured having this touched by indifferent hands." And then she sobs, "And now, tell me how I am going to manage to live? I know that I must, but how shall I do it? How can I do it?"[1]

These are not rhetorical questions. The cry is in earnest. Tragedy has ripped Marie from a familiar journey to a lonely exile in a foreign place. With no regard for her fragile state of mind, questions are flooding the senses with these startling new realities she must face. Marie writes, "I do not have a happy or serene soul by nature, and I latched onto Pierre's sweet serenity in order to find courage. And this source has gone."[2]

"And this source has gone." is a repeating swell of anguish as Marie must face each dimension of her old life that has been swept away. Marie has lost someone who understood her. Private insecurities, dislikes, frustrations, as well as strength of opinions and insights—were safe in Pierre's confidence. Marie has lost someone who defended her. Pierre believed in her from the beginning of their research, when she knew there was an element and decided to find it. In a misogynist world that wanted to deny Marie the Nobel Prize, Pierre pushed back and won. Pierre, who had repeated Marie's name in the Nobel acceptance speech, will never again say Marie's name. She will write his biography, stressing again and again his noble character. She wants the world to know he was a great man of science and a great man of character. But now she must figure out how she will go on without him.

"Before meeting you, I had never met a man like you, and never since then have I seen as perfect a human being. If I hadn't known you, I would never have known that it was possible to know of it."[3] Marie Curie

Jacques writes a gentle note of encouragement, "I hope… that you have found the energy to overcome your despondency; you are the center of a little world and your responsibility is great. You must revive and carry on in spite of everything."[4]

Marie will revive. We can thank Lord Kelvin. In the months following Pierre's death, Kelvin is challenging Marie's work.

Lord Kelvin, who had come to visit Pierre in his lab, who had requested Pierre send copies of his equipment so Kelvin himself could use it, who had sat beside Marie while Pierre gave his speech in London, and who has just attended Pierre's funeral…that Lord Kelvin. He has published an argument claiming that radium is not an element.

To disagree, critique, or question is not what is disturbing. Lord Kelvin, world renowned scientist and a member of science societies, knows that when writing a rebuttal to scientific claims the statement is to be published in a scientific journal. This puts the article in front of a jury of peers who have an educated eye to evaluate the merits of the arguments. Instead Kelvin, using his name/influence has his rebuttal printed in the *Times* of London. Capturing the frenzy of radium, Kelvin states that the radium is only a compound of lead and helium.[5] He claims the Curies made a mistake in calling this a new element and implies the Curies did not deserve the Nobel Prize. If this is true–the Curie's work is nothing.

The back-story for Kelvin making this claim: If the Curies' work on radium is true, it contradicts Kelvin's work. Kelvin has previously stated that the age of the Earth is twenty million years old. Marie's work makes Kelvin's proclamation incorrect. (Ernest Rutherford defends the Curies' work and challenges Kelvin with an article in the publication *Nature*.) Marie doesn't respond to Lord Kelvin with a written dispute. She goes to the laboratory and will crush the debate there.

Marie, the woman who sifted through tons of pitchblende and extracted a quarter teaspoon of radium, now reclaims from the ashes of her life the will to follow Pierre's directive, "one must work just the same." To refute Kelvin's claim against the findings of their research, Marie must produce a perfectly pure metallic radium sample.

Marie is back in the laboratory. With Debierne's help, the work will take three years and the result is a tiny square of shiny white metal. Marie explains, it "has never been repeated...because it involves a serious danger of loss of radium which can be avoided only with utmost care. At last I saw the mysterious white metal, but I could not keep it in this state, for it was required for further experiment."[6] This experiment is so difficult it has never been repeated.

Lord Kelvin won't be able to apologize. One year after his allegations, he dies. As for Marie, some critics had also doubted polonium, so she puts that argument to rest also. Marie and Debierne produce enough polonium to identify that it is indeed its own element.

In 1906, a scholarship fund to support the Curie's research is set up by Andrew Carnegie. Mr. Carnegie does not want the scholarship in his own name. It will be called "The Curie Foundation." He stipulates that Marie is to be given full control. Marie uses the funds to recruit student scientists, men and women, from around the world to come and study under her direction.

The grace and generosity of Marie's character will reach as far as China. At the temple of Confucius at Taiyuan-fu, there is a portrait of Marie hanging as one of the 'benefactors of humanity.' Alongside her portrait are Descartes, Newton, the Buddhas, and the emperors of China.[7]

November 5, 1906–Marie is scheduled to start teaching her

class at the Sorbonne. It's an historic moment. She is the first woman to ever lecture from these glorified halls. A crowd is packing the auditorium by noon. Marie's lecture is not scheduled to start until one-thirty. Most of the audience are gawkers and won't understand the class but they will be able to claim, "I was there!"

Marie is not at the Sorbonne. Marie is at the cemetery in Sceaux, standing by Pierre's grave. Is Marie reminiscing that a mere fifteen years ago she was crossing the Sorbonne courtyard for the first time? Does Marie murmur to Pierre the memory from three years earlier when they had ridden their bicycles to the Sorbonne on the day she gave her doctoral defense? Now she must go to the Sorbonne alone. Her journal entries are empty. For this private moment at Pierre's tombstone, Marie is silent.

Customarily, the first day of class is opened by the Dean of Faculty, Paul Appell, introducing the new person to hold the chair. Included in the introduction is a small speech extolling the previous chair person. Marie has requested that Appell make no mention of Pierre and instead simply introduce her.

Crowds unable to fit in the grand hall are spilling down the corridors. The audience includes Sorbonne students and Marie's students from the Sevres. The Polish community has turned out as an expression of pride in their fellow Pole. Irene and Dr. Curie are in the sea of faces. Photographers are ready with their cameras pointed at the grand entrance. Journalists have pencils poised to describe the moment when Marie extols a tearful tribute to her belated husband.

Marie does not come in through the usual door. She enters through a side door. With heads cranked in the wrong direction, most of the spectators don't even notice that Marie, wearing her usual black dress, is already at the lecture table.

As unassuming as her entrance, Marie does not succumb to any desire for attention or playing to the audience's petty expectations. She starts her lecture in a poignant quiet voice at the exact point in the notes where Pierre had left off. "When one considers the progress that has been made in physics in the past ten years…"[8] The room is transfixed in this noble moment. Do they comprehend how perfectly poignant is the scene? Marie's voice is breathing life into Pierre's notes. When Marie finishes her lecture, the crowd erupts into applause. Marie collects her notes and leaves through the side door.

After the first day, Marie writes in her journal, "You would have been happy to see me as a professor at the Sorbonne, and I myself would have so willingly done it for you. But to do it in your place, my Pierre, could one dream of a thing more cruel…I really feel that all my will to live is dead in me, and I only have my duty to bring up my children and also to continue on the path I have accepted. Perhaps, also the wish to prove to the world and especially to myself that the one that you have loved so much really has some value. I also have the vague hope…that you might know about my life of pain and effort and that you would be grateful. And so that I might, perhaps, find you more easily in the other life, if there is one."[9] Marie adds, "Tomorrow I will be 39…"[10]

When Marie expresses the desire to "prove to the world" her value, the proving will need to be to women as well as men. Women have a vested interested in **not** wanting an example to be available to themselves or their daughters of how they too can reach for the stars. A few months after Marie's first lecture at the Sorbonne a popular novelist, Colette Yvert, has a book release, *Princesses of Science*. It is a huge success and is awarded, by an all female panel, the Prix Femina Award. Here's the story line:

> *The heroine is a doctor's daughter who becomes a doctor and practices medicine. All seems to be going well, she marries and has a child. Tragedy hits when the cook quits and the collars of her husband's shirts are not properly starched. The drama ramps up when their infant child dies and then the inevitable demise of every woman who would dare to have a life, her husband runs to the arms of another woman. The heroine comes to her senses, realizes she should not try to live up to what her father wants and instead live the traditional role of a mother and wife.*

This is the society backlash that Marie is facing, with no Pierre at her side.

Marie is once again consumed with her work in the laboratory. Staying late into the night, she is returning to the lab early each morning. She is completing experiments Pierre had been pursuing for his book. Marie writes the second half of the manuscript and gives no credit to herself for the six hundred page book, *Works of Pierre Curie*.

Neglecting her health, Marie can't keep up the pace. When she faints and falls in the laboratory, her family is called. Eve writes, "Jacques and Marie's brother and sister, Joseph and Bronya, observed with terror the movements of this black-robed woman, the automaton Marie had become: stiff, absent-minded, the wife who had not joined the dead seemed already to have abandoned the living."[11]

For Irene, there are nights she wakes up from nightmares and is worried that her mother might be dead too. Eve remembers seeing her mother staring into space or another time she sees her mother collapse. A step out of this fog of grief is when Marie decides to move from her house in Paris. Dr. Curie, the girls, a Polish housekeeper, and Marie move to Sceaux.

For the back garden of their new house, Marie has gymnastic equipment built for Irene and Eve. The daily regimen of the daughters includes exercise and swimming lessons. The girls go for hikes, take bicycle trips, and learn to ride a horse. They also learn to cook and sew, and when they each turn eleven, they are allowed to walk the streets by themselves. The tragedy of their father's death does not make Marie an overprotective mother. Instead, Marie insists her daughters be able to live independent lives when they grow up.

Marie, Eve and Irene in the back garden of their house, 1908,
Musée Curie (coll. ACJC)

Irene writes about those years, "My mother tried to give us every chance to exercise. We swam, rowed, and skated. We did gymnastics, cycling, and riding on horseback…Regarding thunderstorms–she got us interested in what thunderstorms consisted of–teaching us, for example, to count the number of seconds which elapsed between the lightning and the thunder's noise: this enabled us to estimate…I suppose her own daily behaviour was what influenced us. She had always taken chances to accomplish what she intended to do and she was not, by nature, a prudent person."[12]

Marie, although a working, single mom, has family support. Bronya suggests a sister-in-law from Poland come to live with Marie in the role of a governess for the girls. Not only does this keep the children surrounded with loving family, it ensures the girls learn to speak Polish.

Dr. Curie, his serene spirit, is a peaceful presence in the house. He is the one to talk with the girls and tell them stories about their father. (Marie will always find it too painful to talk about Pierre.) Providing the girls with a semblance of standing in for their father, Eve writes of their grandfather, "He would talk and laugh and he was absolute joy to the children. Especially Irene, whom he understood so well because she was so much like her father, his son."[13]

The summer of 1906 when Irene is away visiting friends, Dr. Curie writes to her, "My dear Irene, my dear big grandchild, this letter from Eve is a thank you for your postcards. I think you will recognize her style." He writes the sounds, "Eu, eu, eu, eu."[14] Later Irene sends her grandfather a letter and she signs, "Your little Irene of nothing at all." Grandfather writes back, "No, you are not a little Irene of nothing at all. You are…my big Irene. Irene of everything. My big Irene of six slices of bread and butter who would smother a little Irene of nothing at all…"[15]

Within the family circle is André Debierne. Continuing as Marie's assistant, he visits on Sundays bringing treats for the girls. Eve delights in drawing pictures with André and Irene wants to do algebra problems. The differences between the girls are clear.

Marie writes of Eve, "She begins at three years and four months to pick out an air, 'Au Clair de la Lune,' on the piano… At four years, she knows how to play around thirty airs and songs." Marie later asks Paderewski to listen to Eve play, wanting to know if he thinks Eve has an exceptional ability. Marie writes in her journal, "I had intuition about it, I who understand nothing of music. I felt very much that she didn't play like just anyone."[16]

For Irene, it is abundantly clear that her talent is math not music. Irene will later be asked if Marie forced her to pursue science. Irene gives this response, "That one must do some work seriously and must be independent and not merely amuse oneself in life–this our mother has told us always, but never that science was the only career worth following."[17]

Marie is determined to see that her daughters' education is nothing short of exceptional. She expresses her misgivings about regular school in a letter to her sister Hela. "I sometimes have the feeling that it would be better to drown the children than to shut them up in the sort of schools we have now."[18] Marie devises a plan for not only her daughters but also the children of several professors of the Sorbonne. Marie arranges that each professor has one day of the week to teach the children.

Thursday is Marie's day to teach science to the young students. She sets up experiments for them to learn through experience. Challenging their critical thinking skills, Marie asks the children how to keep a pan of boiling water hot. After hearing several elaborate answers, Marie demonstrates the simple answer. She places a lid on the pot. Marie insists her students keep the same standards for a clean laboratory as her adult students. She scolds them, "Don't tell me you will clean it afterward. One must never dirty a table during an experiment."[19] Marie instills other life lessons too. She tells the children, "You must get so that you never make a mistake. The secret is in not going too fast."[20]

In the continual struggle Marie has with the media; when the press gets wind of the classes for the children they spin a story. One article reads, "This little company which hardly know how to read or write, has permission to make manipulations, to engage in experiments...The Sorbonne...has not exploded yet, but all hope is not yet lost."[21] Yes, it is hoped this deviation from the norm 'explodes' so the experiment fails and society will not be challenged. The Sorbonne isn't blown up by careless children, although time constraints of the professors force the classes to come to an end after two years.

As Irene and Eve continue to grow, they share a love of literature, just as Marie had with her siblings. The family tradition of women being financially responsible also continues. This is still a novel idea for women. Eve remembers Marie instilling, "an instinct of independence which convinced us both that in any combination of circumstances, we should know how to get along without help."[22] Infusing an 'instinct of independence' includes Marie's indifference to money, materialism, and social protocols. Marie abides by each style of her daughters. For Eve, Marie sees the outgoing people person, who enjoys fashion and uses her natural charm. Marie knows that Irene is content with a book or the solitude of the laboratory. Irene doesn't see the need to greet people, so she doesn't. As understanding as any mother can be, there are still 'days' with her children.

Marie is tutoring Irene at home for entrance exams to a school. A parent trying to teach their own child is usually not a good idea. When Irene is distracted and doesn't answer a math problem quickly, Marie takes Irene's notebook and throws it out the window. Irene, like her father, is unperturbed. Irene gets up, walks downstairs and goes outside and retrieves her notebook. Going back inside, Irene marches up the stairs, sits down, and answers the question.

And there are ways that Marie's style is not what is best for the girls. Marie keeps the mood of the house calm and never raises her voice. This is fine for Irene, but this is not what Eve needs. Eve later writes that Marie "would not allow anybody to raise their voice, whether in anger or in joy."[23] During Eve's growing years, Marie is in her forties and struggling with the balance of home and work. Eve writes of Marie, "In spite of the help my mother tried to give me, my young years were not happy ones."[24]

A frustration both daughters experience is they must share their mother. The demands of teaching and being world famous, take Marie away from home. Irene is annoyed when a female student comes to visit for tea. Irene tells Marie, "You must take notice of me."[25]

When the three are apart, there are daily letters going back and forth. While the letters usually describe the simple details of life, on one occasion Irene writes to her mother, "When it rains, I think that these dark moments spent waiting for light would be much nicer if you were in a chair next to me. And when I see the sun shine in the sky and make beautiful reflections on the water in the streams, I think that everything would be nicer if a Sweet Me' (the girls' pet name for their mother) were there, near me, to look at them."[26]

9

Invasion of Privacy

Marie continues her teaching and has finished the meticulous work of verifying radium and polonium. By 1908, she completes the book, *Works of Pierre Curie*. During the next two years Marie writes and publishes a nine hundred and seventy-one page text, *Treatise of Radioactivity*. Ensuring that Pierre is not forgotten, Marie has his picture opposite the title page. In this book, Marie explains everything known about radioactivity. *Treatise of Radioactivity* is still used as the most accurate account of the beginning years of radioactivity.

Marie's British colleague, Ernest Rutherford gives Marie's book a positive review in the international scientific press, but privately he can't contain his petty annoyance with Marie's work. Rutherford writes to a fellow scientist, Bertram Boltwood, "Reading her book, I would have thought I was rereading something I myself had written, supplemented by some research done in the last few years. It is very funny to see the trouble she goes to at certain points to claim that French science was first, or rather that she herself and her husband were first...And yet I can sense that the poor thing has worked enormously hard..."[1] Boltwood is a sympathetic ear to Rutherford's grousing.

Bertram Boltwood is a Yale University graduate and teacher at his alma mater from 1897-1900. Boltwood is considered an American pioneer of radiochemistry and the first to measure the age of rocks by the decay of radium to lead. He befriends Rutherford, but despises Marie despite his interest branching from Marie's work. He got his nose put out of joint with her when he wrote and asked to compare the standard she uses for radium with his own standard. Agreeing on how to measure radium, the standard to be used, is the coming debate. For the sake of having a precise standard, Marie tells Boltwood, no. Miffed with Marie's answer, Boltwood writes to Rutherford, "The Madame is not at all desirous of having any such comparison carried out, the reason, I suspect, being her constitutional unwillingness to do anything that might directly or indirectly assist any worker in radioactivity outside her own laboratory."[2] Considering the largesses which both Pierre and Marie have given of their time and information freely, his accusation is merely a reflection of his frustration at being told–no.

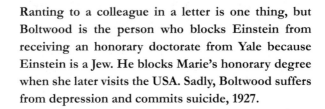

Ranting to a colleague in a letter is one thing, but Boltwood is the person who blocks Einstein from receiving an honorary doctorate from Yale because Einstein is a Jew. He blocks Marie's honorary degree when she later visits the USA. Sadly, Boltwood suffers from depression and commits suicide, 1927.

Unable to control how the media extols radiation, what Marie is able to keep is an ethical guideline by insisting her standard of measure be used to measure radium's strength. Her meticulous writing in the *Treatise* earning Rutherford's remarks, "the poor thing has worked enormously hard" is ignoring the length men have gone to trying to keep Marie out of their science circle. Whether Rutherford knew or not the fabrication of the first Nobel nomination to exclude Marie, Rutherford is certainly aware that Marie is not a member of the Academy of Science in Paris. (Rutherford enjoys his membership to the Royal Society of London and will later be president, 1925-1930.) Marie is not taking any chances that her name and work will be misrepresented or erased in the field of radiology.

The continued myth, Pierre the genius with Marie the support, is wearing on Marie's acquaintance from England, Hertha Ayrton. British papers have continued to credit the discovery of radium to just Pierre. In March 1909, Ayrton writes to the *Westminster Gazette*, "Errors are notoriously hard to kill, but an error that ascribes to a man what was actually the work of a woman has more lives than a cat."[3] Her protest does nothing to dispel the error.

Developing the processes to work on radium and polonium has put Marie at the forefront of metrology, the science of measurement. This knowledge becomes the core to atomic research, which is what leads to supporting Rutherford's theory of transmutation. Rutherford had thought his theory might not be able to be proved, but now Marie's work makes that possible. Rutherford writes, "Apart from the interest of obtaining a weighable quantity of polonium in pure state, the real importance of the present investigations of Mme Curie lies in the probable solution to the question of the nature of the substance into which the polonium is transformed…It was a matter of very great interest and importance to settle definitively whether polonium changes into lead…The experiment of Mme. Curie and Debierne has settled this question conclusively. "[4]

Marie and the girls have spent the last four years learning to restructure their family. They will need to regroup again. Dr. Curie has been ill for a year with lung congestion and pneumonia. Marie is his constant nurse. In February of 1910, Dr Curie, eighty-two years old, dies. This is an enormous loss for Irene, Eve and Marie. Marie writes of Irene, her "pain is deep. She saw her grandfather dead and was present at his burial.

She worried about losing me, too, attached herself to me even more than ever. She suffers and matures."[5]

Dr. Curie is buried at the family burial plot in Sceaux. Marie has Pierre's coffin lifted and placed on top of Dr. Curie's. She ensures that when her coffin is next, she will be beside Pierre.

During this year Marie sends a picture of her and the girls to Jacques. He writes back, "The two girls were a pleasure to see, but you look so sad. My wife cried so much when she saw how thin and drained you were. You must rally, if it is only for your children who need you to live a long time."[6]

Lonely for challenging science conversations, missing the security that comes with being understood in a friendship, Marie is reawakening her heart. The person Marie has been spending time with is certainly on academic par with Pierre. Pierre had been his teacher.

Later that year, Marie always dressed in dark clothes whether for her practical reasons of working in the lab or that she has been in mourning, arrives at a dinner party at the Borel's. Marie is wearing a white blouse and a skirt. Marguerite Borel (daughter of Paul Appell who is dean of the Sorbonne's Faculty of Sciences) notices that Marie has a rose tucked in her belt. While this is not an unusual accent for other ladies, it is unusual for Marie.

"Without your affection, I can't live." Paul Langevin to Marie[7]

Paul Langevin, Pierre's former student and long time family friend to the Curies, has been working with Marie to help her prepare course lectures at the Sorbonne. Marie, five years his senior, enjoys Paul's brilliance and insights as a peer. Their professional talks turn personal. Paul writes his feelings, being drawn to Marie "as to a light…and I began to seek from her a little of the tenderness which I missed at home."[8]

Marie knows Paul's wife Jeanne. Marie has visited their home, knows their four children and has heard Jeanne's stream of complaints about Paul. Jeanne's chief grudge is Paul staying within the field of pure research and not taking a position in industry that would increase his income and afford the family more of the finer things in life. Marie, at some point, has even interceded to Paul on Jeanne's behalf. Hearing this, Paul shows Marie the gash in his head where Jeanne had broken a bottle over his head.

It is common knowledge within the science community that Paul has an unhappy marriage. Marie has talked with Henriette Perrin (the neighbor who had watched the girls at the time of Pierre's death.) Marie asks Henriette, "When you know that a man is one of the most intelligent there is…should you refuse to do what you can to help him?"[9]

Marie and Paul's relationship has moved beyond friendship and she is getting caught up in the Langevin turmoil.

The summer of 1910, Marie is away with her daughters. She and Paul are corresponding. Marie is worried Paul will not stand up to his wife and break free. Reminiscent of the time she was waiting for Casimir to stand up to his parents, Marie writes to Paul, "If she were to have another child that would mean a final separation because I couldn't accept this dishonor to myself, to you and to other people I respect. If your wife understands this she will make use of it. So I beg you not to make me wait too long for you to stop sleeping in her bed."[10]

When Marie has not heard from Paul for a couple days, she asks Jean Perrin to check on him. The danger for Marie is that her letters will end up in Jeanne's possession. Marie's concerns are not unfounded. When Perrin arrives at the Langevin's home, Jeanne has the letters and is threatening to expose the affair. In the unfolding scene, the Langevin's eleven year-old son is in the room and Jeanne pulls him into the drama. She asks him if he plans on having a mistress when he grows up. Perrin tries to calm the situation. Over the next week he visits several times to keep everyone in check.

When Perrin is leaving one night from the Langevin's, he is shocked to see Marie coming down the sidewalk toward him. Marie explains to Perrin that Mme Langevin and her sister had followed her and confronted her in the street. Jeanne made several insulting remarks, after which she threatened to kill Marie unless she leaves France.

Perrin's continued visits to the Langevin's' home resolves nothing except to hear Jeanne's repeated threats to kill Marie unless she is gone from France in eight days. Perrin coordinates a meeting to try and bring some resolution to the situation. The meeting includes Jeanne's brother-in-law Henri Bourgeois. Bourgeois is an editor of a newspaper, *Petit Journal*, known for being a disreputable source of information. The meeting results in Paul promising to never again see Marie. Jeanne promises to stop threatening Marie and to not have the scandal go public.

The agreement buys some time.

Marie is attending the World Congress of Radiology and Electricity in Brussels, Belgium. Jean Perrin is there along with Ernest Rutherford from England. The use of radium in medicine, industry, and research is making it imperative that a uniform measurement for the element be established. This meeting is to choose an International Radium Standard. Since hospitals are using radium as a treatment of cancer, they need to know its purity so they can determine an optimum dosage to treat tumors. Following many arguments and accusations, Marie is appointed to "prepare the primary standard."[11] Marie has this perspective, "In France the control of radium tubes, by the measurement of their radiation, takes place in my laboratory, where anyone may come to bring the radium to be tested."[12]

Aside from multiple languages, ego priorities and behind-the-scenes science politics, the committee manages to agree that the word 'Curie' will be the term for the measurement.

{
Naming the measurement after the discoverer is a common courtesy. Ohm, watt, volt, farad, coulomb, henry and ampere are all named after the inventor. Marie is the only woman so honored.
}

December 1910, Marie is offered the Legion of Honor award. Comparable to France offering the pension after Pierre's death rather than the position at the Sorbonne, the Legion of Honor is tempting bait to divert from the real prize. Marie, like Pierre, declines the award. Like Pierre who really wanted a laboratory, Marie wants membership to the Academy of Sciences, the assembly that sets policy for science. She has won a Nobel Prize and published the nine-hundred-page *Treatise on Radioactivity*. One Academy member writes, "Where would the Academy find a scientist with greater authority than Madame Curie to give it an opinion on these works about radioactivity whose number is growing so rapidly?"[13] There are three living Nobel Prize winners in France. The others have been long time members of the Academy, but not Marie. Marie applies for membership.

"Women cannot be part of the Institute of France."[4] Academy of Science Member (1911)

Reporters, covering the story of the upcoming Academy vote, are showing up to hear Marie's lectures. Finding fault with anything, they write derisively that her students applaud when Marie enters the lecture hall. Their assessment that Marie's lectures are boring is more an indictment on their lack of understanding the subject matter. (Marie will never be the one to point out that the hyped criticism is being fueled by some of the science professors from the Sorbonne.)

A newspaper article tugs on the fear factor that Marie is 'foreign born.' The photo of Marie, more like a mug shot, is not so subtle. A quoted character assessment of Marie is based on evidence from a handwriting expert and a physiognomist (a person who bases character traits on the shape of one's skull). Pulling out all stops, the press is also pushing the slant that having women in the Academy will destroy the feminine ideal and will be the downfall of families.

The backlash is not only from men. Threatened by Marie's challenge to their status quo, women are saying "Science is useless to women." and "One must not try to make woman the equal of man."[15] It is suggested to Marie that she withdraw her candidacy in order for an older man to have the position. Marie will not step aside.

Bending the ear of Academy members to keep their 245 year male membership intact, are conservatives, Catholics, chauvinists, and anti-Semites. Worse than not being pure French, Catholics are claiming that Marie is a freethinker. Add to this, they play on bigoted, anti-Semitic sympathies and infer that Marie is a Jew. {This is after the Dreyfus affair. In spite of

Dreyfus being exonerated, hatred of Jews runs rampant and many in France still refer to Dreyfus as the "Jewish traitor."[16]}

Support from some liberal papers and colleagues like Gabriel Lippmann won't be enough to stem the negative tide. It won't be enough that the respected newspaper *Le Figaro* names Marie the nation's most famous physicist. It won't be enough that Marie fulfills the duties of family life and is the one to provide financial support for herself and her children. A woman will never be 'enough.'

Marie is making waves by having the audacity to apply for membership to the Academy. The waves are rocking the boat called *Status Quo*. Meetings for voting in new members usually garner sixty some members showing up. With Marie's name on the ballot, all one hundred sixty three members are in attendance.

January 23, 1911 is the vote. The meeting starts with the door keeper announcing, "Let everybody come in, women excepted."[17] Male journalists and photographers are even allowed in with the members, just no women.

For the first vote, Marie loses by one. Those voting against Marie are shocked at how close they came to having their male influence challenged. There is a call for a revote. In the next round, Marie loses by two votes. Marie is denied a membership to the Academy of Science. Marie will never again apply.

Seeing this close call, members who voted against Marie demand a different vote. This vote is to decide whether a woman can ever be admitted to the academy. The vote, 90 to 52, decides no women forever.

"Forever" is going to be sixty-eight years. In 1962 the first woman is voted into the Academy of Science. Marguerite

Perey, one of Marie's students, breaks the 296 year old tradition of men-only membership.

> Marguerite Perey, as a young student, is unable to study medicine due to financial hardship. At age nineteen, Marguerite applies for a job with Marie. Marie hires her. She becomes Marie's student and receives a grant to finish her PhD. Marguerite discovers the element "francium." She will be the first woman to be elected to the French Academy of Sciences, 1962.

One member, Charles-Edouard Guillaume (a Swiss physicist who wins a Nobel Prize in Physics, 1920) writes that the vote "was achieved by methods that would make monkeys blush."[18] Later, Marie receives a letter of support saying, "I think you are too noble a character to be affected the least bit by this affair at the Institute..."[19] However, none of the members that support Marie quit the Academy in protest.

Marie is at the laboratory the day of the vote. Her students have a bouquet of flowers ready to give her when she gets the call with the good news. When Marie takes the call, her students take the bouquet away so she won't see it. They were so sure the vote would be a 'yes.'

The Academy keeps their priority of 'men only' at the cost of losing the wealth of information Marie can bring to their esteemed gathering. If Marie wants her papers presented at the Academy, she will need to have a member do the presenting. Marie will not bow to this. While less read by the science community, for the next eleven years she will instead have her work published in science journals.

The professional snub is a tremor to a fault line in Marie's life that is about to crack wide open.

Spring 1911, Marie has a visitor. It's Mme Langevin's brother-in-law, the newspaper editor. Henri Bourgeois tells Marie that Mme Langevin has asked him to relay to Marie that someone has entered Paul Langevin's apartment and taken personal letters from the desk. Bourgeois' message to Marie is that her life is at risk and she should leave the country.

> Of note, for the upcoming scandal: the letters are certainly personal in nature; however, no letter is ever made public. What is made public are out of context selected sentences with the wording altered.

Marie goes to Jean Perrin with this latest development. Perrin takes the threat seriously since he has witnessed the evidence of bruises from previous encounters that Paul has suffered from his wife. (In one instance Mme Langevin, her mother, and sister throw an iron chair at Paul.) The Perrins inform Paul that his wife is no longer welcome at their house. "Your wife has recently made threats of murder serious enough so that we all have been afraid that she is capable of acting on them."[20] Perrin is tired of the never ending drama and advices Marie she should leave town.

The situation is quiet for eight months.

Marie does have the opportunity to leave town temporarily. Emile Borel (French mathematician) and his wife, Marguerite Borel (who noticed the flower tucked in Marie's belt) invite Marie and her daughters to go with them for a science conference in Italy. Marie and Emile attend the conference while Marguerite spends time with Irene and Eve.

One of the evenings in Italy, Marie talks to Marguerite privately. It can be understood that some of Marie's concern is self serving because she is in love with Paul, but Marie is equally concerned about science. Marie explains that she is afraid Paul will succumb to his wife's demand to leave science and earn more money in industry. Marie tells Marguerite, "Save him from himself. He is weak. You and I are tough. He needs understanding, he needs gentleness and affection."[21] Marguerite records this conversation later and writes about Marie, "under the austere scientist, [was a] tender and lively woman capable of walking through fire for those she loves."[22]

Back in Paris, Langevin is spending nights at the Perrins' home. When he discovers one of his sons is ill Paul goes home. A fight starts between Paul and his wife. Mme Langevin threatens to expose the letters. Paul, who had been planning a trip to London with two of his sons, leaves immediately. This action plays into Mme Langevin's hand and she charges Paul with abandoning his home and taking their sons.

The strain on friendships continues with the circle of scientists when Marie's assistant, Debierne meets with Marguerite and asks her to speak with Paul and tell him to put an end to his relationship with Marie. Debierne tells Marguerite, "He is worrying her. She can't bear to see him so despondent."[23] Marguerite tells Debierne that Langevin complains of these things to her too. Debierne replies, "Complaining to you is not as dangerous."[24] Debierne will also confront Langevin directly. He blames Paul for Marie's bad health, distraught emotions, and not being able to concentrate on her daughters. They argue.

> There is also the quiet quandary of some of Marie's male colleagues. How can they defend or advise Marie when they have mistresses of their own?

Marie sends the girls to Poland to stay with Bronya and Casimir. Marie will join them, but first, she goes to Holland. Marie is there to meet a physicist, Heike Kamerlingh Onnes, who studies how radioactive bodies behave at very low temperatures. (Onnes is awarded a Nobel Prize for physics in 1913.)

Marie and the girls enjoy a stay with family in Poland. Eve, an energetic six-year-old, can keep up on the long hikes. Marie writes, "Eve very much adored by everybody and very happy. She goes into the mountains with us…She bears up well and walks well… She carries her backpack and is very happy with the excursion and the camping."[25] Marie describes Eve's sensitive side, "I had just reproached Irene for I don't know what, and Eve dissolved into tears."[26] Irene, in typical fourteen year old fashion, informs her mother that she loves Poland, the countryside, the people and the language but makes it clear she likes France more.

Marie leaves in October for Brussels for a veritable 'Who's Who' gathering of the top physicists in the world. It's the first Solvay Conference. Marie's colleagues/friends Jean Perrin (Nobel Prize, Physics 1926) and Ernest Rutherford (Nobel Prize, Chemistry 1908) are amidst the attendees along with Max Planck (Nobel Prize, Physics 1918). There is a new kid on the block, Albert Einstein (Nobel Prize, Physics, 1921). The group includes Paul Langevin.

1911 Solvay Conference, *Musée Curie (coll. ACJC)*

Marie Curie seated second from right, Ernest Rutherford standing directly behind Marie, Albert Einstein standing second from right, Paul Langevin standing to right of Einstein.

> The Solvay Conference (invitation-only) is established by the Belgian industrialist, Conseil Solvay. The conference is devoted to preeminent open problems in physics and chemistry. The subject of this first conference is *Radiation and the Quanta.*

Aside from scientific discussions about Beta-rays, meetings are also to decide where to keep the official international unit of radium, the Curie. Since it is Marie who discovered radium, and Marie produced the sample now being used as the standard, she sees no problem with keeping the radium permanently in her laboratory.

Protests erupt. Others explain the sample should be kept at the Office of Weights and Measurements in Sevres. Rutherford attempts to explain, "I am sure it is going to be ticklish business to get the matter arranged satisfactorily as Mme Curie is rather a difficult person to deal with. She has the advantage and at the same time the disadvantage of being a woman."[27]

Marie leaves several meetings complaining of headaches and exhaustion. Whether Marie's ailments are in light of the personal turmoil she is experiencing or not, these confrontations with colleagues are a cakewalk compared to what is coming.

The media has been brewing, and an unnamed Sorbonne academician is stirring the pot. He writes, "Madame Curie, since the death of her illustrious husband has not accomplished anything by herself. She has stood by the wayside while others are unraveling the mysteries of the atom."[28] Another paper declares, "The recent work of the Curie Laboratory illustrates...

the absence of true innovation…it is busy work."[29] Marie's 'busy work,' obtaining pure samples of radium and polonium, is a scientific feat no one else could achieve. There is no acknowledgement for finishing the book about Pierre's work and her 900+ treatise she has published on radiation, a text still used today.

November 4th, Marie is still attending the Solvay Conference. As she crosses the hotel lobby reporters are waving newspapers in front of her and shouting questions. Marie doesn't understand the confusion until one reporter shoves the paper in front of her. The headlines read, "A Love Story: Mme Curie and Professor Langevin."[30] Marie is stunned. She turns and leaves.

Accusing Marie of being a husband snatcher, the article reads, "The fires of radium which so mysteriously warms everything around them, had a surprise in store for us: They have just kindled a blaze in the hearts of the scientists who are studying their behavior with such tenacity—and the wife and children of one of these scientists are in tears."[31] The article's source is an interview with Mme Langevin's mother who is falsely claiming no one knows where the 'lovers' are at this time. A picture of Marie is featured in the newspaper, but the article fails to have a picture of Paul.

Marie responds to the article with a letter to a reputable newspaper. Aside from the accusations being false, Marie points out that anyone in Paris knows she is in Belgium for the Solvay Conference. Marie stays at the conference.

It's November 7, Marie's forty-fourth birthday. She is handed a telegram. As she opens the message, is she filled with trepidation for what might be another announcement of bad news? She can breathe a sigh of relief. She reads:

"You have been awarded the Nobel Prize in Chemistry. Letter follows, Aurivillius."

Marie is being honored for "producing sufficiently pure samples of polonium and radium to establish their atomic weight, facts confirmed by other scientists, and for her feat of producing radium as pure metal."[32] This second Nobel Prize is in her name alone. (Marie is the only person to date to received two Nobel Prizes in two different categories of science.)

The Paris papers hardly mention that Marie is being awarded a second Nobel Prize. The glory of this honor is crushed with the priority for scandal. Marie returns to Paris and the drama is both public and private.

Timing for the story to break cannot be worse. Technology upgrades: linotype, the electric telegraph, telephones, and photos have reporters busier than ever stirring up a 'need to know' for their readers in order to sell more papers. Ravenous after the feeding frenzy of the Dreyfus Affair, reporters are quick to latch on to another storyline that sells: adultery. And for masses of people in marginal lives, readers relish the theme, 'how the mighty have fallen.' No matter that Marie never wanted to be 'mighty.' Another square the story fits is Marie, not Paul, being a foreigner. Xenophobia, the unreasonable fear and hatred of foreigners, is in full swing with the Langevin affair. A journalist writes, "France in the grip of the bunch of dirty foreigners who pillage it, soil it and dishonor it."[33] And considering the numbers of papers sold with the character assassination of Captain Dreyfus, anti-Semitism is always a popular twist. The rumor is reignited that Marie is a Jew.

Another publication hits the stands with the title, "The Truth About the Langevin-Curie Scandal: For A Mother."[34] The choice of color for the cover is red. Following this is a gossip paper with an article that is filled in with quotes and accusations from Mme Langevin. Marie is portrayed as "the vestal virgin of radium" who "deliberately, methodically, scien-

tifically, set about alienating Paul Langevin from his wife and separating her from her children..."[35]

The media incitement has its effect. Crowds are circling around Marie's home every day. They are throwing stones at the windows and shouting, "Get out, foreigner!" and "Husband snatcher!" [36] "Go home to Poland!"[37]

> **Silent Double Standard: The crowds do not go to Paul's house to condemn him, nor are any quotes (warped or otherwise) released from his letters to Marie, only Marie's letters to Paul.**

One more article appears, this time printed in the *Le Petit Journal* where Mme Langevin's brother-in-law is the editor. The headline reads, "A novel in a Laboratory–the Affair of Mme Curie and M Langevin." Mme Langevin gives details of the last fight "over a badly made fruit compote"[38] and that M Langevin became violent, he hit her and then disappeared with two of their sons. In reference to the letters, Mme Langevin is outraged that Mme Curie has suggested Paul break off his marriage. In this orchestrated story, Mme Langevin proclaims she is still hoping her husband will return.

Carefully playing to the reader's sympathies, there is no mention that Mme Langevin knew Paul went to London with the boys and nothing is said of the previous violence to Paul on her part. And finally, the article plays to its readers and upholds society standards by ensuring the point of contention is **not** that her husband has a mistress.

Paul, in line with the status quo of the day, had mistresses in the past. The wife's role is to tolerate these indiscretions as long as the husband sticks by the rules of the game. One rule is a mistress is not supposed to break up a marriage. Another rule is the mistress is supposed to be a shadow in the world of society. Paul and Marie are breaking the rules.

And the egregious letters? What is written? Here are some excerpts of Marie's letters:

"There are very deep affinities between us which only required a fertile piece of ground in order to develop. We sometimes sensed this in the past but we did not become fully aware of it until we found ourselves face to face with each other at a time when I was mourning the beautiful life I had made for myself, and you had the feeling you had completely lacked this sort of family life."[39]

"My Paul, I embrace with all my tenderness."[40]

"It would be so good to gain the freedom to see each other as much as our various occupations permit, to work together, to talk or to travel together when conditions lend themselves."[41]

And Marie reminds Paul of the risk she is taking: "Think of that, my Paul, when you feel too invaded by fear of wronging your children; they will never risk as much as my poor little girls, who become orphans between one day and the next if we don't arrive at a stable solution."[42]

Written by a woman in love? Yes. Advice written by a caring friend? Yes.

An accusatory letter-to-the-editor in the newspapers leads to a challenge to Langevin, and this leads to a duel. While the duel comes to nothing, the firestorm continues. Counter accusations to the slanderous articles comes from Emile Borel. He points out that Mme Langevin knew all along that M Langevin and the two sons were in England or that Paul was staying with the Borels. While this is supportive of Marie, the publicity is about to strike at Marie's Achilles heel.

The rumor mill is churning out the spin that Marie and Paul, while teaching at the same school, were involved when Pierre was still alive. This leads to the suggestion that Pierre's death was a purposeful act. It is a loud whisper in the grapevine that Pierre, in despair over his love betrayed, purposely threw himself in front of the horse cart. Jacques tries to stop the nonsense and writes to the press to make clear that Marie and his brother Pierre were truly in love and that he sees Marie as a sister.

Marie writes to the paper, "I find all these intrusions of the press and the public into my private life abominable...This is why I am going to take strong action against the publication of any documents attributed to me. Also, I have a right to demand large sums of money in reparation, and I will use this money in the interests of science."[43]

At this point the reporter, who first exposed the story, sends a letter to Marie and apologizes. He admits to using unreliable sources. He writes, "Madame, I am filled with despair and I offer you my humblest apologies. I was relying on similar information from different sources when I wrote the article that you know about. I was wrong. And now I can hardly understand how my professional enthusiasm could have led me to commit such a detestable act...I am left with only one consoling thought–that such a humble journalist as I am could never, by any of his writings, tarnish the glory that halos you nor the esteem that surrounds you...Your, very distressed, Fernand Hauser."[44]

The story will be retracted. But the damage is done. The public, quick to vilify, is not willing to step into the age of enlightenment and see they are wrong.

When one article makes headlines, Marguerite Borel and Debierne go to Marie's house to bring Marie and her daughters back to Borel's apartment for privacy. Arriving at Marie's house, there is a mob at the gate. Marie and Eve are hurried out to the car. Irene is at school and a friend has already shown Irene the newspaper. Debierne goes to the school and brings Irene to the Borel's home as well.

The Sorbonne is under public pressure to remove Marie from her position. What the Sorbonne is bowing to is one of the paper headlines asking, "Will Mme Curie Remain a Professor at the Sorbonne?" The article justifies its query, "As is our custom, we would have said nothing about this if it involved only the private lives of the people concerned. But something more is involved here. Mme Curie occupies a public teaching position which she obtained in circumstances that give public opinion the right to form a judgment, and her students and their families the right to demand that the teacher be what the English call "respectable.""[45]

When the minister of education hears Marie is staying with the Borels, he is furious. Emile Borel has the apartment as part of his teaching position with the Sorbonne. The minister tells Borel he is discrediting the Sorbonne and threatens to fire him if he persists. Borel replies, "All right, I will persist."[46] The minister backs down and gives Borel time to think about it.

Other men are staunch allies and friends for Marie. Gabriel Lippmann stands by Marie and for this he is labeled "the Jew of color photography."[47] Jean Perrin will defend Marie and he is tagged, "a fanatic Dreyfusard."[48]

In the meantime, Emile's wife, Marguerite, has gotten a message from her father to come at once. (Reminder: Marguerite's father, Paul Appell, is the dean of the Sorbonne's Faculty of Sciences, Marie's doctoral advisor, part of the effort to deny Marie the first Nobel Prize, and the one to notify Marie of Pierre's death.) Marguerite is under the impression her father wants to meet and be sympathetic to Marie's situation. She is wrong.

When Marguerite comes into the room her father is putting on his shoes and he pauses to tell his daughter that she cannot have Marie stay at her place. He states that it is ruining the reputation of the Sorbonne. When Marguerite argues, Appell gets angry and recounts his previous support for Marie (he put forward her name for membership to the Academy) and adds, "but I cannot hold back the flood now engulfing her."[49] Appell informs his daughter that he is going to fire Marie from her position of chair, he wants Marie to resign from the Sorbonne and return to Poland. He has backed this position the day before with a group of Sorbonne professors who are demanding Marie leave France.[50]

Marguerite knows this is only happening because Marie is a woman. No one is gathering at Langevin's house to throw stones at him because 'boys will be boys' and are not to be held accountable to the same standards as girls. Does Marguerite remind her father there is a history professor at the Sorbonne who is having an affair with the wife of a high official? Nothing is done to him. There is a professor at the Polytechnique sleeping with the wife of the mathematician. Nothing is done to him.[51] Nor are these scandals unusual. Parisian courts register thirty-nine declarations of adultery every day and twenty-four of every one hundred births in Paris are illegitimate.[52] Einstein has an illegitimate child (presumably put up for adoption), has an affair with his cousin Elsa, divorces his wife, and marries Elsa. Any moral outrage?

If society wants to make Marie an outcast, Marguerite will not. Marguerite sees Marie as an emancipated woman. Marie, providing her own financial support, isn't chasing Paul for money. Marie's letters reveal a woman of passion, which is the other element that shakes tradition. Women who are wives are respectable not passionate. Passion is the job of a prostitute. Later, when Marguerite is asked if she associates with 'this' type of woman, Marguerite responds unabashedly, "We associate with her to such an extent that she lives with us. Yes, at the Ecolé."[53]

Marguerite begs her father to not go through with his plan. When Appell refuses, Marguerite tells him, "If you give in to that idiotic nationalist movement and insist that Marie should leave France you will never see me again!"[54]

Appell, who still hasn't put on his shoes, is so exasperated he throws his shoe at the wall. He concedes to his daughter's threat.

By November 16th, Marie's lawyer convinces the French press to hold off on any further articles. The only paper who does not comply is *L'Action Francaise*. This is the same paper that churned the attack on Capt. Dreyfus. Their bigotry includes; Protestants, Jews, Freemasons, the liberal intelligentsia and scientists.

A voice of reason is in an editorial of the *New York Times*. It is a rebuttal to the insinuation that Marie's actions have tarnished science and the Sorbonne. "Assailed by a jealous woman who accuses her of estranging a husband from wife and children… There are hints of deliberate mischief making in the case. The letters quoted by Mme Langevin's complaint may not be genuine. In any case neither science nor the Sorbonne can suffer at all from social scandals affecting the lives of scientists."[55]

Mme Langevin's demands include full custody of the children and to be paid one thousand francs a month or she will give the letters to the newspapers. When Paul refuses, she charges him with "consorting with a concubine"[56] Although Marie is not specifically named, the charge means the case will be heard in a criminal court, which means more publicity. Marie's bank accounts during these months show large sums of money being given to Paul. It is possible Jeanne is blackmailing him.

Bronya, Hela and Joseph arrive from Poland to give Marie their support. They are encouraging Marie to come back to Poland. Paderewski, the Polish pianist, also comes to visit Marie. Charles-Edouard Guillaume writes to Marie, "We share your sadness and your joys. We were with you during the painful days you have just gone through; we still are with you. There are people who cannot forgive your superiority: they proved it during your presentation at the academy. The same base jealousy has animated them again…The campaign the last few days is proof that the same people have not given up yet."[57]

Albert Einstein writes to Marie, he is "so incensed over the way in which the rabble dares to react to you that I absolutely had to vent these feelings. I am convinced, however, that you hold the rabble in contempt, whether they feign reverence or seek to satisfy their lust for excitement through you. I feel the need to tell you how much I have come to admire your spirit, your energy and your honesty. I consider myself fortunate to have made your personal acquaintance in Brussels…I will always be grateful that we have among us people like you–as well as Langevin–genuine human beings, in whose company one can rejoice. If the rabble continues to be occupied with you, simply stop reading the drivel. Leave it to the vipers it was fabricated for. With cordial regards to you, Langevin and Perrin. A. Einstein"[58] In a letter to a friend, Einstein's sentiments are modified. He writes, [Marie] isn't "attractive enough to become dangerous for anyone."[59]

Georges Urbain, Sorbonne professor, expresses some understanding when he writes to a fellow scientist, "In Mme Curie's letter to Langevin, who was so unhappy at home, she gives him advice on how to free himself. I think that Perrin or myself could have given him the same advice, but the fact that it was given by a woman and that the woman used affectionate terms are a sign of guilt in the eyes of the world."[60] He later writes, "I am very sorry about the general cowardice I see. Among Marie Curie's greatest admirers are those who throw stones at her today."[61]

Marie, under the barrage of character assassination shots, is unsure she will survive. She writes to Georges Gouy, Pierre's confidante, and asks for his help to plan for the disposition of her affairs. Gouy responds to Marie, "Needless to say you can count on me to follow all the recommendations you will make. But the time has not come for that, and you will live long enough to arrange everything as you deem right. Perrin writes, "I witnessed the emotion that this…produced on Madame Curie, an emotion so powerful that we feared for her life."[62] Marie is forty-four.

Unbeknownst to Marie, there are members from the Nobel committee suggesting that Marie not come to Stockholm the next month to receive the prize. Their reason, *thoughtful of course*, is to spare Marie embarrassing herself and the king. One writes, "It would be very desirable that Mme Curie should not come to Stockholm to receive the prize from the hand of King Gustave. It could bring a lot of unpleasantness to the Academy and Science and mostly to herself."[63]

Paul Langevin steps in with a letter to those pressuring Marie to not attend the Nobel Prize ceremony. He writes, "One cannot judge…, the correspondence which is reproduced in a distorted fashion–by alterations and omissions…if one does not know the condition in which I lived for thirteen years, nor from what kind of people these attacks came…It hurts me to have to shout with all my strength that such a woman did not do what she is accused of…"[64]

As for the relationship between Marie and Paul Langevin, any romantic interest is over. They will remain friends and professional colleagues the rest of their lives. Paul later has a separation decree from his wife although he will return to her in a few years. One of his students, Eliane Montel, becomes his mistress, and Paul asks Marie to help Eliane have a position at the laboratory. Marie does. Paul has a son by Eliane, named Paul-Gilbert. In an interesting twist of history, Marie's granddaughter, Irene's daughter Helene, marries Michel Langevin, a grandson to Paul. The two grandchildren are unaware of the scandal until late in life.

Marie receives the no-attendance request letter from the ss, the Academy that has denied Marie membership. They want Marie to worry about their "esteem." She reads, "All my colleagues replied that they do not want you to come here on December 10…I, too, beg you to stay in France; because nobody can predict what would happen during the prize-giving…The honor, the esteem for our Academy, as well as for Science, and for your fatherland, seem to demand that under such circumstances you abandon the idea of coming here to get the prize."[65]

Even in her weakened state, Marie will not be cowed. She writes back, "You suggest to me…that the Academy of Stockholm, if it had been forewarned would probably have decided not to give me the Prize. Unless, I could publicly explain the attacks of which I have been the object…I must therefore act according to my conviction…The action that you advise would appear to be a grave error on my part. In fact, the Prize has been awarded for discovery of Radium and Polonium. I believe that there is no connection between my scientific work and the facts of private life…I cannot accept the idea in principle that the appreciation of the value of scientific work should be influenced by libel and slander concerning private life. I am convinced that this opinion is shared by many people."[66]

Bronya and Irene (fourteen-years-old) accompany Marie for the forty-eight-hour train trip to Sweden. Although confident her decision is correct, Marie has reason to wonder, "What will happen?"

Marie is greeted with a warm reception, complete with respect and affection. The Swedish Association of University Women hosts a banquet in Marie's honor. Three hundred women attend. During the Nobel Prize ceremonial speeches the extraordinary accomplishment of Marie is mentioned, "During the eleven years in which Nobel Prizes have been awarded, this is the first time that the distinction has been conferred upon a previous prizewinner." Any fears of causing embarrassment are unfounded. King Gustaf awards the prize to Marie, and she becomes the first woman to address the Nobel Academy. Among the society women with their gowns and jewels, Marie is in her usual subdued black dress. She gives her lecture "Radium and the New Concept in Chemistry."

Marie honors her fellow scientists giving credit to those that helped her: Becquerel, Rutherford, Soddy, Debierne, Han, and even Boltwood. Marie includes praise of Pierre, but she makes it clear that she alone carried out the significant discoveries. Marie makes clear who discovered these elements and who created and performed the process to isolate these elements as proof of her hypothesis. She uses throughout her speech, "I called," "I used," "I carried out," "I found," "I obtained...."[67]

Sitting in the audience, Irene watches and listens to her mother give the presentation. Irene will be the next woman to receive a Nobel Prize in science, in 1935.

When Marie returns to Paris after receiving her second Nobel

Prize the headlines of the *L'Oeuvre* reads:

THE INVASION OF FOREIGNERS

"The invasion has infiltrated the Sorbonne, the Ecolé Centrale, the Institute Pasteur, the Faculty of Medicay...Everywhere."

"Foreigners at the Sorbonne. Laboratories invaded by a mob mostly made up of foreign individuals. The numbers of women are constantly increasing, the most commendable of them are there because they are looking for husbands..."[68]

The emphasis would have been better spent on the looming war, the invasion of Germans.

10

"...wounds are not painful."

Paris papers are giving front page coverage to the Frenchman who wins the Nobel Prize in literature. Marie, having won her second Nobel Prize in science, is scarcely acknowledged. The tabloids are espousing worries of being invaded with foreigners at the Sorbonne and the accusations continue that the foreign female students are enrolled in husband hunting.

Marie, returning to the classroom of the Sorbonne to teach, will only last a couple weeks. By the end of December she is in debilitating pain. Using an assumed name, she is taken to a hospital and treated for fever and kidney infection. The press catches wind of Marie's stay and the rumor mill purports that she went to the hospital to have Langevin's baby. Wanting to squash the continued revilement, Marie agrees to have her medical condition made public.

The strain is taking a toll on Marie, and she needs a kidney operation. The doctors believe Marie is too weak to survive surgery. She is sent home to rest, but there is no rest. Marie's home in Sceaux is no longer private. It is a public spectacle, and Marie decides to sell and move to an apartment in Paris.

Marie has the operation in February. She is so ill she can't stand by herself, and her weight has dropped from 123 pounds to 103. She gives instructions to Debierne and Gouy for what to do with the radium that is in her possession should she die. Debierne is handling all her personal affairs. Marie will later tell her daughter Eve that during this time she was on the brink of suicide and madness.[1] The concerted effort to publicly humiliate and crush her might be working.

In spite of her ill health, Marie agrees to see a delegation from Poland. They want Marie to leave Paris, come home to Warsaw and be the director for the Radium Institute being built. They tell Marie, "Our people admire you, but they would like to see you work here in your native city. This is the ardent desire of the whole country. If we have you in Warsaw, we will feel stronger, we will lift up our heads, which have been bowed down by the weight of so many misfortunes. May our prayer be answered. Do not push away the hands that are reaching out toward you."[2]

The Polish delegation is led by Henry Sienkiewicz, also a recipient of a Nobel Prize. Marie, because of her daughters, will not leave France. She promises to direct the institute but still live in France. She sends two of her best assistants, both Polish, to provide the day to day guidance.

Demands don't stop because Marie is ill. Settling the debate about the 'unit of measure' is requiring her attention. Decisions are overdue to have a means of controlling the quality, purity, and procedure for how radium is being used. International mines and facilities are providing materials that register varying levels of strength. With no checks and balances in place, the degree of strength being advertised is not the same as what is in the substance sold. Having a standard would allow doctors to prescribe a consistent dosage. Marie has stipulated, "For measurements dealing with new questions, only my laboratory…is in a position to solve the problems which arise."[3]

The meeting to discuss establishing the standard is in Paris, the spring of 1912. Marie is too ill to attend, so Debierne goes in her place. Decisions are made for a definitive process and a standard is agreed upon. The measurement, a Curie, is the amount of radon expended by one gram of radium per one second. This is used for medicine, industry, and research. Marie agrees that her original measured sample of radium will be moved to the Bureau of Weights and Standards in Sevres. In return, she insists on being paid or given a replacement for both samples, the sample she is sending and the replacement.

Marie's tough side also applies to running the lab. Still not having the new laboratory promised years ago, Marie keeps a sharp eye on the work of her staff and running the current lab. She learns that one of her assistants is planning on opening a separate laboratory. Although this assistant had worked for years with Pierre, Marie writes to him, "Having considered your current situation and the needs of the laboratory, I feel that it is no longer possible for you to do the things I need done, and I ask you to resign from your post as an assistant immediately..."[4]

That summer Bronya urges Marie to rent a place in the country to get away and rest. Only close friends know Marie's whereabouts and she uses an assumed name to avoid any publicity. Eve and Irene are either visiting their mother or they are with Jacques and his family. Marie continues her convalescing with a visit to Hertha Ayrton in England.

Hertha is a leader in the National Suffrage League. Her recent work is to promote a law that will allow a wife to keep her salary rather than having to give it to her husband. Hertha attends demonstrations, and is one of the women arrested in the first march by the English suffragettes. Sentenced to nine months in prison, Hertha goes on a hunger strike. Due to an international petition, she is released.

> Unlike Hertha, Marie is never an outspoken proponent for women's rights. Marie supports women through education, positions at the laboratory, and references for jobs. Hertha later asks Marie to sign a petition that demands the release of three imprisoned British suffragettes. Marie agrees and explains this exception to her normal stance, "I accept your using my name for the petition because I have great confidence in your judgment, and I am convinced that your sympathy must be justified."[5]

Hertha has nursed back to health many of her fellow suffragettes who were released from prison after their hunger strike. (Previously, women were tied down and force fed. 'Luckily' the authorities have stopped this tactic.) Bringing them back from the brink of despair and death, Hertha helps them heal but she doesn't coddle. Hertha will help Marie.

Area locals and the press do not realize that Hertha's guest is the famous Madame Curie. Marie takes this time to gather her strength and to recover from the shock of having her private life smeared across the tabloids. A turn in the tide comes with good news about the court hearings for the Langevin case. Marie's name is kept out, and she hopes this will give sway to the Sorbonne that she can continue to teach and work in the laboratory.

While Marie is away, the separation from her daughters is difficult. Plans are for Irene and Eve to come visit their mother in England. Marie arranges a piano teacher for Eve and a math tutor for Irene.

For the times the girls are not with their mother, the three of them have a stream of letters traversing back and forth. The girls describe hiking and cycling trips and express their worries about their mother's health or the health of the goldfish. If they are at the shore, the girls write descriptions of the waves. Irene is starting to feel more independent and is referring to her mother as "My dearest" rather than, "My sweet Me."[6] Being the older sister, Irene gives account for her younger sister. Irene writes, "Eve and I are well and I have been swimming as much as possible…I only missed once since you left. These days the sea is rough but I still swim. It's fun." And Irene will always have questions about her math, "I couldn't answer problem no. 2, the 2 equations with 2 unknowns, but I'm sending you nos. 3 and 4. Mr. Hornois helped me with 3, but I did 4 by myself."[7]

In Oct 1912, Marie is back in the laboratory in Paris. Here Marie can find sanctuary to concentrate, to measure and make notes, all with no interruptions. And Marie must once again defend her work.

Sir William Ramsay (Nobel Prize Chemistry 1904) has published his work on the atomic weight of radium. He published an experiment where he states his results prove Marie's work false. Marie writes to Rutherford her astonishment after reading Ramsay's article. "…He concludes that his work is the first good work on the subject!!! I must say that I was astounded. Moreover [he] made some malicious and incorrect comments [about] my experiments on atomic weights."[8] Keep in mind that Ramsay is the same person that said to the media, "all eminent women scientists have achieved their best work when collaborating with a male colleague."[9] Ramsay is peeved because he wanted to control the radium standard and lost out. Marie, a woman, has control of the radium standard and she will prove Ramsay assertions wrong.

Spring 1913 and Marie is back to teaching at the Sorbonne.

Since their promise to Pierre, the Sorbonne still hasn't come through with the money for a new laboratory. When the Pasteur Institute offers Marie a position, Marie threatens to accept and quit the Sorbonne. More impetus comes when Austria also offers to create a state-of-the-art laboratory for Marie. These offers move the Sorbonne to make the money and land available to begin building. The laboratory will be known as the Radium Institute with an additional building for medical research.

Marie is intimately involved with the planning and building. Workers become accustomed to Marie climbing up the scaffolding to ask questions. She will fulfill Pierre's vision to have a first class laboratory. The budget covers a salary for the gardener because her plans include a garden with lime trees and rambler roses.

One spring afternoon, Petit, the Curies' assistant from the old days at the shack, comes to talk to Marie. He tells her there are workers who will be tearing down the shack, and he is wondering if she might like to come and see their old place one last time. Marie goes.

In the seven years since the Curies vacated the run down building, it has not been used and nothing has changed. The blackboard still bears chalk notes written by Pierre. Marie writes, "I made my last pilgrimage there, alas, alone. On the blackboard there was still the writing of him who had been the soul of the place; the humble refuge for his research was all impregnated with his memory. The cruel reality seemed some bad dream; I almost expected to see the tall figure appear, and to hear the sound of the familiar voice."[10]

It will always be difficult for Marie to even say his name.

Albert Einstein is in town to speak for the French Society of Physics. Einstein's wife, Mileva is with him. The Curie and Einstein families enjoy time together so well that they decide to share their summer vacation in the Swiss Alps.

> Albert's friendship with Marie includes the practical as well as theoretical discussions. Albert needs a reference letter for a new position at the Zurich Polytechnic. Marie offers to write the letter and Einstein accepts.

Albert Einstein, Marie Curie, 1925, *Musée Curie (coll. ACJC)*

Two weeks of hikes in the Alps includes Einstein's eldest son Hans Albert and Marie's two daughters. On one occasion the three youngsters burst out laughing when they hear Albert saying to Marie, "You see, Madame, what I need to know is exactly what happens to the passengers in an elevator when it falls through the air."[11]

Albert hasn't figured this out yet. But he will.

In November 1913, Marie is coming home to her country, Poland. In Warsaw, Marie attends the dedication of the radium institute built in her honor. This is a far cry from attending the underground "Flying University" so many years ago. One ceremony is at the Museum of Industry and Agriculture, where she had first found her love of chemistry experiments. Another moment of poignant nostalgia follows.

Marie sees a familiar face in the audience. It's Jadwiga Sikorska, the elementary school director who had risked her life to teach Polish children about Poland. Marie goes to her and kisses her. It is difficult to fathom the pride Mlle Sikorska experiences on this occasion as she can see the results of her devotion to her students. Her student, Marie Sklodowska Curie, has been awarded two Nobel Prizes.

> After World War II the name of the institute is changed to the Maria Sklodowska-Curie Institute of Oncology. To date it is the leading cancer research and treatment center in the country.

Despite the joy in being able to give lectures in her native language, the fact remains that Poland is still under Russian domination. Marie's nephew, her brother Joseph's son, is a factory worker. During Marie's visit, he has been in prison for fifteen days. His crime is writing patriotic poetry.[12]

Returning to Paris, Marie is absorbed with building details of the laboratory. The site is on the Rue de Pierre Curie and Marie is seen slogging through the mud at the site checking on progress. Part of the Curie laboratory is to house the largest collection of natural radioactive elements. This collection from around the globe is also the international center for measuring radium samples for medicine and industry. For years the Curie laboratory has been the 'go to' institution for the certification of radium for industry, medicine, and private requests. Now this will be a state of the art facility. Most important for Marie is the laboratory will provide space for research.

July, 1914, Marie is touring the new laboratory with André Debierne. Did they both look at each other and laugh at memories of their work in the shack? Debierne, who has stood by the Curies, is he relieved at how far Marie has come in less than three years? Are they wistful that Pierre is not there to see his dream of a laboratory finally come true? The words engraved in stone over the entrance are "Institut Du Radium, Pavillon Curie."[13]

In the coming weeks, the institute is ready but empty of scientists. Debierne, Langevin, Marie's nephew Maurice Curie, and a large number of students, are being called up. Marie writes, "The few men of the laboratory staff and the students were mobilized, and I was left alone with our mechanic who could not join the army because of heart trouble.[14]

World War I, the Great War, has commenced. Germany is invading Luxembourg and Belgium. French casualties in the first month average ten thousand per day.

Marie's unclouded vision to assess new circumstance sets the course for the next chapter of her life. When other celebrities or wealthy citizens abandon France for the more secure countries of England or the United States, Marie remains. We see her stamina, perseverance, and resourcefulness fully engaged to alleviate the suffering of millions of wounded. For the nation that so recently was making media fodder of Marie's life, she will be risking her life to help them.

In a war that starts on horses and ends with tanks, the new weapons are mangling a soldier's body faster than his brain can catch up. Boys, never having seen a plane, are trying to grasp, "What is air support?" Sending a radio message is iffy. Use a homing pigeon instead.

Media proclamations of war glory are invoked to cover the incoming reports of insidious gore. In the first six weeks of war the tally of killed or wounded for the Germans is 747,000 and 845,000 for the French.[15]

Changes are affecting all facets of the war–equipment, technology, medicine, and weapons. What is hardest to change is people's minds, even when it can save lives. Helmets, requested for the French soldiers in 1914, are denied on the grounds "it would look too German."[16] French soldiers are not issued helmets until the following year, although they do have red trousers to wear as they start their march off to war.

Earlier in the summer of 1914, Marie sent the girls, the cook, and the governess to Brittany for their summer holiday. Marie's train ticket is for August 1. She never uses it.

Irene writes to her mother, "Eve works a lot. She doesn't want to do arithmetic, but one shouldn't bother her about that because she puts really a lot of good will into doing other things, even German." Marie, with appreciation for Irene's thoughtfulness, writes back, "I feel already, how much you have become a companion and friend to me."[17] Irene will soon be sixteen and reads books in English, German and Polish. Like her grandfather, Vladislav, Irene loves Charles Dickens. Having finished her entrance exams, she expects to be starting at the Sorbonne this October.

As the war becomes an immediate reality, their letters turn from gentle concerns of daily life to legitimate fears of being separated. Irene is begging her mother to be able to return to

Paris. Marie worries that Paris will be invaded and says 'no.' Marie writes her daughters to warn them, that if Paris is under siege, their communication might be cut off and they may not hear from her. She adds, "If that should happen, endure it with courage, for our personal desires are nothing in comparison with the great struggle that is now under way. You must feel responsible for your sister and take care of her if we should be separated for a longer time than I expected."[18]

Marie writes again the next day, "I'm afraid you're going to worry because of my letter of yesterday..." More letters from Marie say, "I'm burning to kiss you. The days go by without giving me that chance." and "I have just received your sweet letter...and I wanted so much to kiss you that I almost cried. Things are not going very well and we are all heavyhearted... We need great courage, and I hope that we shall not lack it. We must keep our certainty that after the bad days the good days will come again. It is in this hope that I press you to my heart my beloved daughter."[19]

With rumblings of the front reaching Paris, grocery shelves are turning bare. Wives are stockpiling. Practicality prevails as shoe stores are sold out of walking shoes instead of high heels. Headlines in the newspaper extol, "The storm has begun, but our ship is seaworthy...Each man is at his post, and we are standing by. Hoist the flag!"[20]

Marie is anxious. If the Germans take Paris, a list of casualties could include her name. Who will care for her daughters? Marie can't count on her siblings in Poland. She has no news of them and won't until the end of the war. Watching over the girls now is a Polish governess and a maid, who are not able to quell the girls' fear as they see men in the village receiving notices to report to duty.

The girls still want to come back to Paris, but Marie insists they stay put. In typical Marie fashion, she writes them, we must "try to make ourselves useful."[21] She instructs them, "If you cannot work for France just now, work for its future. Many people will be gone, alas, after this war, and their places must be taken. Do your mathematics and physics as well as you can."[22] But the strain is ever there of wanting to be with her daughters. Marie writes, "I am dying to come and hug you. I don't have the time...There are moments when I don't know what to do. I want to hold you close so badly."[23] The girls write every day to reassure their mother. Irene adds, her pleas to return to Paris stating, "We must be together in this time of trial."[24]

"All [wounded] agree that the wounds are not pain-ful." Press Release from the Ministry of War

By November 1st, three months into the war, 310,000 men (approx. 3,500 men per day) have died and 300,000 (3,300 men per day) are wounded. The Ministry of War is determined to keep a positive spin on the gruesome facts. They announce in the press, "All [wounded] agree that the wounds are not painful. The speed with which they are inflicted, as well as their heat, ensure that there is no danger of infection, and the disorders caused by them are for the most part insignificant."[25] (Clearly whoever has written this has never been shot.)

Marie believes the Germans will eventually lose, but she knows the war will not end quickly, and in spite of what the Ministry of War tries to have citizens believe, the wounded are in pain and they are suffering. With new weapons available, the death toll and number of wounded will be greater than previous wars, and what Marie understands is that not having x-ray equipment at the front line, soldiers are suffering needlessly. Doctors, unable to see where bullets are lodged in the patient, are blindly probing in the bloody flesh. Limbs are cut off and bodies are disfigured.

Marie writes of the beginning months, "The lack of equipment and the lack of information at the beginning of the war permitted operations without radiological exam which, later, would have been considered criminal. The custom was to have X-rays at the main centers, which were at the rear of the front, miles away."[26]

Marie challenges the Military Health Service to have X-rays available at the front. They are not jumping to acknowledge, let alone resolve, the problem. X-rays are new and seen as a luxury. The Health Services' perspective is that x-rays are only for the wounded who are transported back to Paris. Bringing technicians and x-ray equipment to the front line is simply not a consideration.

Marie fights to breakthrough this roadblock. Less than two weeks into the war, by August 12th, the Ministry of War appoints Marie to the position of 'Director of the French Red Cross's Radiological Service.' They give her orders to form a fleet of cars supplied with the x-ray equipment and staff necessary to be a mobile unit in the field and at the front. The orders state the wounded are to be given radiological examinations right away.

As Marie attacked the mountains of pitchblende to find radium, she must find equipment and personnel in a time of war. Marie envisions having a fleet of mobile x-ray units, staffed with trained technicians, to be driven to any active battlefront hospital with wounded soldiers. The first two such vehicles are donated by the Red Cross of France. Clearly this is not enough for 3,000 men per day being wounded.

Marie starts by collecting the unused X-ray equipment from laboratories, from offices of doctors and from the companies that manufacture scientific instruments. Next Marie needs to acquire the cars, which she does by visiting the well-to-do women and asking them to donate their car. Marie promises them, "I'll give it back to you after the war."[27] Many ladies give their car and they give money. Motivation might be that a German plane has dropped three bombs on Paris. They are also dropping leaflets claiming, "The German Army is at the gates of Paris. The only thing for you to do is give yourselves up."[28]

The next step for Marie is to visit body-mechanic shops to see if they will turn the cars into vans. The vans have no front doors and they are painted regulation gray with the Red Cross emblem on its sides. The vans will have a battery to generate enough electrical current to produce X-rays. Additional equipment includes a folding table for the patient, photographic plates, a screen, heavy curtains, cotton gloves and a lead filled apron as protection from the X-ray tube on the movable stand. The fleet of vans will rise to twenty. The vans become known as a "La Petite Curie."

Marie takes a crash course in anatomy and x-ray techniques. Not satisfied with the training, Marie develops a class herself. Next, Marie needs to train staff in nursing and how to operate the equipment. Students come to realize they must learn more than medical steps.

The new technicians will have their sensibilities challenged with the sounds of groans and the sights of gashing wounds, to say nothing of seeing naked men. Many of Marie's students are middle class women coming from a sheltered life.

One woman wrote, "I had never before seen a nude woman. I had scarcely looked at myself in the mirror."[29] The field technicians will have no support for their moments of tears and distress. Any problems with equipment they must solve on their own while they handle the tidal wave of incoming wounded. For the Battle of Somme, the British will have sixty thousand casualties, the first day.

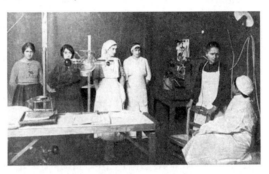

Nurses in training with Marie Curie, *Musée Curie (coll. ACJC)*

One hundred fifty women go through Marie's two month training.[30] They learn the equipment, and how to read the information. Eve admires her mother's teaching style and writes of Marie's "ability to bring science down to the level for a chambermaid to understand."[31] The training is a time consuming effort for Marie to develop the curriculum as well as teach the classes. Later, both Italy and the American Expeditionary Forces will request Marie's help in developing these training classes.

"Civilians mustn't bother us!" [32]

When all the logistical obstacles are resolved, there is still the resistance from the front-line surgeons that Marie must overcome. Medical personnel are resentful of having their practice challenged by a civilian, especially a woman. Patients are clinging to life as doctors cling to their stubborn mentality of "We've always done it this way." It is only due to "Madame Curie" and her authority that she can override their objections. When the doctors finally become accustom to using the X-ray procedure, they streamline the process even more by taking out the step of having the picture developed. They can perform the operation from the radiological screen.

Marie is trained and equipped with the first Petit Curie. She is notified by telegram or telephone calls with the details of when and where wounded are arriving. On her way out the door, she picks up her black briefcase with a few toiletries. The only extra she has with her are a few photographs of her parents. Marie has gotten her driver's license so she can drive without a military chauffeur. Day or night, through any weather, she drives twenty-miles-an-hour to the field hospitals of the battlefields.

> **The battlefields where Marie attends the wounded include: the Battles of Amiens, Ypres, and Verdun.**

Marie is called to some sites that require her to travel by train. Officials at the station tell Marie it can take up to three days to have her equipment loaded and to the front. Marie (and later Irene) won't accept this answer. Marie writes, "Many a time I loaded my apparatus on to the train myself, with the help of the employees, to make sure that it would go forward instead of remaining behind several days at the station. And on arrival, I also went to extract them from the encumbered station."[33]

"The way of progress was neither swift nor easy." Marie Curie

Early September the Germans are closing in on Paris. Residents can see the flashes of artillery. The government and citizens are crowding on trains going south as they abandon the city. September 6th, the Battle of Marne has begun, and there is fear that Paris will be captured. Officials know Marie's radium is a national asset and this cannot fall into the hands of the Germans. Marie is instructed to take the radium south to Bordeaux for safety.

Marie is one of the passengers on a train leaving Paris. She has a forty-five pound lead box at her feet. In the box she has packed the one gram of radium. Arriving at Bordeaux, the next day, Marie rents a safe-deposit box and leaves her radium there. She can only hope it will be out of reach of the Germans. She takes the train back to Paris that same day.

No civilians are on the train going back to Paris, only soldiers reporting for duty and Marie. One soldier shares his sandwich with her. He asks, "Are you not Madame Curie?" Marie gives her usual response, "No. You must be mistaken."[34]

Marie could have stayed safely in Bordeaux or she could have traveled to be with her daughters. Instead, Marie returns to Paris where the Germans are closing in and the wounded need x-rays.

Irene is desperate to be in Paris, and she writes her mother about their latest distress. The country people in the village are suspecting the Curie girls of being German spies. Hearing them speak to their maid and governess in Polish, the villagers assume they are speaking German. On one occasion, a man bursts into their house and accuses the girls of being spies.

Irene informs Marie she is going to discuss the issue with

the mayor. Irene is also giving French lessons to the maid and governess to help them not stand out. Irene writes, "It means more because you yourself were accused of being a foreigner and we haven't anyone in the army…They say I'm a German spy…I'm not very frightened about all this but I'm very upset. It makes me sad to think people take me for a foreigner when I'm so profoundly French and I love France more than anything else. I can't help crying every time I think about it…"[35]

Marie writes back to Irene, "I was sorry to hear that you're having trouble over your nationality. Don't take these things too much to heart, but do your best to explain it to the people you see. Remember, also, that not only should you endure these little miseries with patience, but that it is actually your duty to protect Josephine and Valentine, (Polish housekeeper and governess) who are foreigners. This would be your duty even if they were German, because even in that case they would have a right to live in Brittany. Darling, try to be more fully aware of exactly what your duty is, as a Frenchwoman, to yourself and to others."[36]

In Paris, there is insufficient transportation to get the troops to the front line. With the Battle of Marne raging, the Paris taxis step up and rush six thousand troops to the front line. The effort causes the French to win, but the cost is 250,000 troops are killed. The British loose 13,000. The Germans lose 250,000.

By Sept 12th, Irene's birthday, Marie writes and says, "The invading forces are withdrawing and soon you'll be able to return to Paris without too much trouble."[37] Finally, on the twentieth, Marie writes, "You have my permission to come back by yourself…If you can bring luggage, take the leather-covered hamper. There isn't much time for taking care of one's clothes here, so if you can, bring them."[38]

Back in Paris, Eve and Irene return to classes. Irene begins training at the Red Cross to be a nurse, and she starts classes at the Sorbonne in mathematics and physics. The French government is appealing for gold and silver to pay for the war. Marie offers her medals, including the Nobel Prize medals. The government declines so Marie uses most of her Nobel Prize money. What could have been the inheritance for her daughters, Marie uses to buy war bonds, knowing they will be worth next to nothing at the end of the war.

When the threat of Germany overrunning Paris is over, Marie goes to Bordeaux to retrieve the gram of radium.

Marie has perfected her skills for using x-ray machinery. As a driver she learns how to repair cars, change a tire, and clean a dirty carburetor. On her way to the front line, when a sentry refuses her passing, Marie finds a different road to get through. Along with driving, Marie will load, unload, pack and load again the equipment. Never requiring special treatment, she sleeps in a nurse's room, a hospital room, or a tent. During the whole war only one kidney attack keeps her in bed for a few days. Otherwise, Marie can be found at the front line or in one of the French or Belgian hospitals as a mere technician performing x-rays or teaching a training program for more nurses and technicians.

When working at the field hospitals, Marie is wearing her usual worn black dress with a Red Cross band on her arm. Society women visiting the hospitals don't recognize that this nondescript and unassuming woman is Madame Curie, the famous twice Nobel Laureate. She hears their comments about her and doesn't bother with any indignance.

Marie is with the Belgian Ambulance Service for several occasions when King Albert and Queen Elizabeth are visiting. She makes no record of their visit. Instead she records, "But nothing was so moving as to be with the wounded and to take care of them…Almost everyone did his best to facilitate the X-ray examination; notwithstanding the pain caused by any displacement…I can never forget the terrible impression of all that destruction of human life and health…men and boys… in a mixture of mud and blood, many of them dying of their injuries, many others recovering but slowly through months of pain and suffering."[39]

Marie remains implacable in the face of caring for ten wounded or hundreds wounded in one day. The patients range from those with the calm of being near death to those overcome with abject fear of having an X-ray. Marie reassures frightened soldiers, "You'll see, it's just the same as a photograph."[40] If the time with patients is three hours or twenty, Marie stays till all the wounded have received an X-ray. If the field site demands repeated visits, Marie will make the location a permanent installation to have X-rays. By the end of the war there will be over two hundred X-ray installations.

Marie's comments during the war are subdued and uncomplaining. She writes, "Of the hospital life of those years, we keep many remembrances, my daughter and I. Traveling conditions were extraordinarily difficult; we were often not sure of being able to press forward, to say nothing of the uncertainty of finding lodgings and food."[41]

Eve records one of Marie's visits to the front, "The melancholy procession began. The surgeon shut himself and

Mme Curie into the darkroom, where the apparatus in action was surrounded by a mysterious halo. One after the other the stretchers laden with suffering bodies were brought in. The wounded man would be extended on the radiological table. Marie regulated the apparatus focused on the torn flesh so as to obtain a clear view. The bones and organs showed their precise outlines, and in the midst of them appeared a thick dark fragment: the shot or piece of shell."[42] A doctor writes Marie, "I am on the go from morning to night. I manage to carry out 588 examinations during the month of July...I don't think I can go on assuming this kind of responsibility much longer."[43]

Marie writes later, "To hate the very idea of war, it ought to be enough to see just once what I saw so often during all those years. Men and boys brought to the ambulance behind the lines filthy and covered with blood."[44]

These memories are shared with her daughter, Irene. At seventeen, Irene is as calm as her mother, and she has inherited her mother's dry wit. She knows she must not laugh when she watches her mother use charm with the inspector general of the Military Health Service who has come to inspect the radiological posts. Marie informs the inspector that these are posts he has authorized. Another time Marie and Irene are stopped by sentries who forbid women to enter dangerous territories. Marie and Irene can sometimes talk their way past the sentry. Other times they must go a different, longer route.

Irene records in her journal about a doctor who wouldn't believe her as to the location of the shrapnel. Irene writes, "After carrying out the task–not an easy one–of teaching the methods of localizing projectiles to a Belgian military doctor who was opposed to the most elementary notions of geometry."[45] To anyone with doubts of Irene's abilities, Irene responds, "My mother had just as much confidence in me as she had in herself."[46]

By the next year, Irene is on her own to install an X-ray facility at the military hospital at Amiens. She is also responsible for the facility at Ypres. Irene has learned how to repair equipment and train nurses. She lives alongside her mother without complaint like a soldier in battlefields. Marie calls her, "my companion and friend."[47] Guns and cannon fire are the backdrop to her days and in a few months she will be in charge of her own field radiological facility in Belgium. Up to this time, Irene has been enrolled at the Sorbonne and has graduated with honors in mathematics, physics, and chemistry.

Irene, when she turns eighteen, is at a field hospital. She writes her mother, "I spent my birthday admirable…except that you weren't there. Ma Cherie."[48]

On the streets of Paris, women are working in jobs that previously were only for men. The tram has conductresses and female ticket takers. Women are watering public gardens, delivering the mail, and becoming car mechanics. Marguerite Borel is conducting aptitude tests for women and running a recruiting station. She is in charge of sending women off to jobs in gunpowder factories, airplane factories, railways, and mail delivery. Marguerite will later be running a hospital and Henriette Perrin, (Marie's backyard neighbor, friend) is a volunteer nurse.

The shift for the woman's role is slower in the hospital wards. The French, unlike the British, do not have the women's auxiliaries of the armed services. In fact, there is a movement to take young women from the French hospital wards "on the grounds that the sights they saw there are not fit for 'well-brought-up young girls.'"[49]

If Marie had ever cared about fashion, she should now be pleased that her style is in fashion. Coco Chanel has declared the new style is 'comfortable.' For workplace clothes, skirts are going up; hair is pulled back in buns or cropped. However, Marie is focused on other recent developments.

Jan 1, 1915–Marie writes to Paul Langevin, who is an army sergeant, "I have had a letter saying that the radiological car working in the Saint-Pol region has been damaged. This means that the whole north is without any radiological service! I am taking the necessary steps to hasten my departure. I am resolved to put all my strength at the service of my adopted country, since I cannot do anything for my unfortunate native country just now, bathed as it is in blood after a century of suffering."[50]

Over a year has gone by and there is no word from her Polish family. She writes on August 6th, "Poland is partly occupied by the Germans. What will be left of it after their passage? I know nothing about my family."[51]

The Curie side of Marie's family is suffering too. Marie's nephew, Maurice Curie, is determined to fight for his country. He walks from the Battle of Marne heading north to the front near Reims. Maurice writes, "one hundred and thirty kilometers (eighty-one miles) on foot, sack on back, rain and mud, hardly any food, across the mass graves of Epernay, Montmirail, etc. It is unbearable." He will spend a year near Verdun (north border of France). Of Verdun, one infantryman remembers, "As soon as I saw the battlefield, even though I had already spent fourteen months at the front, I thought; 'If you haven't seen Verdun, you haven't seen anything of war.'"[52]

Later Maurice writes his sentiments, an echo of so many, "This war which never ends."[53]

The war years press on. During 1916 there is a rallying cry "They shall not pass" as the Germans once again are pushing to invade France. The Battle of Verdun begins in February 1916 and won't end until December. The French hold the Germans, but the cost is more than 700,000 troops killed or wounded. French casualties are 337,231 of which 162,308 are dead or missing.

Holding the line at Verdun, there is only one road, the "Sacred Way," to get in and out. It has twelve thousand vehicles passing through to keep the lifeline of supplies into Verdun. The stream of traffic averages one vehicle passing every fourteen seconds for days and nights.[54] Men who were not deemed strong enough or young enough to fight instead have driving shifts of up to seventy-five hours at the wheel.

One driver remembers, "For a week, I was driving–day and night without lights–on unbelievable roads, often with a load twice too heavy for my truck. And yet you couldn't drag along [slow down], because shells were flying all around…One of them, an Austrian 130, sent the residue of its powder right into my face."[55]

Marie corresponds with soldiers throughout the war. Letters from her nephew describe the wretched circumstances. Maurice writes of his life in the trenches; for weeks and months on end he contends with freezing rains, rats and lice. All this is aside from the fact; they are under constant enemy fire. The situation worsens in April 1915. The Germans start using poisonous gas.

André Debierne becomes the director of Chemical Warfare Service to find ways to combat the chlorine-gas shells being launched to the trenches of the French and British troops. Men are filling the hospitals, half-blind and coughing up their lungs from mustard gas. Marie's friend from England, Hertha Ayrton, invents a fan that clears the poison gases from the trenches.

Paul Langevin is transferred from digging ditches and making earthworks as an army sergeant, to being back in the laboratory as a physicist. Using quartz from Pierre's collection, Paul is fine-tuning the ability to use ultrasound to detect the enemy submarines that are wreaking havoc on the seas. In 1916, 936 allied ships are sunk. In 1917, the number reaches 2,681. This is not only a loss of crew and ships, but a dire loss of cargo, food, and fuel for England. Winston Churchill writes "the hanging by a thread, a very slender thread, and one that is in great danger."[56]

A small reason for joy comes for Marie when Jean Perrin is assigned to her service. In January 1915, they are traveling north together. On this one trip they have two flat tires, crash into a tree, and stop for a cup of tea.

For another trip, Marie has a driver, and they are returning to Paris. A sudden turn by the driver throws Marie from the car (no doors) into a ditch. The boxes of equipment are in the ditch too. The driver frantically looks for Marie among the boxes and is calling "Madame! Madame! Are you dead?"[57] Marie never tells the girls of the incident, but they see the blood stained linens in her dressing room. They also get the details when the story hits the newspapers. Marie's wounds are mild compared to the injuries in battles.

From July 1 through November 1 of 1916, the Battle of Somme ensues. One medic wrote, "Hunting for the dead–horrible deliveries of wretches battered to pulp–blood flows–the very sheds are groaning."[58] Noted as one of the bloodiest military battles in history, 1.5 million casualties are recorded.

From 1916 through the end of 1917, there are no bombs dropped on Paris. That reprieve comes to an end in January of 1918 when the Germans throw their entire military strength into the Western Front. Supply lines into the city are cut putting gas in short supply and bread is rationed. Parisians are freezing for lack of coal. Worse than people suffering the cold is the scarcity of water due to frozen pipes. All the while, the death toll of soldiers continues to rise.

Rutherford is visiting Paris in 1917 to give a lecture. Perrin, Langevin and Debierne are working in the laboratories on war research. Marie is also in town. They gather to hear Rutherford give his lecture, and then Marie has her colleagues over for tea. Rutherford remarks about Marie that she is "rather gray, worn out and tired."[59]

Thanks Ernest for that astute observation.

Marie looks tired because she is tired. Aside from twenty years of being exposed to more radiation than any other human being, Marie continues to be exposed due to the X-ray work she is providing. For three years Marie has given complete dedication to the wounded. She travels in any weather, in cars that have no doors and are started by cranking the engine. She sleeps wherever she can find a spot and eats whatever is available at the moment. Add to this, Marie continues to watch over the new laboratory. She moved all the laboratory equipment from the old building to the new building in 1915. She does this with no money or help. Using one of the radiologic cars, she makes trip after trip after trip, loading and unloading and then setting up the equipment in the new laboratory. Marie wants the new laboratory to be up and ready when the war is done. Add to this, Marie is a mother. Watching over her daughters, she must see to their safety, their education, and their well being.

Aside from Marie's trips to the front, she prepares radon tubes to be used in the medical field. Marie called these tubes, emanation bulbs. Marie has no assistants and makes the emanation bulbs herself. Marie writes, "I proceeded to place at the disposal of the Health Service not the radium itself, but the emanation which can be obtained from it at regular intervals."[60] Marie provides this service past the end of the war. The tubes are used to treat the wounded and sick, both military and civilian.

1918 will see the end of the war, but not without a fight–literally. On January 30th, thirty planes fly over Paris and drop 144 bombs, equivalent to 7,000 pounds of explosives. This raid is the largest so far of the war. The Germans see this as a means of softening up the target before putting their full force into an attack on the Western Front. By March the aerial assault increases. The Germans have a siege gun dubbed, the Paris gun. This gun is capable of hurling two-hundred pound shells from seventy-five miles away. With no warning sound of a plane engine overhead, the shell comes arcing down from twenty-five miles up in the sky. Meant to break the morale of civilians, the Paris gun is effective. On the first day of the siege, Parisians who have survived nearly four years of war must withstand twenty-one of these shells landing in Paris. In the following days, the

Parisians withstand an average of twenty shells per day.

There is no reprieve for a religious holiday. On Good Friday a church is hit. The roof collapses, along with a stone vault and a support pillar. Eighty-eight people are killed, sixty-eight are wounded. The gun isn't withdrawn until August, just ahead of the advancing Allied forces.[61]

The Germans must be held back. From January through May, they are less than forty miles from Paris. Writer Helen Pearl Adam records, "The worst days of 1914 seemed come again. After four years of heroism and endurance, after four years of civilian patience, after four years of tested faith in victory, the solid ground beneath our feet threatened to fail. The people who remained in Paris kept their flag flying."[62] Parisians "held furtive consultations as to what arrangements we could make if we had to walk out of Paris at one gate while the Germans walked in at another."[63]

The Germans are pushed back, but the next assault is from within the city. That autumn there is a global flu pandemic sweeping through France. For 1918, after four years of war, personal suffering and loss for millions, another 237,509 French citizens die from the flu pandemic.

By November of 1918, the war statistics are as grim as the photos. Of the 8.4 million mobilized French forces, approximately 1.4 million are killed, 4.3 million are wounded, and 537,000 are prisoners /missing. The casualty count is 6.2 million. So, if you are active duty in this war, you have a 73.3% chance of getting killed or wounded. Not good odds and it would be higher if not for a petite woman who insisted on having X-ray facilities at the front. Records from just 1917-1918 show over 1.1 million wounded soldiers receive X-rays.[64]

Edith Wharton writes of 1918, on the eleventh day, of the eleventh month, at the eleventh hour, "Through the deep expectant hush, we heard, one after another, the bells of Paris calling to each other…our hearts wavered and doubted. Then, like the bells, they swelled to bursting, and we knew the war was over."[65] After 1,561 days of war, on November 11, 1918, the guns are quiet.

Marie and Irene are working in the laboratory when they hear cannons roar at 11:00 a.m. and church bells ringing. The two women go to stores to buy French flags, but they are sold out. They hurry to a fabric store to buy blue, white and red cloth. Marie and Irene make a flag and hang it across the Pavillon Curie. Marie and thousands of others go to the Champs-Elysees to celebrate.

Marie has more reason to celebrate.

With the end of the war, Poland is a free country. Under the domination of outside rule for over one hundred and fifty years, Marie writes her brother Joseph, "…we have seen that resurrection of our country which has been our dream. We did not hope to live to this moment ourselves…"[66]

Marie has not yet heard from Bronya and there is a political tangle in alliances for whether Poland will keep its freedom. When reporters ask Marie about "the Polish question," Marie keeps her answer vague. Nicholas II has announced that after his victory of Austria, he will "re-form Poland under his authority."[67] Regardless of what Nicholas says, Marie is making plans to go and see her family in Poland. She hasn't seen them in years.

The end of the war isn't a return to the 'good ol days.' Eve records of her mother, "The memory of the thousands of hacked-up bodies she had seen, of the groans and shrieks she had heard, was to darken her life for a long time."[68] Families must come to grips with the fact that their sons, husbands, and fathers are not among the men coming home. One in ten able bodied men have been killed. For the student population, this decimates half of the students of 1911, 1912, 1913. Many surviving students are scooped up by industry where their salaries outdo any potential income in research. For the French economy, the salaries increase but not exceeding inflation. During the 1920s there are strikes and civil unrest.

The competition for jobs adds to the pressure for women to get back in the house and leave the jobs for the men. The freedom that was growing for females is reversed. Women who had gone to work as factory workers, nurses, technicians, teachers, farmhands, and mechanics relinquish their rights. It will take another twenty-seven years and another world war for women to even have the right to vote.

For the Curie family–Irene is appointed as assistant in the lab. This insures an income for her. Marie is offered a state pension again and she accepts. The income is necessary relief because Marie has given much of her money for war bonds. Marie is close to broke.

11

"...her family and her work."

Everyone knows it is a matter of time until there is a WWII.
The League of Nations is crippled when the United States
refuses to join, and Germany is being forced to pay exorbitant
reparations. Einstein signs a petition that will outlaw war. Marie declines to sign with this explanation, "I entirely share your
aspirations for the reign of peace and fraternity. Certainly, I
have a horror of war, and I deplore, like you, the subjection
of intelligence to brute force. But the highest cultivation of
intellect is not a guarantee of a just view of national and social
problems...."[1]

Marie is busy with the laboratory, and she writes the book
Radiology in War. Like millions of others, Marie wants to put the
war years behind her. Her willingness does not include an immediate change of heart toward the Germans and particularly
the scientists who gave them support.

During the war, a group of ninety-three intellectuals had
signed a manifesto, "Appeal to the Cultured World" that
supported the German excuse of invading neutral Belgium
as a military necessity. Among the ninety-three intellectuals
(hence the name, The Manifesto of the Ninety-Three) who
signed are fifteen scientists, and Marie despises them. After
the war, when Marie meets a foreign scientist, she asks them
if they had signed the appeal. If they did sign, Marie barely
speaks to them, and she will not have them work in her
laboratory.

Marie returns to her research and she hasn't lost her touch. An assistant gives this description of Marie working, "The series of operations–opening the apparatus, starting the chronometer, lifting the weight, etc.–was affected by Mme Curie with the admirable discipline and harmony of movement. No pianist could accomplish what Mme Curie's hands accomplished with greater virtuosity. It was a perfect technique, which tended to reduce the coefficient of personal error to zero."[2]

Marie might be thinking the rest of her days will be spent in the solitude of her new laboratory. Marie might also think the last person on earth she will talk to, let alone trust, is a journalist. Changes are coming.

For a scientist of her stature, Marie has no secretary and the typewriter she uses is the one she bought from a war surplus sale. The Curie Institute, Marie's new laboratory, should be equipped with modern apparatus but suffers for lack of funds. Monetary donations are given to the medical research side of the institute, not Marie's science side. There is also a shortage of radium. Marie and her team continue to make do with her original small sample.

A suggestion is made that Marie make a public appeal to raise funds. Considering the media circus portraying Marie as an 'assistant' or a husband stealing foreigner, she says 'no.' Any request for media interviews are on Marie's terms. She gives interviews only on Tuesdays and Fridays and the guidelines for these conversations are specific. Questions are for scientific matters, nothing personal.

Into this arena steps Marie Mattingly Meloney, who everyone calls, Missy. She will earn the love and trust of Marie Curie.

> Missy later earns the admiration of First Lady, Eleanor Roosevelt. Eleanor describes Missy as "fine lace made of cable wire."[3]

Born in Kentucky, Missy's mother is a progressive college graduate who challenges the status quo by establishing a school for freed black slaves in 1876. Missy's plans to become a concert pianist are thrown off when a horseback riding accident leaves her with a limp, and then, she gets a diagnosis of having a bad lung. Missy claims, "I have been lame since fifteen, and had a bad lung since seventeen and have done the work of three men ever since."[4]

At seventeen, Missy is a full-time reporter for the *Washington Post*. She becomes the *Denver Post*'s bureau chief in Washington, D. C., and she is the first woman to have a seat in the Senate press gallery. By the time she is meeting Marie, she is a well known American journalist and editor of the *Delineator*, a popular women's magazine. Long before Barbara Walters, Missy will have a list of famous interviews–Hitler, Mussolini, H.G. Wells, and Eleanor Roosevelt.

Missy's earned reputation comes from her commitment to inform her readers of current events and make them aware of their civic duties to their country. After the ravages of WWI, getting her readers to 'care' when what they really want to do is pull back and take a break, is a difficult goal. Missy is searching for the next great story for her readers. A hint of the story is the fact that cancer has surpassed tuberculosis as the chief cause of death. Missy will soon have her "aha" moment for a story, but first she is walking in to meet Madame Curie.

Missy has been requesting an interview with Marie, and the request is always denied. Missy tries using her influence with the editor of a French magazine, but Missy is told, "She will see no one. She does nothing but work. Few things in life are more distasteful to her than publicity. Her mind is as exact and logical as science itself. There are but two things for her–her family and her work."[5]

Using the power of networking, Missy contacts her friend Henri-Pierre Roches. Roches is a Paris society art collector. Roche is friends with Marie (through mutual visits to the home of French sculptor, Auguste Rodin). Missy asks Roche to speak with Marie. He agrees Assuaging concerns for being misrepresented, Roche suggests to Marie she meet with this American journalist. Marie agrees.

Missy records her thoughts prior to meeting Marie. "I had been in Mr. Edison's laboratory a few weeks before sailing from home. Edison is rich in material things–as he should be. Every kind of equipment is at his command. He is a power in the financial as well as the scientific world. In my childhood I had lived near Alexander Graham Bell; had admired his great house and his fine horse. A short time before, I had been in Pittsburgh, where the sky is plumed by the tall smokestacks of the greatest radium reduction plants in the world. I remembered that millions of dollars had been spent on radium watches and radium gun sights. Several millions of dollars' worth of radium was even then stored in various parts of the United States. I had been prepared to meet a woman of the world enriched by her own efforts and established in one of the white palaces of the Champs d'Elysees or some other beautiful boulevard of Paris."[6]

Instead Missy records Marie's office, "the small bare office which might have been furnished from Grand Rapids, Michigan."[7] Missy continues, "I found a simple woman, working in an inadequate laboratory and living in an inexpensive apartment, on the meager pay of a French professor."[8] Missy remembers, "The door opened and I saw a pale, timid little woman in a black cotton dress, with the saddest face I had ever looked upon. Her kind, patient, beautiful face had the detached expression of a scholar. Suddenly I felt like an intruder."[9]

On that day in May, 1920 a friendship begins.

Marie explains to Missy her difficulties in expanding her research when she only has one gram of radium. Missy is astonished and responds, "You have only a gram?" Marie corrects her and replies, "I? Oh, I have none. It belongs to the laboratory."[10]

As their conversation continues, Missy realizes that Marie knows the location of every gram of radium in the world. Marie tells Missy, "America has about fifty grams of radium. Four of these are in Baltimore, six in Denver, seven in New York..."[11]

Missy suggests Marie use the money from her patents to buy the radium she needs. Marie replies, "There were no patents. We were working in the interests of science. Radium was not to enrich anyone. Radium is an element. It belongs to all people."[12]

Missy goes on, "But you ought to have all the resources in the world to continue your research. Someone must undertake this?" Marie responds, "Who?"[13]

Missy ends the interview with this last question, "If you could have one wish, what would you want most in the world?" Marie has an immediate answer, "A gram of radium."[14]

Missy with core goal of improving the life of mankind through civil service has just found an icon. Marie with a core goal of improving the life of mankind through research has just found a supporter. Missy is going to make Marie's wish come true.

In the following days, the two women meet several times. Missy is proposing she will raise $100,000 dollars (approx 1.5 million in 2016) in America to buy one gram of radium. The plan includes having Marie come to America to be given her gram of radium by the President. The rest of the arrangement is an autobiography to be written, with the royalties going to Marie to help her finances. For Missy, the publishers of her magazine will have exclusive rights to the first articles of Marie's trip to America.

Marie worries about media attention. She does not want the American press to make this a rehash of the Langevin affair. Missy, using her connections, contacts every editor-in-chief of every newspaper she knows and asks them to bury the old story. Missy is so effective, not only do they comply with her request, but some newspapers give donations for the radium cause.

Missy begins her work on finding the right hook for her story. Using the American love of an underdog, the headlines for the fundraising campaign reads:

"THAT MILLIONS SHALL NOT DIE"

The emphasis will be on what is hitting home for so many Americans, cancer. Missy puts the emphasis on Marie's work in support of cancer treatment, for in truth radium therapy is made possible due to Marie's research. The pitch in the campaign reads, "The great Curie is getting older, and the world losing, God alone knows, what great secret. And millions are dying of cancer every year."[15] Missy reminds her readers that Marie Curie, "has contributed to the progress of science and the relief of human suffering, and yet, in the prime of her life she [is] without tools which would enable her to make further contribution of her genius."[16]

Marie is beginning to comprehend that the prestige of her name and her presence (going to America) will help garner support for research and laboratories. As for an autobiography about her life, Marie doubts it will be of interest. She tells Missy, "But it will not be much of a book. It is such an uneventful, simple little story. I was born in Warsaw of a family of teachers. I married Pierre Curie and had two children. I have done my work in France."[17]

Missy's all women organizing committee is a progressive mark for the day. However, progress only goes so far when committee member names are listed in the traditional style of the time of using their husband's first name, not their own. The committee includes Mrs. John D. Rockefeller (oil baron, husband), Mrs. Calvin Coolidge (Vice-President, husband), and the founder of the American Society for the Control of Cancer, Mrs. Robert Mead.

With Missy's return to the states, telegrams are clicking back and forth across the Atlantic as details continue to be hammered out. In order to ensure privacy, Missy and Marie have developed code words for different topics, the Langevin affair being one of the topics. Missy's telegram address in New York is IDEALISM.[18] She is living up to the name.

Some details being cleared up are hilarious. Missy, in her telegrams uses the term grain and/or gram for the amount of radium. Marie wants to clarify this and telegrams, "Grain insufficient to justify absence from laboratory because equal to fifteenth of gram." [19]

When the Paris papers get wind of the story of the gram of radium, they announce that the United States is giving the gram to the University of Paris, the Sorbonne. Marie is furious. What might be perceived as a 'control issue' would be accurate–she wants control of the radium. For her own self? Hardly. If she had wanted to be greedy she could have started that a long time ago. Missy writes and confirms to Marie, "The gram of radium is for you, for your personal use, and you will be the one to decide how it is used after your death."[20] Missy adds this thoughtful touch, "I would be happy to be of some use to the University of Paris if it needs help, but for the moment I am devoting all my time and energy to your interests."[21]

With a lack of donations from big donors, Missy switches gears and goes to a grassroots effort. What today is called 'crowd sourcing,' Missy is requesting one or five dollar donations from her readers. The cause catches on with college women who start support campaigns to raise money. A member of the "Marie Curie Radium Fund" writes, "We witness in her research one of the most complete pieces of detective work that ever unearthed a hidden mystery...It is the privilege of the women of this country to lay this tribute at her feet–a gift of radium–instead of a wreath of laurel–with which she can and will give back to them a thousand fold more in value, a hoped-for revelation of the medical power, when its forces can be tamed and used in cancer–that dread scourge."[22]

The itinerary for the trip to America is shaping up and includes eighteen college lectures and seven honorary degrees. There will be a tour of Niagara Falls and the Grand Canyon. Around these dates are sprinkled luncheons and dinners. The main event is at the steps of the White House. President Harding will be awarding Marie one gram of radium.

Marie tells Missy she can stay only two weeks, explaining she will miss her daughters too much. Missy immediately tells Marie to bring the girls. Eve takes Marie shopping for the upcoming trip. Her new dresses are still black, but at least Eve convinces her mother to leave the worn dresses at home.

The date is set for boarding the ship on May 7, 1921.

In March, a French journalist, Stephane Lauzanne is startled when his receptionist tells him he has a call and, "Madame Curie wishes to speak to you."

Good grief! What on earth could this be? The last time he heard Madam Curie's voice was November 1906, her first day teaching at the Sorbonne.

The editor remembers of the call, "This great woman—the greatest woman in France—was speaking haltingly, tremblingly, and almost like a little girl. She, who handles daily a particle of radium more dangerous than lightning, was afraid when confronted by the necessity of appearing before the public."[23] Marie is telling him, "I wanted to tell you that I am going to America. It was very hard for me to decide to go because America is so far and so big. If someone did not come for me, I should probably never have made the trip. I should have been too frightened. But to this fear is added a great joy. I have devoted my life to the science of radioactivity, and I know all we owe to America in the field of science. I am told you are among those who strongly favor this distant trip, so I wanted to tell you I have decided to go, but please don't let anyone know about it."[24]

France is caught off guard with the clamor for Marie's attention from the United States, and that the President will be the one to give Marie the gift of Radium. Begrudging financial support for the laboratory finally comes through; however, Marie still doesn't have a secretary. The French minister of public education offers Marie the Legion of Honor, for the second time. For the second time, Marie declines. The French offer to have a bon voyage party at the Paris Opera. Marie agrees when she knows the money raised by the event will benefit the Radium Institute. Missy is back in Paris for the gala.

There is an irony in this evening, when ten years earlier, Marie was roasted in the press. Jean Perrin, who had come to her defense during the dark times, is a speaker for the gala. He extols to the audience Marie's great contributions to science.

The day to set sail on the *Olympic* is nearing. Marie is fifty-four years old. Eve and Irene have always known their mother as a scientist, but they have no idea their mother is so famous. They are beginning to understand.

The president of the White Star Line escorts Marie and her daughters to their rooms, the honeymoon suite. Marie does not bask in this lap of luxury, she is uncomfortable. She writes a friend, "I left France to go on this distant frolic, so little to my taste and habits." Marie added about Missy, that she "is more of a friend than I can tell you, and I don't think she's doing this for personal advantage; she is an idealist and seems very disinterested."[25] Aside from the uncertainties and no staff that is overseeing the details, Marie is struggling with a constant humming in her ears (tinnitus) and her vision is becoming cloudier. Marie has double cataracts. Missy has arranged for an eye specialist to see Marie once they arrive in the states. The voyage is rough and causes Marie dizzy spells.

When the ship docks in New York City, Marie is deluged with reporters and photographers who meet her on the upper deck. Marie thought she could hand the reporters a typed statement she has written. Clearly they want more.

Seeing Marie will be interviewed before she gets off the ship, someone brings her a chair. Questions come from all sides and voices call out to her, "Look this way, Madame Curie!²⁶" Both Marie and Irene, dressed in plain clothes and sensible shoes, aren't exactly camera ready. It is Eve in her silk stockings, high-heeled shoes and a flowered hat that catches the photographers. The reporters dub her, "Miss Radium Eyes."²⁷

Thousands have gathered to welcome Marie. A band is playing the anthems of France, the United States, and Poland. In the crowds are Girl Scouts, nurses, doctors, and college students, each with their own connection to this iconic woman, a scientist, a teacher. Groups of Polish immigrants have come waving their national flag. Eve and Irene are astonished at the attention. Marie is overwhelmed. She is handed bouquets of flowers and stays to hear several speeches. They are finally able to leave in a limousine, which has been made available, compliments of Mrs. Andrew Carnegie.

When the car arrives at Missy's home, Marie sees the pathway to the house is lined with roses. This expression of gratitude is from a horticulturist, who had been cured of cancer by radium treatments.

So many Americans truly want to show their love and appreciation to the famous Madame Curie. They admire her for her integrity to not have made financial gain, and to serve mankind. There are also those who are curious to see a woman scientist. Marie will never grow accustomed to this attention. On a later trip, Marie writes to Eve, "I am seeking, however, to surmount my extreme repulsion for this whole situation and keep my eye on the real issue which is to gather the necessary funds to allow me to pursue my work."[28] Marie makes a constant effort to escape the press. She records, "I came down the service stairs to avoid sixty reporters waiting at the main entrance."[29]

Marie is cautious to never give advice in any correspondence or interview. Just as Einstein would not suggest how to run electrical wire in a house, Marie will continually remind anyone that she cannot give advice on medical treatments for cancer. Marie talks to crowds of her role in science and tries to keep the focus on the benefits of pure research. She says, "When radium was discovered, no one knew that it would prove useful in hospitals. The work was one of pure science. And this is a proof that scientific work must not be considered from the point of view of the direct usefulness of it. It must be done for itself, for the beauty of science, and then there is always the chance that a scientific discovery may become, like radium, a benefit for humanity."[30] In spite of her efforts, exaggerated claims continue. Headlines from the *New York Times* declare– "Mme Curie Plans to End All Cancer." Or there is the triple alliteration that is a catchy false cry.

"CURIE CURES CANCER!"

Eve later writes about the trip, "Americans had surrounded Mme Curie with an almost religious devotion and had placed her in the first rank of living men and women."[31] Aside from outrageous medical claims, the press is handling Marie better than in the past. The *New York Times* reports, "She works for science, not for money, and it might be said with truth that she will be the trustee rather than the owner of this American gift."[32]

A small hiccup at the beginning of the trip is Marie not having a cap and gown. Since she is the only woman on the faculty of the Sorbonne, the men have gowns, she doesn't. Missy calls in a tailor to quickly make a cap and gown for Marie. No one argues with Marie when she refuses to wear the mortarboard cap saying it looks hideous and it keeps falling off.

The teas and ceremonies are unavoidable. What Marie enjoys most is her time spent meeting women students in their labs and discussing their work. The tour of schools includes: Smith, Simmons, Wellesley, Radcliffe, Bryn Mawr—all women's colleges. At the Smith College, she thanks them for the beautiful reception. In the remarks made by Professor Neilson, Marie is described as "first among women of all ages…" Those are nice words, except Neilson goes on to tell this story. He relays that Marie is so engrossed in her lab that when a maid comes in crying, saying she has swallowed a pin, Marie replies, "Never mind, here's another." When it's Marie's turn at the podium she answers, "It's a good story, but unfortunately, it never happened."[33]

Events are scheduled for the Waldorf-Astoria, the National Academy of Sciences, and The American Museum of Natural History. One memorable event is May 18th at Carnegie Hall. The International Federation of University Women has 3, 500 members gathered to honor Marie. The ceremony includes the French and Polish ambassadors. Marie is thrilled to see her old friend, pianist, and former Polish Prime Minister, Ignace Paderewski.

The media attention, the constant stares, and shaking hands are exhausting to Marie. One man shakes Marie's hand so hard he sprains her wrist. Now her arm is in a sling.

On the eve of the White House ceremony, Missy shows Marie the document she will receive the next day. Marie looks over the paper and says, "We have to add something."[34] Marie wants the wording to explicitly state not only her ownership of the radium, but that it will be her decision of how to leave the radium in her will. Marie wants to ensure that when she dies, the gram of radium will be the property of the Curie Laboratory. Missy agrees and says they will have the wording checked by a lawyer. Marie wants it done, now. Missy explains to Marie this means having the donors agree. Marie says fine. Have the donors agree, now.

A lawyer is found to make the changes that night, and two of the women are contacted to represent the donors. Marie explains to Missy, "The act of the gift will soon be valid, and I may die in a few hours."[35] Marie also wants the money being donated to come under her control and not answer to the donors. Marie holds to this in spite of the money being tied up for several years in a bank. Marie does not chance having to bow to whims of donors when it comes to spending the money for the laboratory.

May 20, 1921 Marie is walking down the White House steps on the arm of President Warren Harding. His remarks for the occasion extol Marie as the "soul of radium" and a "noble woman, devoted wife, a loving mother who, along with her crushing work, performed all the duties a woman must perform."[36] President Harding places a ribbon around Marie's neck with a gold key hanging from it. The key is for the small mahogany box on the table serving as a decoy for the actual box that is being guarded. Harding declares, "As a nation whose womanhood has been exalted to fullest participation in citizenship, we are proud to honor in you a woman whose work has earned universal acclaim and attested women's equality in every intellectual and spiritual activity."[37]

Finally, Marie will have access to another gram of radium. The radium, less than half a teaspoon, is divided into a dozen different portions in sealed glass vials and then secured in a lead casket with a wall two inches thick. (The casket is on display at the Curie Museum in Paris. It weighs 130 pounds, 60,000 times the weight of the radium itself.[38])

At the White House reception, Irene and Eve are in line shaking hands and greeting guests in English, French, or Polish. Marie is wearing the same black dress she wore ten years earlier for her second Nobel Prize.

Another stop on the Curie tour is the Canonsburg Company in Pennsylvania. This is the facility that prepared the gram of radium for Marie. They used the same process that Marie used, except she did this in a shack for a laboratory.

Marie at the Canonsburg Company,
1921, *Musée Curie (coll. ACJC)*

Marie isn't able to keep up with the schedule of events. She is suffering with hypertension and a kidney infection. Missy is also exhausted and near the point of collapse. Keeping up with the relentless schedule, has caused Missy's tuberculosis to recur. Marie sends her daughters to represent her at ceremonies. There are some events where the daughters literally stand in for Marie, wearing the honorary cap and gown to receive the honorary degree. No one ever knows.

Irene is bored and finds this a trying time. Eve comes through as the needed balance since she enjoys the social chatter about jazz and fashion. As Irene settles into her role at events, she is the one to talk with the scientists.

In Chicago there are large groups of Polish men and women gathered to see Marie. These touching occasions are also meaningful for Marie. The women simply want to be near Marie. Marie is the woman who represents their beloved country. They reach out to kiss her hands and touch her dress.

In the midst of the celebrity attention, Marie is still unassuming and takes care of her own needs. Missy writes about Marie, "Once during our American travels, we stayed in a home where there were several other house guests besides our party of five. I entered Madame Curie's room and found her washing her under clothes. Marie explained, "It is nothing at all. I know perfectly well how to do it, and with all of these extra guests in the house, the servants have enough to do."[39] Lavish and luxurious will not ever be descriptors for Marie. When Marie sees a small house with a garden from the train window she says, "I have always wanted such a little home."[40]

While many colleges are lining up to give honorary degrees to Marie, some schools resent that Marie is taking from their 'rice bowl.' They want to protect their private funds and not give their donors any reason to divert money to Marie. (Marie, receiving generous donations from Andrew Carnegie, being an example.)

There is also backdoor politics for not honoring Marie. At Yale University, Boltwood has pressured the school to not grant Marie a degree. Marie is in good company because Boltwood will also block Einstein from receiving an honorary degree. Misogyny and anti-Semitism isn't erased with academic intelligence. Boltwood later meets with Marie at the famous Sloane Laboratory for Yale. After spending a couple hours with Marie he describes her as "touching" and "unusually amiable." He has the delayed epiphany of "her great interest in scientific subjects."[41]

Harvard's current president will compare Marie to Sir Isaac Newton except the retired president, Charles Eliot, thinks differently. Charles refuses to meet Marie at a formal reception held in her honor. He writes, "The credit for the discovery of radium did not belong entirely to her and that, furthermore, she had done nothing of great importance since her husband died in 1906."[42]

Marie joins the girls for the train trip across the US to see the Grand Canyon. This is a memorable time for Marie and her daughters. As they visit the national park, could Marie have imagined that the Marie Curie Cancer Care (United Kingdom charity, est. 1948) would have a yearly fundraiser trek in the canyon to raise money to provide care for people with cancer and support to their families.

The day arrives when the Curie ladies must leave the United States. This trip will redefine the rest of Marie's life. Whether she wants it or not, she is a celebrity. Irene and Eve must share their "sweet Me" with the world. Her cabin is filled with flowers and telegrams of well wishers. Saying goodbye to Missy is difficult. Marie tells her, "Let me look at you one more time, my dear dear friend…This may be the last time I will ever see you."[43]

Marie has found a kindred spirit who has survived in a world dominated by men, and they both are struggling with the frustrations of poor health. Missy has tuberculosis and Marie is sure she herself is going blind. Both women also share a trait of remaining 'disinterested' in any personal gain from their chosen profession. The next fifteen years will include a continuous flow of correspondence. Honest and revealing, Marie later writes to Missy asking her to destroy their letters. Marie explains, "They are part of me and you know how reserved I am in my feelings."[44] More so, Marie knows how poorly the world tries to understand her.

July 2, 1921, their ship arrives in France. There are no throngs of adoration at the dock, two reporters. Two lab assistants have come to help with the luggage and to take the radium to the lab. The media preoccupation is with the Carpentier (French)-Dempsey (American) boxing match. Reporters ask Marie her opinion of the fight, and she responds that she has no opinion in this matter. Marie and the girls are not able to get a ride. All the cabs are all parked near loudspeakers that are broadcasting the fight. The Curie ladies walk home. After the public fuss in the States, this might have been a relief.

Marie brings back from this trip the gram of radium worth $100,000, equipment given to her from the Sloane Laboratory, $22,000 worth of mesothorium, $7,000 in speaker's fees, and an extra $52,000 that Missy has raised. Marie has promised to write the biography of Pierre Curie and that earns $50,000.[45]

Marie writes a thank you to her "American Women" for their gifts. "I was very thankful to my sisters of America for this genuine proof of their affection."[46] What Marie also takes home is a satisfaction in seeing the number of scientific laboratories and hospitals using Curie therapy. It is more than she could have imagined for France.

Marie is exhausted and takes a vacation to rest, swim in the ocean, read and putter in the garden. The village on the French coast has become so popular for the yearly gathering of science families it has been dubbed "Sorbonne-by-the-Sea." The Curie family friends are there–the Borels and the Perrins. Eve and Irene are with Marie. For a time, Marie can relax and enjoy being a mother.

"It is the lesson I learned from my mother."[47]

Eve's relationship with her mother has always been different than Irene's. Eve writes, "My mother was thirty-seven years old when I was born. When I was big enough to know her well, she was already an aging woman who had passed the summit of renown. And yet it is the celebrated scientist who is strangest to me-probably because the idea that she was a "celebrated scientist" did not occupy the mind of Marie Curie."[48]

Through Eve's childhood, Marie recognizes Eve's talents. She writes that Eve has "astonishing musical abilities."[49] When Eve is three and a half, Marie buys her a grand piano and hires a piano tutor. During Eve's growing years, Marie's letters to her are not comments about polonium's reaction to nickel but, "I think it is unsatisfactory to let all one's interests in life depend on feelings as stormy as the feeling of love."[50] In later years, Eve pursues journalism. Considering her mother's aversion to journalists, Marie supports Eve's decision.

> Eve's chief complaints of Marie's parenting were wishing her mother had been more authoritarian so Eve would have had something to rebel against.

During Eve's teenage years Marie comes in to chat with her as she is getting ready for a night out. Marie, with no desire for makeup says, "I have no objection in principle to this daubing.

I can only say one thing to you: I find it frightful...To console myself, I will come kiss you in your bed tomorrow morning, before you have time to put these horrors on your face. And now, off you go, my little child. Goodnight. Oh! Do you have anything I can read?"[51] Considering black is Marie's 'go to' color of choice, it is a shame Eve's response isn't recorded when Marie tells Eve, "You wear black too much."[52]

Eve has her mother's ability to banter with wry wit. She responds to journalists, "You see I am the only one of the family not to have won a Nobel Prize." And later Eve's husband, a French diplomat Henry R. Labouisse, wins a Nobel Peace Prize for the United Nations Children's Emergency Fund in 1965. Now Eve tells a journalist, "There were five Nobel Prizes in my family. Two for my mother, one for my father, one for my sister and brother-in-law, and one for my husband. Only I was not successful."[53]

Eve leaves the route of playing for piano concerts, and instead writes music reviews. She becomes a film and theater critic for Paris magazines using a pseudonym so as not to gain from her famous family name. As Eve moves into her role as a journalist, she interviews dignitaries around the world. Before the US joins in WWII, Eve does use her name and her platform to tour the United States and encourage the US to be a part of the war. Eve meets Eleanor Roosevelt and has dinner at the White House. Eleanor writes about Eve in her My Day column.[54]

Eve Curie giving a lecture in NYC April 1940 *"We discovered that peace at any price is no peace at all. We discovered that life at any price has no value whatever; that life is nothing without the privileges, the prides, the rights, the joys that make it worth living and also worth giving. And we also discovered that there is something more hideous, more atrocious than war or than death; and that is to live in fear."[55]*

During WWII, Eve joins the French Resistance. And because she knows German, Eve becomes a "Special War Correspondent" and travels to Iran, Iraq, India, China, Burma, and North Africa. Her book, *Journey Among Warriors*, is published in 1943, and it is nominated for a Pulitzer Prize for Correspondence in 1944.[56] Proceeds from book sales are given in support of French prisoners of war. When giving an interview about her strength and courage during WWII, Eve responds, "It is the lesson I learned from my mother."[57]

Public opinion will be slow to catch on to encouraging their daughters to be self reliant as Marie has done with Eve and Irene.

Public opinion will also be slow to acknowledging the dangers of radium.

Marie always reminds people that she is not a medical doctor. She and Pierre had accepted the risks associated with radium, and they were willing to pay the price for their research.

Post WWI, after millions had been X-rayed, many people who had been exposed to radiation are beginning to suffer from a variety of ailments. In Marie's book, *Radiology and the War,* she states that radiodermatitis could lead to death. As a counter-balance, over 8,319 patients (1919-1935) are cared for at the Radium Institute. Patients are being saved from suffering and death by the use of X-rays and radiation treatments.

In 1925, a report recommends that radioactive material be enclosed in a thick, heavy metal box. Workers are to be protected with lead screens, ventilation hoods are in place to remove radioactive gases, and tongs are used to handle radioactive material. Marie insists that her workers have periodic blood tests, although she will rarely follow the protocol herself.

Marie's personal friends benefit from radium. Missy undergoes radium treatment and a tumor is successfully treated. The dancer, Loie Fuller, also has radium therapy for breast cancer and writes Marie, "Dear, dear friend. Once again in your debt."[58]

One reason it takes so long to understand the harmful effects of radiation is radioactive material is silent and invisible. If a person gets hit with a bullet, there is a bang and blood. Radiation is different from anything they have ever seen (not seen) before. It affects different people in different ways, and then, there is the question of how much radiation is harmful.

And yet–staff from Marie's lab are falling ill and dying. Marie organizes a fund to raise money for the widows.

When Marie is away, Irene writes to Marie about a chemist at the Radium Institute, "in very bad health…she has stomach troubles, and extremely rapid loss of hair…"[59] The chemist has been working with polonium. Marie releases a statement warning research colleagues about the possible dangers affiliated with handling radioactive materials.

The time Marie is happiest is in her laboratory although this joy is now clouded, literally, with her fading vision. She doesn't want workers in the lab to know her eyesight is deteriorating. She tells her daughters, "Nobody needs to know that I have ruined eyes." As Marie struggles with aging and poor health, she writes to Bronya, "Nor do I know whether, even by writing scientific books, I could live without the laboratory."[60]

Deeply contemplative for how to spend whatever is left of her life, Marie tells Bronya, "I have suffered so much in my life that I have no more suffering left in me. Only a real catastrophe could affect me now. I've learned what it is to be resigned and I try to find a few small joys in the grayness of daily life…Tell yourself you can build houses, plant trees, cultivate flowers, watch them grow and not think of anything else. We haven't much life left ahead of us, so why go on tormenting ourselves."[61]

It is the introspection of a tired woman.

12

"I am going home."

"I will never forget the expression of intense joy that came over her face." [1] Irene describing Marie in the laboratory

Marie is at work in the laboratory and aside from the Curie Institute being world renown; the students are from around the world. Over the years the staff and students are from Norway, Sweden, Russia, Poland, England, Germany, Belgium, China, Iran, India, Austria, Portugal, Switzerland, and Greece.[2] Marie's pragmatic style, vision for science and priority of attention to students makes her a masterful leader in her position as director of the Laboratory. One student recalls, "Marie Curie came every day and spent hours and hours there… There was no question that she was good at administration… But what was most important and most precious was the close contact between the students and the heads…She had a thorough knowledge of the work each student was doing, and was always very interested in all the details. In the laboratory, her face, which was usually closed and slightly sad, became animated, she smiled often, and she even laughed with a fresh, young laugh…And every student was struck, from time to time, by the extent of her knowledge, the luminous clarity of her mind, as she always grasped the essence of a problem, no matter how complicated it was."[3]

A daily ritual has developed at the laboratory. The students wait at the stairs for Marie to arrive each morning. As Marie approaches the steps, the students start asking their questions. Marie stops and sits down on the steps with the young scholars gathered around her. One student recalls, "We called these occasions 'the study of science of radioactivity on the staircase.'"[4]

Marie answers her students' questions and can refer to all the publications connected with their experiments that have been performed at the institute, in any of the five languages. The students refer to Marie as "the boss." Marie also takes an interest in their personal lives and her reputation is considered tough but fair.

Those who will not be allowed to continue as one of her 'laboratory children' are students who are not serious about their work. Marie spots anyone who is there only to later claim they had worked under the guidance of Madame Curie. If this is the case and they do not measure up, they are dismissed from the program. In one notebook, Marie writes beside the name of a student '…idiot.'[5] And not all Marie's staff adores her. There is an instance of her chief of staff who is furious (the reason remains unknown) and he is seen banging on her locked office door shouting "Bitch! Bitch!"[6]

Regardless of the work with students and directing staff, Marie finds time for her research. A student writes this apt description of Marie: "The workday isn't long enough for the separation [of a radioactive element]. Mme Curie stays in the laboratory during the evening, skipping dinner. But the separation of this element is taking a long time: we will therefore spend all night working…It's two o'clock in the morning, and there is still one more operation to be done: the centrifuging of a liquid for an hour around a special support. The centrifuge turns with a wearying noise, but Mme Curie stays next to it, not wanting to leave the room. She contemplates the machine as though her ardent desire to succeed in the experiment could cause the actinium X to precipitate by the power of suggestion alone. For Mme Curie, nothing exists right now except this centrifuge–not her life, the next day, not her fatigue. This is a total depersonalization, a concentration of her whole soul in the work she is doing."[7]

The Paris Academy of Medicine (different from the Academy of Science) has been in place for two hundred and twenty four years. No woman has been a member. In February 1922, Marie's name is recommended for membership, for the discovery of radium and introducing Curie-therapy as a new medical treatment. In a gracious show of support, the other candidates who are being considered for the open seat, resign in Marie's favor. The academy's president announces, "You are the first woman of France to enter an academy, but what other woman could have been so worthy?"[8]

The summer of 1923, Marie has a cataract operation. Her eyes are bandaged for several days and she will eventually have three more operations. Marie needs a magnifying glass to read. She writes her lecture notes in large bold letters, and her equipment at the lab has color coded labels. Marie has continual humming in her ears. She tells her doctor, "Radium may have had something to do with these problems, but we can't be certain of that…"[9] Eve is with Marie during this time.

In December of the same year, Hela, Bronya and Joseph come to Paris to attend the twenty-five year anniversary for the discovery of radium. Complete with a brass band, the Sorbonne is surrounded with crowds. Guests include: Alexandre Millerand who had been her lawyer during the Langevin affair, Paul Appell (the man who threw his shoe), and president of the Curie Foundation, Jean Perrin who had fought for Marie to stay, and of course, André Debierne who is still working with Marie. The French government agrees to give Marie an annual pension of forty thousand francs, and the pension will carry on to her daughters after her death.

In March 1925, there is a scurry again at the Sorbonne caused by a Curie. Irene is about to give her doctoral thesis. The event has been covered by the *New York Times* and a thousand people are cramming into the amphitheater. Marie, wanting to keep the attention on Irene, does not attend.

Irene, like her mother twenty years earlier, is dressed simply. She dedicates her thesis to, "Mme Curie by her daughter and her pupil." Eve remembers this day and that Irene went "calmly off to the Sorbonne, came back confident of having passed, and waited without any great emotion for the result that was guaranteed in advance."[10] Paul Langevin, who had been supervised by Irene's father, is Irene's doctoral professor.

Marie arranges a tea and champagne celebration for guests at the institute's garden. In a display of physicists being playful, tea is brewed in laboratory flasks, heated on bunsen burners, and served in the lab beakers.

Irene is quietly referred to as the "crown princess" of the laboratory, and she has the brains to back it up. The Sorbonne had appointed Irene as Marie's assistant after the war.

Parts of Irene's duties include giving direction to new assistants and one of them is Frederic Joliot. He has come up through the lesser ranks much like Pierre and Paul Langevin. In fact, Langevin was Frederic's teacher and mentor. It is Langevin who recommended Frederic to Marie. Frederic has been enamored with the Curies since he was an eight year old. As a child, seeing a picture of the Curies in a magazine, he cut it out, put it in a homemade frame and hung the picture in his bedroom. Frederic once asked Irene, "What is it like to be the daughter of such famous parents?" Irene responds that she simply doesn't understand the question.[11]

Later, Frederic writes about Irene, "I saw that inside this girl, whom others looked on as pretty much a rough block of stone, there was an extraordinarily sensitive and poetic creature who in many ways was like a living example of what her father had been...I saw in his daughter the same purity, the same good sense, the same calm."[12] Irene has also taken notice of Frederic.

Eve recalls, "One morning [at breakfast] Irene calmly announced to her family her engagement to Frederic Joliot, the most brilliant and most high-spirited of the workers at the Institute of Radium. The existence of the household was turned upside down...A young man suddenly appeared in the female household where except for a few familiars, nobody ever penetrated."[13]

Marie comments to Jean Perrin, "This boy is full of fireworks."[14] She introduces Frederic for the next two years as, "The man who married Irene."[15] Since French law gives husbands control of the property, Marie insists on a prenuptial agreement making certain that only Irene will have control of the Curie Institute and the radioactive substances. Irene, always protective of her name 'Curie,' will sign her name on separate documents as Irene Curie. Together they are Irene and Frederic Joliot-Curie.

Frederic defends his doctoral thesis on March 17, 1930. Marie once again hosts a celebration tea in the garden of the institute.

Irene and Frederic have a baby girl, Helene, born the year after their wedding, 1927. The doctor has told Irene she has tuberculosis and to cut back on work and not have any more children. The week after Helene is born, Irene is back in the laboratory and in five years, they have a son, Pierre. Marie is delighted with grandchildren. Eve recalls, "Stories about her granddaughter…, a quotation from the child's talk, could make her suddenly laugh to the point of tears, with an unexpected laugh of youth."[16]

Helene, the granddaughter, remembers her parents speaking of her grandmother Marie, frequently when she was growing up. She remembers that her grandmother loved to garden and doesn't know her grandmother is famous until later as a young woman. Both Helene and her brother Pierre become physicists. Helene is the one to later marry Paul Langevin's grandson.

During the 1920s, Bronya decides that Warsaw should also have a radium institute. Bronya and Marie start a fundraising campaign, "Buy a brick for the Marie Sklodowska-Curie Institute."

Marie and Irene go to Warsaw in 1925 to lay the cornerstone of the Marie Sklodowska-Curie Institute. Marie meets the President of the Polish Republic. He had met Marie thirty-three years earlier when he was in exile in Paris. While he and Marie are chatting at the event, he remembers the traveling cushion Marie had loaned him for his secret trip back to the

Russian-controlled Poland. Marie reminds him that he has never returned the cushion.[17]

On this trip, Marie attends the theater. The show is starring the actor M. Kotarbinsk. (This is the same man for whom Marie, as a teenager, and her cousins made a wreath of flowers and tossed it to him.) When Kotarbinsk is on the stage, he sees Marie in the audience. He bows to acknowledge her.[18]

Marie is suffering constant problems with her health. Aside from her struggle to cope with blurry vision, Marie is afflicted with anemia, fatigue, a running low-grade fever and a drop in her blood pressure. Still wary of media attention, Marie uses assumed names when she checks into hospitals for treatment. She writes to Bronya, "Sometimes my courage fails me and I think I ought to stop working, live in the country and devote myself to gardening. But I am held by a thousand bonds, and I don't know when I shall be able to arrange things otherwise. Nor do I know whether, even by writing scientific books, I could live without the laboratory."[19]

One of the 'thousand bonds," is the 1927 Solvay Conference.

Marie is the only woman among twenty-eight men invited to the 1927 Solvay Conference. Of the twenty-nine attendees, seventeen were or will be Nobel Prize winners. Marie ranks alone in having two Nobel Prizes, in two different science categories.

Another of the 'thousand bonds' is Missy, who is on her way back from an interview with Mussolini in Italy. Missy stops in Paris to see Marie and to be awarded the Legion of Honor from

France. It's 1928 and Missy, like Marie, is tired and struggling with poor health. Missy has received radiation treatment for a malignant tumor. She is disillusioned with business and politics, and her husband has died of tuberculosis. As the two women catch up, Missy realizes that Marie is using her own funds to supply Warsaw with a sample of radium. Missy offers to raise money, a sequel to the first U.S. trip. Missy says, "I don't see much in life anymore that is worth the trouble, but to serve a great cause, even by performing humble tasks, brings me real rewards."[20]

Marie wants to make the trip as a Polish woman, and she wants Bronya to come with her. Missy says—no. She believes the campaign will be successful only if the emphasis is on Marie, the world's greatest scientist, needing radium to research cancer treatments. Understanding how to successfully leverage Marie's notoriety, Missy tells Marie she must go as neither a citizen of France or Poland but of Radium.

Marie agrees, but insists there will be no interviews, autograph sessions, picture taking or handshaking events. Missy agrees and organizes an itinerary of visits exclusively to laboratories, scientific conferences, a few official receptions and a banquet honoring Thomas Edison. The presentation of the radium will be done by the President again. This time it is President Hoover.

October 15, 1929, the ship docks in New York City. The New York Times article claims "Mme Curie Arrives, Happy to Be Back." [21] The truth is, Marie is tired, frail and wearing thick dark glasses.

As Marie makes her tour stops, she is impressed with how far laboratories have progressed. The physics department at Columbia University is a thirteen-story building, almost solely devoted to the study of the atom. In comparison, Marie's laboratory is three stories, including the basement. Marie is also amazed with the large number of female students, although there is a burden for these young women.

There is growing public pressure for female scientists to maintain Madame Curie's standard. Marie tries to dissuade this by telling them, "It isn't necessary to lead such an antinatural existence as mine, I have given a great deal of time to science because I wanted to, because I loved research…What I want for women and young girls is a simple family life and some work that will interest them."[22]

When Marie tours General Electric, the company shuts down the plant so Marie can examine all the pieces of equipment. She is amazed at the endless rows of precision instruments and the massive assembly lines. She is equally amazed that there are no women workers.

Marie's visit to the White House has the additional honor of her being an official guest. No foreigner had ever been given this privilege. On Wednesday, October 30, 1929, the day after what becomes known as Black Tuesday, President Hoover presents Marie with the gift of radium. It is a glowing tribute against the coming dark days of The Depression.

July of 1930 Marie is in Geneva for the League of Nations. She is shifting her opinion and realizing the necessity of scientists having patents on their work. Reconciling to the fact that more research is driven by the profit of the industry, she works on the League of Nations' International Committee on Intellectual Cooperation. In the next few years, Marie insists that governments establish a royalty payment for scientists whose discoveries benefit humankind.

Marie writes to Eve about being in the committee… "However imperfect it may be, Geneva's creation has a greatness that deserves to be supported."[23] Einstein is a member for awhile and writes, "Its members may be efficient, but this is the most inefficient enterprise I've ever been associated with."[24] In the turmoil of the times and the rising anti-Semitism, Einstein quits for political reasons. Einstein tells fellow physicist, Max Planck, "I am on the nationalists' list to be assassinated."[25]

During the trip in 1930 to Geneva, Marie learns that Jacques, Pierre's brother, is seriously ill. Marie leaves immediately to help care for him. At the same time, Marie receives news from Poland that Bronya's husband, Casimir, has died. This coincides with the recent tragedy that Hela, Bronya's daughter has died. (Hela had been living in Chicago, and the cause of death is possibly suicide.) Marie writes to Eve about Bronya, "What I fear most for her is the moment when she must step down from her activities because she could let herself get overwhelmed by the past that haunts her."[26]

During 1930, Marie has her fourth cataract operation. Marie writes Eve that she is pleased with the results. She can go for walks again on mountain trails without wearing her glasses. Missy comes to visit during the fourth operation. Missy encourages Marie to come to the United States one more time. Marie is unsure about making the trip. When Missy bids Marie goodbye, this will be the last time the two friends are together.

Marie is the icon of science. Her shift from research to promoting science is certainly less intellectually stimulating. Marie writes to Irene: "I am stupefied at the life I'm leading and I can't say anything intelligent to you. I ask myself what fundamental defect in the human organization makes this kind of agitation to a certain extent necessary: We are dignifying science, Mrs. Meloney (Missy) would say. And what can't be denied is the sincerity of everyone doing these things and their conviction that they have to do them."[27]

In July of 1932, Marie will 'dignify science' with her presence at the inauguration of the Marie Sklodowska-Curie Institute in Warsaw. Marie cannot deny the immediate impact of her second trip to the United States. The gift of radium to Warsaw means cancer patients are receiving radiation treatments.

"Marie Curie is, of all celebrated beings, the only one whom fame has not corrupted." Albert Einstein

Marie, who will always cringe at the thought of public appearances, is sacrificing her time to make trips to Holland, Brazil, Italy, Denmark, Czechoslovakia, Spain, Scotland, and of course, Poland. She travels to Geneva to be a voice in the League of Nations in her position on the 'Commission for the Intellectual Cooperation.' At a conference in Spain, Marie speaks on, "The Future of Culture." Marie states, "I believe that Science has great beauty. A scientist in the laboratory is not a mere technician; he is also a child confronting natural phenomena that impress him as though they were fairy tales. We mustn't let anyone think that all scientific progress has been reduced to mechanisms, machines, gear boxes…though these things, too, have their own beauty…I also don't think that the spirit of adventure is in danger of disappearing from our world. If I see anything vital around me, it is this very spirit of adventure, which seems ineradicable and is very closely related to curiosity."[28]

In October 1933, for the seventh Solvay Conference in Brussels, the attendees will include Marie, Irene and Frederic. A third woman at the conference is Lise Meitner. It will be the first conference dedicated to nuclear physics.

1933 Solvay Conference–Front Row includes Lise Meitner, Marie Curie, and Irene Joliot-Curie, *Musée Curie (coll. ACJC)*

Marie works in the laboratory every workday and gives lectures at the Sorbonne twice a week. Jean Perrin is in the building next door, at the Institute of Physical Chemistry. Henri Poincare is across the courtyard at the Institute of Mathematics and Mathematical Physics, which is headed by Emile Borel. And now the Academy of Sciences, that keeps a death grip on their all-male policy, is seeing their funding gradually maneuvered away by Jean Perrin. Money is instead going to the Centre National of Research Scientifique, or known today as CRNS.

Marie's priority of the laboratory continues. When a student reported to her the results of an experiment, the student remembers, "Madame Curie turned around abruptly, removed her glasses, and gazed at me with her most beautiful smile, which lit up her tired face,..."[29] For anyone traveling to a remote location, Marie reminds them to bring back minerals. The lab has one of the most extensive collections.

Marie falls in the laboratory and breaks her wrist. Complications hold her back from returning to work right away. She is weak, feverish, and having dizzy spells. She still contends with constant ringing in her ears and her fingers are sore. She overcomes all this and is back to work and making trips for the sake of science.

Eve meets Marie at the train after one of her many trips. Eve has given up on changing her mother's dress preference. She wants the simplest dress and the cheapest hat. Marie still carries the same brown leather handbag, given to her by an association of Polish women.

Eve knows how draining trips and public attention are for her mother and writes, "We have seen Marie Curie in the evening of her life at the mercy of the admiration of crowds, received by presidents, ambassadors, and kings in all latitudes. One picture, always the same, dominates the memory of these fetes and processions for me; the bloodless, expressionless, almost indifferent face."[30]

Marie continues as the chair of general physics at the Sorbonne, she teaches on Mondays and Wednesdays at five o'clock. Every morning, Marie is at the laboratory. Irene is taking on more and more of the lab responsibilities, but Marie is still there. Staff in the laboratory is aware of her frail condition, and her difficulty in seeing.

André Debierne is still at Marie's side to give her support. He has worked with Marie for almost forty years. Irene and Fred come to Marie's apartment for lunch several times a week. And Marie continues to keep her personal life, personal. Her driver recalls having stopped at a crowded restaurant and the owner brings over the guest book and announces loudly Marie's name and asks her to sign the book. The driver remembers, "Madame Curie got up, without a word laid down money for the uneaten meals, and we left."[31] And yet another time, after a dinner, Marie walked in the hotel's flower garden. The next morning, Marie finds freshly cut roses lay on her table. She asks for the guest book and signs her name.

In the winter of 1933-1934, Marie spends time on vacation in the French Alps with Irene and her seven-year-old granddaughter, Helene. Marie is busy skiing, skating, and snowshoeing. One evening Irene is worried when her mother hasn't returned. Marie is fine. She stayed out to see the sunset.

January 15, 1934, Marie goes to the laboratory to see Irene and Frederic's work. They give Marie a tube containing the first sample of an artificially created radioactive isotope. Marie holds the Geiger counter up to the sample and the clicks confirm the radioactivity. Irene remembers, "I will never forget the expression of intense joy that came over her face."[32] This will be the final thrill of Marie's life, in the laboratory.

> A scientific journal that year will call artificial radio-activity "One of the most important discoveries of the century."[33] Irene and Frederic will be awarded the Nobel Prize in Chemistry the following year for their discovery. At the reception, the King of Sweden asks Frederic where Irene is and Frederic finds her in a quiet corner, reading a book.

Society has inched forward when an article about Irene and Frederic in *Time* magazine reads, "Husband and wife work like one person with two heads, four hands and twenty fingers."[34] The struggle to be equal is far from over. Other press stories will continue to attribute Frederic with the brains and Irene as the assistant.

Irene and Frederic will both apply for membership in the Academy of Sciences. Frederic is accepted and Irene is not. Irene will apply two more times and be denied. Irene comments, "Well at least they are consistent in their thinking."[35]

Marie and Missy continue to write. Marie asks Missy to come and take a vacation with her, but Missy is too ill. Marie also writes asking for reassurance that when she dies, the radium will remain in the laboratory under Irene's control. She also asks Missy again to destroy their correspondence over these last several years. Missy assures Marie of both concerns. Marie has also cleared material from her own files that she doesn't ever want to be made public.

Bronya comes to visit in the spring of 1934. The two sisters have five weeks together and take a road trip. Before Marie leaves she writes to Irene: "I have written a provisional resolution on the subject of the gram of Ra which can serve as a will and I have put it with the documents from America in a packet: the contents are indicated in red on the outside. All this is in the drawer of the chest in the drawing room, below the locked drawers."[36]

Cold days during the trip cause Marie to catch a chill. Marie worries she will not be able to finish the second edition of her book on radioactivity or finish the new country home she is having built in Sceaux. After Bronya leaves, Marie writes to her, "I feel the need of a house with a garden more and more and I ardently hope that this will succeed…"[37]

Marie, not recovering, is taken to a clinic. Jacques, still the ever caring brother-in-law, writes to Marie, "When you are back on your feet you must resolve to follow a more serious and less debilitating regime. Tenderest wishes and affection."[38]

In May, Marie is at the laboratory, but she is struggling. She quietly says, "I have a fever, I'm going home."[39] It will be the last day she is in a laboratory. When she is walking through the garden she sees a rose bush that needs attention and tells a staff person to make sure the plant has care.

Marie needs care too, and it's Eve who is staying with her. When a few friends come to visit or when Marie chats with Eve, Marie is pleased that proofreading of her book is finished and she talks about the new house being built in Sceaux.

Marie has a doctor's visit. She has continual humming in her ears, and she is nearly blind in spite of the cataract operations. Her diagnosis is tubercular lesions. Eve consults four other doctors. They agree. The doctor recommends Marie go to a sanatorium for the fresh air.

In this next episode of family support, the plan is for Eve to stay with her mother the first few weeks, and then some of the family from Poland will come, followed by Irene. Marie, Eve and a nurse leave in a train. The journey is exhausting. Marie faints in Eve's arms on the train.

Once they arrive at the sanatorium, Marie is using an assumed name, "Mme Pierre." The doctors take X-rays of her lungs and there is no sign of tuberculosis. This is disheartening, realizing now the trip was worthless. The doctor, diagnosing extreme pernicious anemia, also tells Eve that Marie's condition is hopeless. He explains, "aplastic pernicious anemia... The bone marrow cannot react probably because it had been injured by a long accumulation of radiation."[40] Marie's temperature is 104 degrees.

As Eve sits with her mother and holds her hand, Eve remembers her mother telling the stories of the carefree teenage year. Eve writes, "Many years later my mother sometimes evoked those happy days for me. I looked at her tired face, worn out by nearly half a century of care and immense toil. And I thanked the destiny which, before it dictated this woman's austere and inexorable summons, had allowed her to follow by sleigh after the wildest kuligs (sleigh ride party), and to use up her shoes of russet leather in one night of dancing."[41]

Eve makes the decision to spare Marie the emotional suffering of knowing the prognosis. Eve also decides not to call the family to the bedside and not to allow any treatment that would prolong Marie's life. Irene and Frederic arrive July 2. When Irene comes to her mother's room, the situation is so shattering to Irene she cannot bear to be in the room. Much like when Marie lost Pierre, Irene is losing more than her mother.

July 3rd, Marie is taking her own temperature. She is happy to see her temperature has dropped. Marie looks out the window to the sunny day and tells Eve, "It wasn't the medicines that made me better. It was the pure air…"[42] The drop in temperature is an indication that she is dying.

By the end of the day, Marie is too weak to stir her tea. The doctor comes in to give Marie a shot. Marie refuses saying, "I don't want it. I want to be left in peace."[43] Eve remembers this as her mother's last coherent words.

Eve records of her mother, "All in white, her white hair laying bare the immense forehead, the face at peace, as grave and valiant as a knight in armor, she was, at this moment, the noblest and most beautiful thing on earth. Her rough hands, calloused, hardened, deeply burned by radium, had lost their familiar nervous movement. They were stretched out on the sheet, stiff and fearfully motionless-those hands which had worked so much."[44]

July 4th, 1934, Marie's journey on earth ends and she joins Pierre.

Marie Curie 1930, *Musée Curie (coll. ACJC)*

EPILOGUE

"We have lost everything."
Georges Fournier, one of Marie's favorite students[1]

M arie was only sixty-six when she died. She didn't want a priest or prayers and certainly not a state funeral. Family, friends and her co workers gathered at the cemetery in Sceaux. Wreaths of flowers arrived from dignitaries around the world. The most notable wreath for Marie would have been the one sent from the president of Poland. A rose was given to each of the mourners to place on top of Marie's casket as they passed by.

Jacques, Marie's supportive brother-in-law for forty years, was too weak to attend the funeral. Bronya and Joseph arrived from Poland. They each brought, unbeknownst to the other, a handful of soil from their homeland. As the casket was lowered, Bronya and Joseph threw the soil on top of it. Marie's casket rested above Pierre's, together again.

The gates of the cemetery were closed to keep the crowds out. The press, uninvited, at least stayed at a distance.

One French paper, *Le Journal*, still found a way to be critical of Marie. Taking a swipe at Marie's funeral they wrote, "... the supreme pride which takes the form of voluntary efface-ment, of refusal of honors, of excessive simplicity."[2] Eve ex-plained, "My sister and I believed that we were respecting the intimate wishes of our mother, in burying her in the cemetery in Sceaux, in the tomb where Pierre Curie rests, and also in giving the ceremony a simple character."[3]

Fellow scientists wrote:

Ernest Rutherford: *"brilliance, her scholarship, and lifelong devotion to her work, [which] played a most important part in the origination of an entirely new science. Her work will go on."*[4]

Nikola Tesla: *"She leaves among her contemporaries an impression akin to that of a rare, ethereal phenomenon. By sheer force of mind she managed to sustain her frail body through years of concentrated effort."*[5]

Jean Perrin: *"Mme Curie is not only a famous physicist: she is the greatest laboratory director I have ever known."*[6]

In 1935, Marie's book RADIOACTIVITY (the book she was worried about finishing) becomes part of the library collection at the Radium Institute. Marie never referred to the Radium Institute as "My Laboratory" it was always "The Laboratory." As the director, she developed and maintained the laboratory, secured radioactive substances for research, kept the laboratory financially sound, and ensured scholarships for the students. From 1919 through 1934, four hundred and eighty-three scientific communications were published. Marie was the author of thirty-one of these publications.

André Debierne, a pillar to Marie's life, was the successor to the Laboratory that was renamed the Curie Institute. Debierne died in 1949. Irene was named the head of the Curie Institute.

December 1935–Irene and Frederic received the Nobel Prize for Chemistry. Irene gave the acceptance speech first. Frederic acknowledged Marie in his speech, "It was certainly a satisfaction for our late lamented teacher, Marie Curie, to have seen the list of radioactive elements that she had the honor to inaugurate with Pierre Curie so extended."[7] Irene, who doesn't mention Marie in her speech, wrote to Missy and explained, "I do not understand how I could speak of her to journalists."[8]

Until the late 1930s, Irene and Frederic followed the protocol of Marie and Pierre, publishing everything they discovered. Not wanting to have their research in the hands of Nazis, Irene and Frederic put all their documents on nuclear fission in a sealed envelope in a safe at the Academy of Sciences. The documents remained sealed until 1949.[9]

Irene Curie died in 1956, and Frederic was devastated. She was fifty-nine, and her death was from Leukemia, caused by exposure to radioactive substances. This exposure was mainly from the X-ray work she performed during WWI. Irene and Frederic had worked together for thirty years. He was offered Irene's chair at the Sorbonne. He accepted, and he became the head of the Curie Institute. This wasn't for long. Frederic died two years later from exposure to radium and polonium.

Helene, daughter to Irene and Frederic, lived in the Curie home in Sceaux. Helene said of her mother, Irene, "My mother told me she had the most interesting life one could imagine. It was my grandmother (Marie) who made her feel that way."[10] Helene confirmed the family tradition, "My brother and I are both physicists, but our parents never pushed that on us. Their point was that we have to choose something interesting to do. It didn't matter if it was related to science."[11]

Paul Langevin became president of the Human Rights League, 1944-1946. He was under house arrest during much of WWII and escaped to Switzerland. Langevin died in December 1946 and France gave him a state funeral. He was buried at the Pantheon. Frederic said of Langevin, he "determined my destiny when he said he had a job for me with Madame Curie."

Jean Perrin who could explain why stars shine or envision using rockets for space travel could just as easily burst into song for their gatherings of the 'Sorbonne at the Sea.' As a social activist Jean had signed the petition on behalf of Capt. Dreyfus, as did Langevin. In the close friendship with the Curies of backyard neighbors, Jean's wife Henriette was the only one to call Marie by her first name. The Perrins escaped France during WWII and went to live in the United States. Jean Perrin died the following year.

Eve Curie agreed to write a biography of her mother. She explained, "I'd never written a book before. I wasn't sure I could do it, but I needed to write this book because it was inevitable that people would write about her, so few knew her at all.".…"I called the book *Madame Curie* by Eve Curie. I didn't think it right to call it *Marie Curie* by Eve Curie; that would have been too intimate."[12]

Eve's biography of Marie, published in 1937, was a best seller. Eve married Henry Labouisse Jr. in 1954. He was an American attorney and diplomat, dedicated to helping the poor. His work as executive director of the United Nations Children's Fund (UNICEF) garnered him the Nobel Peace Prize in 1965. Eve, journalist, author, and dedicated to the work of UNICEF became a US citizen in 1958 and died October 22, 2007.

On April 20, 1995, the remains of both Pierre and Marie were transferred to France's national mausoleum, the Pantheon in Paris. Marie was the first woman to be buried here for her own accomplishments.

Readers can make their own conclusion as to whether Marie and Pierre would have preferred to remain at rest in the cemetery at Sceaux.

Marie, born into a world lit only by fire, brings change to society and science. Her sheer will rose higher than the thousand year old dam of resistance that was determined to hold her back.

For the generations to come, Marie reminds us:

"We must have perseverance...We must believe that we are gifted for something, and that this thing, at whatever cost, must be attained." Marie Curie

BIBLIOGRAPHY

Abir-Am, P. and Outram, D. (1987). *Uneasy Careers and Intimate Lives, Women in Science, 1789-1979*, Rutgers University Press.

Atkins, A. (2011). *Eleanor Roosevelt ~ Unleashed.* Flash History Press.

Atkins, A. (2014). Golda Meir ~ True Grit. Flash History Press.

Birch, B. and Birmingham, C. (1996). *Marie Curie's Search for Radium*, Barron's Educational Series, Inc.

Brian, D. (2005). *The Curies, A Biography of the Most Controversial Family in Science*, John Wiley & Sons, Inc.

Bynum, W. (2012). *A Little History of Science*, Yale University Press.

Chesler, E. (1992). *Margaret Sanger and the Birth Control Movement in America*, Simon & Schuster.

Cobb, V. (2008). Marie Curie, A Photographic Story of a Life, DK Publishing.

Curie, E. (1937). *Madame Curie, A Biography,* Doubleday, Doran & Company, Inc.

Curie, M. (1923). *Pierre Curie*, The Macmillian Company.

Emling, S. (2012). *Marie Curie and Her Daughters*, Palgrave & Macmillan.

Enss, C. (2006). *The Doctor Wore Petticoats, Women Physicians of the Old West*, A Twodot Book.

Giroud, F. (1986). *Marie Curie, A Life*, Holmes & Meier Publishers, Inc.

Goldsmith, B. (2005). *Obsessive Genius, The Inner World of Marie Curie*, W.W. Norton & Company, Inc.

Gribbin, J. (2004). *The Scientists*, Random House.

Hall, L. (2007). *Who's Afraid of Marie Curie?*, Seal Press.

Hoff, J. (1991). *Law Gender & Injustice, A Legal History of U.S. Women*, New York University Press.

Isaacson, W. (2009). *American Sketches, Great Leaders, Creative Thinkers, and Heroes of a Hurricane*. Simon & Schuster.

Koblitz, A. H. (1983). *A Convergence of Lives, Sofia Kovalevskaia: Scientist, Writer, Revolutionary*, Rutgers University Press.

Lerner, G. (1993). *The Creation of Feminist Consciousness, From the Middle Ages to Eighteen-seventy*, Oxford University Press.

Lerner, G. (1986). *The Creation of Patriarchy*, Oxford University Press.

Lerner, G. (1997). *Why History Matters*, Oxford University Press.

Macmillan, M. (2001). *Paris 1919*. Random House.

McAuliffe, M. (2011). *Dawn of the Belle Epoque*, Rowman & Littlefield.

McAuliffe, M. (2014). *Twilight of the Belle Epoque*, Rowman & Littlefield.

Mikolajcqyk, S. (1948). *The Rape of Poland, Pattern of Soviet Aggression*, McGraw-Hill Book Company, Inc.

Morgan, E. (1972). *The Descent of Woman, The Classic Study of Evolution*, Souvenir Press.

Ogilvie, M.B. (2011). *Marie Curie, A Biography*, Prometheus Books.

Quinn, S. (1995). *Marie Curie, A Life*, Perseus Books.

Redniss, L. (2011). *Radioactive, Marie & Pierre Curie, A Tale of Love & Fallout*, Harper Collins.

Sheffield, S.L. (2004). *Women and Science, Social Impact and Interaction*, ABC-CLIO, Inc.

Steele, P. (2008). *Marie Curie, The Woman Who Changed The Course of Science*, National Geographic Society.

Trager, J. (1994). The Women's Chronology, Henry Holt and Company.

Winter, A. (1998). Mesmerized, Powers of Mind in Victorian Britain, The University of Chicago Press.

ENDNOTES

Part One

[1] (Quinn, 1995), pg 137

Chapter 1

[1] (Goldsmith, 2005), pg 23/24

[2] (Giroud, 1986), pg 9

[3] (Goldsmith, 2005), pg 20

[4] (Curie E. , 1936), pg 9

[5] (Brian, 2005), pg 20

[6] (Quinn, 1995), pg 44

[7] (Giroud, 1986), pg 10

[8] (Brian, 2005), pg 20

[9] (Curie E. , 1936), pg 13

[10] (Quinn, 1995), pg 38

[11] (Brian, 2005), pg 18

[12] (Quinn, 1995), pg 39

[13] (Quinn, 1995), pg 41

[14] (Quinn, 1995), pg 41

[15] (Quinn, 1995), pg 33

[16] (Quinn, 1995), pg 33

[17] (Giroud, 1986), pg 13

[18] (Quinn, 1995), pg 47

[19] (Quinn, 1995), pg 27

[20] (Quinn, 1995), pg 50

[21] (Brian, 2005), pg 21

[22] (Curie E. , 1936), pg 38

[23] (Curie E. , 1936), pg 34

[24] (Brian, 2005), pg 22

[25] (Curie E. , 1936), pg 34

[26] (Quinn, 1995), pg 50

Chapter 2

[1] (Goldsmith, 2005), pg 31

[2] (Curie E. , 1936), pg 39

[3] (Giroud, 1986), pg 15

[4] (Quinn, 1995), pg 56

[5] (Quinn, 1995), pg 61

[6] (Curie M. , 1923), pg 83

[7] (Giroud, 1986), pg 15

[8] (Brian, 2005), pg 25

[9] (Goldsmith, 2005), pg 37

[10] (Quinn, 1995), pg 67

[11] (Giroud, 1986), pg 22

[12] (Brian, 2005), pg 27

[13] (Goldsmith, 2005), pg 38

[14] (Quinn, 1995), pg 70

[15] (Giroud, 1986), pg 23

[16] (Goldsmith, 2005), pg 37

[17] (Giroud, 1986), pg 23

[18] (Giroud, 1986), pg 23

[19] (Curie E. , 1936), pg 68

[20] (Giroud, 1986), pg 19

[21] (Curie E. , 1936), pg 68

[22] (Curie E. , 1936), pg 67

[23] (Goldsmith, 2005), pg 39

[24] (Quinn, 1995), pg 74

[25] (Quinn, 1995), pg 75

[26] (Goldsmith, 2005), pg 40

[27] (Brian, 2005), pg 33

[28] (Giroud, 1986), pg 25

[29] (Goldsmith, 2005), pg 39

[30] (Goldsmith, 2005), pg 39

[31] (Quinn, 1995), pg 71

[32] (Goldsmith, 2005), pg 39

[33] (Brian, 2005), pg 29

[34] (Curie E. , 1936), pg 78

[35] (Brian, 2005), pg 30

[36] (Quinn, 1995), pg 78

[37] (Quinn, 1995), pg 66

[38] (Quinn, 1995), pg 81

[39] (Curie E. , 1936), pg 83

[40] (Quinn, 1995), pg 79

[41] (Brian, 2005), pg 31

[42] (Brian, 2005), pg 32

[43] (Brian, 2005), pg 32

[44] (Brian, 2005), pg 32

[45] (Curie E. , 1936), pg 88

[46] (Brian, 2005), pg 33

[47] (Curie E. , 1936), pg 88

[48] (Curie E. , 1936), pg 90

Chapter 3

[1] (Curie E. , 1936), pg 94

[2] (Curie E. , 1936), pg 100

[3] (Brian, 2005), pg 34

[4] (Quinn, 1995), pg 88

[5] (Quinn, 1995), pg 102

[6] (Quinn, 1995), pg 91

[7] (Quinn, 1995), pg 90

[8] (Quinn, 1995), pg 92

[9] (Quinn, 1995), pg 96

[10] (Quinn, 1995), pg 93

[11] (Quinn, 1995), pg 92

[12] (Quinn, 1995), pg 95

[13] (Quinn, 1995), pg 97

[14] (Giroud, 1986), pg 41

[15] (Giroud, 1986), pg 49

[16] (Curie E. , 1936), pg 96

[17] (Curie E. , 1936), pg 111

[18] (Goldsmith, 2005), pg 51

Part Two

[1] (Ogilvie, 2011), pg 57

[2] (McAuliffe, Dawn of the Belle Epoque, 2011), pg 2011

[3] (Trager, 1994), pg 354-355

[4] (McAuliffe, Twilight of the Belle Epoque, 2014), pg 86

[5] (Giroud, 1986), pg 104

[6] (McAuliffe, Twilight of the Belle Epoque, 2014), pg 80

[7] (McAuliffe, Twilight of the Belle Epoque, 2014), 85,86

[8] (McAuliffe, Twilight of the Belle Epoque, 2014), pg 259

Chapter 4

[1] (Quinn, 1995), pg 109

[2] (Brian, 2005), pg 6

[3] (Curie M. , 1923), pg 18

[4] Brian, 2005), pg 1-2

[5] (Quinn, 1995), pg 113

[6] (Brian, 2005), pg 9-10

[7] (Brian, 2005), pg 11

[8] (Goldsmith, 2005), pg 54

[9] (Brian, 2005), pg 14

[10] (Curie E. , 1936), pg 120

[11] (Giroud, 1986), pg 49

[12] (Goldsmith, 2005), pg 54

[13] (Goldsmith, 2005),pg 56

[14] (Curie M. , 1923), pg 41

[15] (Curie E. , 1936), pg 127

[16] (Quinn, 1995), pg 116

[17] (Curie E. , 1936), pg 129

[18] (Curie E. , 1936), pg 130

[19] (Brian, 2005), pg 42

[20] (Brian, 2005), pg 43

[21] (Curie E. , 1936), pg 132

[22] (Curie E. , 1936), pg 133

[23] (Curie E. , 1936), pg 122

[24] (Quinn, 1995), pg 121

[25] (Brian, 2005), pg 44

[26] (Curie E. , 1936), 134

[27] (Curie E. , 1936), 129

[28] (Brian, 2005), pg 44

[29] (Quinn, 1995), pg 123

[30] (Giroud, 1986), pg 65

[31] (Curie E. , 1936), pg 135-136

[32] (Brian, 2005), pg 45

[33] (Curie E. , 1936), pg 136

[34] (Brian, 2005), pg 46

[35] (Goldsmith, 2005), pg 59

[36] (Quinn, 1995), pg 127

Chapter 5

[1] (Curie M. , 1923), pg 50

[2] (Giroud, 1986), pg 94

[3] (Brian, 2005), pg 49

[4] (Brian, 2005), pg 49

[5] (Giroud, 1986), pg 73

[6] (Giroud, 1986), pg 74

[7] (Giroud, 1986), pg 74

[8] (Giroud, 1986), pg 74

[9] (Giroud, 1986), pg 75

[10] (Giroud, 1986), pg 75

[11] (Brian, 2005), pg 54

[12] (Brian, 2005), pg 53

[13] (Brian, 2005), pg 56

[14] (Goldsmith, 2005), pg 71

[15] (Goldsmith, 2005), pg 73

[16] (Brian, 2005), pg 57

[17] (Goldsmith, 2005), pg 78

[18] (Goldsmith, 2005), pg 78

[19] (Goldsmith, 2005), pg 79

[20] (Goldsmith, 2005), pg 88

[21] (Curie M. , 1923), pg 89

[22] (Brian, 2005), pg 58

[23] (Goldsmith, 2005), pg 83,84

[24] (Curie E. , 1936), pg 159

[25] (Curie M. , 1923), pg 90

[26] (Goldsmith, 2005), pg 77

[27] (Brian, 2005), pg 76

[28] (Brian, 2005), pg 59

[29] (Goldsmith, 2005), pg 155

[30] (Cobb, 2008), pg 72

[31] (Goldsmith, 2005), pg 69

[32] (Quinn, 1995), pg 153

[33] (Giroud, 1986), pg 85

[34] (Giroud, 1986)pg 85,86

[35] (Curie E. , 1936), pg 188

[36] (Goldsmith, 2005), pg 103

[37] (Brian, 2005), pg 64

Chapter 6

[1] (Goldsmith, 2005), pg 89

[2] (Quinn, 1995), pg 154

[3] (Quinn, 1995), pg 172

[4] (Curie M. , 1923), pg 46

[5] (Curie M. , 1923), pg 91

[6] (Giroud, 1986), pg 90

[7] (Curie E. , 1936), pg 169

[8] (Curie E. , 1936), pg 238

[9] (Brian, 2005), pg 75

[10] (Curie M. , 1923), pg 69

[11] (Giroud, 1986), pg 97

[12] (Goldsmith, 2005), pg 91

[13] (Emling, 2012), pg 64

[14] (Curie M. , 1923), pg 49

[15] (Brian, 2005), pg 64

[16] (Giroud, 1986), pg 94

[17] (Goldsmith, 2005), pg 94

[18] (Goldsmith, 2005), pg 94

[19] (Cobb, 2008), pg 77

[20] (Brian, 2005), pg 68

[21] (Brian, 2005), pg 68

[22] (Quinn, 1995), pg 214

[23] (Giroud, 1986), pg 93,94

[24] (Giroud, 1986), pg 94

[25] (Goldsmith, 2005), pg 102,103

[26] (Cobb, 2008), pg 79

[27] (Giroud, 1986), pg 95

[28] (Giroud, 1986), pg 95

[29] (Brian, 2005), pg 68

[30] (Curie E. , 1936), pg 276

[31] (Sheffield, 2004), pg xix

[32] (Giroud, 1986), pg 101

[33] (Curie E. , 1936), pg 183-184

[34] (Brian, 2005), pg 71

[35] (Curie M. , 1923), pg 70

[36] (Brian, 2005), pg 71

[37] (Goldsmith, 2005), pg 100

[38] (Goldsmith, 2005), pg 100

[39] (Brian, 2005), pg 74

[40] (Giroud, 1986), pg 117

[41] (Ogilvie, 2011), pg 81

[42] (Curie E. , 1936), pg 206

[43] (Quinn, 1995), pg 183

[44] (Curie E. , 1936), pg 202

[45] (Brian, 2005), pg 75

[46] (Goldsmith, 2005), pg 122

[47] (Emling, 2012), pg 76

[48] (Goldsmith, 2005), pg 93

[49] (Brian, 2005), pg 77

[50] (Curie E. , 1936), pg 190-191

[51] (Brian, 2005), pg 75

[52] (Goldsmith, 2005), pg 108

[53] (Brian, 2005), pg 79

[54] (Ogilvie, 2011), pg 184

[55] (Curie E. , 1936), pg 210

[56] (McAuliffe, Twilight of the Belle Epoque, 2014), pg 83

[57] (Quinn, 1995), pg 193

[58] (Steele, 2008), pg xxv

[59] (Brian, 2005), pg 81

[60] (Brian, 2005), pg 81

[61] (Curie E. , 1936), pg 216

[62] (Goldsmith, 2005), pg 114

[63] (Curie E. , 1936), pg 214

[64] (Brian, 2005), pg 84

[65] (Brian, 2005), pg 84

[66] (Giroud, 1986), pg 124

[67] (Curie M. , 1923), pg 63

[68] (Brian, 2005), pg 13

[69] (Curie E. , 1936), pg 235

[70] (Giroud, 1986), pg 132

[71] (Curie E. , 1936), pg 218

[72] (Goldsmith, 2005), pg 131

[73] (Goldsmith, 2005), pg 129

[74] (Brian, 2005), pg 89

[75] (Curie E. , 1936), pg 218-219

[76] (Brian, 2005), pg 14

[77] (Brian, 2005), pg 95

[78] (Goldsmith, 2005), pg 124

[79] (Goldsmith, 2005), pg 117

Chapter 7

[1] (Goldsmith, 2005), pg 59

[2] (Giroud, 1986), pg 123

[3] (Curie E. , 1936), pg 230

[4] (Giroud, 1986), pg 123

[5] (Curie E. , 1936), pg 85232

[6] (Brian, 2005), pg 204

[7] (Emling, 2012), pg 75

[8] (Goldsmith, 2005), pg 112

[9] (Goldsmith, 2005), pg 130

[10] (Goldsmith, 2005), pg 131

[11] (Goldsmith, 2005), pg 137

[12] (Brian, 2005), pg 66

[13] (Goldsmith, 2005), pg 138

[14] (Brian, 2005), pg 95

[15] (Brian, 2005), pg 92

[16] (Goldsmith, 2005), pg 138

[17] (Brian, 2005), pg 93

[18] (Curie E. , 1936), pg191-192

[19] (Goldsmith, 2005), pg 132

[20] (Curie E. , 1936), pg 242

[21] (Brian, 2005), pg 98

[22] (Brian, 2005), pg 100

[23] (Brian, 2005), pg 100

[24] (Curie M. , 1923), pg 67

[25] (Curie M. , 1923), pg 66

[26] (Curie E. , 1936), pg 247

[27] (Curie E. , 1936), pg 250

[28] (Curie E. , 1936), pg 249

[29] (Giroud, 1986), pg 141

[30] (Giroud, 1986), pg 141

[31] (Giroud, 1986), pg 141

[32] (Ogilvie, 2011), pg 100

[33] (Giroud, 1986), pg 140

[34] (Curie E. , 1936), pg 247

[35] (Giroud, 1986), pg 140

[36] (Ogilvie, 2011), pg 97

[37] (Curie E. , 1936), pg 248

[38] (Brian, 2005), pg 104

[39] (Brian, 2005), pg 103

[40] (Brian, 2005), pg 103

[41] (Giroud, 1986), pg 142

[42] (Giroud, 1986), pg 142

[43] (Giroud, 1986), pg 142

[44] (Giroud, 1986), pg 141

[45] (Giroud, 1986), pg 142

[46] (Brian, 2005), pg 103

[47] (Curie E. , 1936), pg 254

[48] (Goldsmith, 2005), pg 140

[49] (Goldsmith, 2005), pg 139

[50] (Brian, 2005), pg 94

[51] (Goldsmith, 2005), pg 52146

[52] (Brian, 2005), pg 113

[53] (Goldsmith, 2005), pg 140

[54] (Goldsmith, 2005), pg 142

[55] (Curie E. , 1936), pg 257

[56] (Brian, 2005), pg 105

[57] (Brian, 2005), pg 115

[58] (Brian, 2005), pg 107

[59] (Giroud, 1986), pg 146

[60] (Brian, 2005), pg 106

[61] (Curie E. , 1936), pg 192

Part Three

[1] (Quinn, 1995), pg 277

[2] (Quinn, 1995), pg 277

Chapter 8

[1] (Curie E. , 1936), pg 256

[2] (Brian, 2005), pg 106

[3] (Brian, 2005), pg 106

[4] (Brian, 2005), pg 108

[5] (Giroud, 1986), pg 147

[6] (Goldsmith, 2005), pg 163

[7] (Sheffield, 2004), pg xiv

[8] (Curie E. , 1936), pg 259

[9] (Brian, 2005), pg 108

[10] (Goldsmith, 2005), pg 144

[11] (Goldsmith, 2005), pg 148

[12] (Brian, 2005), pg 110

[13] (Curie E. , 1936), pg 265

[14] (Brian, 2005), pg 110

[15] (Quinn, 1995), pg 251

[16] (Quinn, 1995), pg 255

[17] (Emling, 2012), pg 206

[18] (Brian, 2005), pg 111

[19] (Brian, 2005), pg 112

[20] (Curie E. , 1936), pg 270

[21] (Curie E. , 1936), pg 271

[22] (Brian, 2005), pg 113

[23] (Goldsmith, 2005), pg 148

[24] (Sheffield, 2004), pg xxvi

[25] (Sheffield, 2004), pg xxvi

[26] (Goldsmith, 2005), pg 151

Chapter 9

[1] (Giroud, 1986), pg 155

[2] (Goldsmith, 2005), pg 160

[3] (Sheffield, 2004), pg xxvi

[4] (Goldsmith, 2005), pg 156

[5] (Brian, 2005), pg 116

[6] (Brian, 2005), pg 116

[7] (Brian, 2005), pg 122

[8] (Goldsmith, 2005), pg 166

[9] (Brian, 2005), pg 122

[10] (Giroud, 1986), pg 180

[11] (Brian, 2005), pg 121

[12] (Brian, 2005), pg 121

[13] (McAuliffe, Twilight of the Belle Epoque, 2014), pg 209

[14] (McAuliffe, Twilight of the Belle Epoque, 2014), pg 210

[15] (Goldsmith, 2005), pg 170

[16] (Giroud, 1986), pg 157

[17] (Curie E. , 1936), pg 278

[18] (Brian, 2005), pg 125

[19] (Quinn, 1995), pg 292

[20] (Quinn, 1995), pg 267

[21] (Brian, 2005), pg 126-127

[22] (Brian, 2005), pg 127

[23] (Brian, 2005), pg 127

[24] (Giroud, 1986), pg 169

[25] (Quinn, 1995), pg 301

[26] (Quinn, 1995), pg 299

[27] (Brian, 2005), pg 129

[28] (Goldsmith, 2005), pg 154

[29] (Goldsmith, 2005), pg 154

[30] (Quinn, 1995), pg 302

[31] (Giroud, 1986), pg 170

[32] (Goldsmith, 2005), pg 172

[33] (McAuliffe, Twilight of the Belle Epoque, 2014), pg 211

[34] (Giroud, 1986), pg 177

[35] (Brian, 2005), pg 134

[36] (Giroud, 1986), pg 177

[37] (Emling, 2012), pg 78

[38] (Giroud, 1986), pg 174

[39] (Giroud, 1986), pg 180

[40] (Goldsmith, 2005), pg 170

[41] (Goldsmith, 2005), pg 167

[42] (Goldsmith, 2005), pg 168

[43] (Giroud, 1986), pg 174

[44] (Giroud, 1986), pg 175

[45] (Giroud, 1986), pg 176

[46] (Giroud, 1986), pg 182

[47] (Goldsmith, 2005), pg 174

[48] (Goldsmith, 2005), pg 174

[49] (Brian, 2005), pg 136

[50] (Emling, 2012), pg 9

[51] (Giroud, 1986), pg 182

[52] (Goldsmith, 2005), pg 175

[53] (Giroud, 1986), pg 182

[54] (Giroud, 1986), pg 182

[55] (Ogilvie, 2011), pg 117

[56] (Ogilvie, 2011), pg 113-114

[57] (Brian, 2005), pg 132

[58] (Quinn, 1995), pg 310

[59] (Emling, 2012), pg 8

[60] (Brian, 2005), pg 139

[61] (Brian, 2005), pg 139

[62] (Quinn, 1995), pg 313

[63] (Brian, 2005), pg 139

[64] (Brian, 2005), pg 140

[65] (Brian, 2005), pg 140

[66] (Goldsmith, 2005), pg 177

[67] (Giroud, 1986), pg 185

[68] (Giroud, 1986), pg 186

Chapter 10

[1] (Emling, 2012), pg 12

[2] (Giroud, 1986), pg 192

[3] (Goldsmith, 2005), pg 158

[4] (Goldsmith, 2005), pg 159

[5] (Brian, 2005), pg 149

[6] (Emling, 2012), pg 18

[7] (Brian, 2005), pg 114

[8] (Brian, 2005), pg 151

[9] (Brian, 2005), pg 151

[10] (Curie M. , 1923), pg 63

[11] (Giroud, 1986), pg 195

[12] (Brian, 2005), pg 151

[13] (Curie E. , 1936), pg 287

[14] (Curie M. , 1923), pg 101

[15] (Brian, 2005), pg 159

[16] (Giroud, 1986), pg 207

[17] (Emling, 2012), pg 23

[18] (Brian, 2005), pg 157

[19] (Brian, 2005), pg 157

[20] (Giroud, 1986), pg 195

[21] (Curie E. , 1936), pg 289

[22] (Curie E. , 1936), pg 292

[23] (Emling, 2012), pg 25

[24] (Emling, 2012), pg 25

[25] (Giroud, 1986), pg 203

[26] (Quinn, 1995), pg 363

[27] (Giroud, 1986), pg 205

[28] (Giroud, 1986), pg 205

[29] (Quinn, 1995), pg 359

[30] (Giroud, 1986), pg 210

[31] (Curie E. , 1936), pg 301

[32] (Curie E. , 1936), pg 295

[33] (Ogilvie, 2011), pg 130

[34] (Goldsmith, 2005), pg 184

[35] (Giroud, 1986), pg 204

[36] (Giroud, 1986), pg 205

[37] (Giroud, 1986), pg 206

[38] (Giroud, 1986), pg 206

[39] (Curie M. , 1923), pg 106

[40] (Curie E. , 1936), pg 304

[41] (Emling, 2012), pg 28

[42] (Curie E. , 1936), pg 296

[43] (Giroud, 1986), pg 209

[44] (Giroud, 1986), pg 207

[45] (Giroud, 1986), pg 207

[46] (Giroud, 1986), pg 207

[47] (Goldsmith, 2005), pg 188

[48] (Goldsmith, 2005), pg 188

[49] (McAuliffe, Twilight of the Belle Epoque, 2014), pg 327

[50] (Brian, 2005), pg 160

[51] (Curie E. , 1936), pg 290

[52] (McAuliffe, Twilight of the Belle Epoque, 2014), pg 303

[53] (McAuliffe, Twilight of the Belle Epoque, 2014), pg 301

[54] (McAuliffe, Twilight of the Belle Epoque, 2014), pg 304

[55] (McAuliffe, Twilight of the Belle Epoque, 2014), pg 304

[56] (Giroud, 1986), pg 213

[57] (Curie E. , 1936), pg 299

[58] (McAuliffe, Twilight of the Belle Epoque, 2014), pg 309

[59] (Giroud, 1986), pg 214

[60] (Curie M. , 1923), pg 107

[61] (McAuliffe, Twilight of the Belle Epoque, 2014), pg 336

[62] (McAuliffe, Twilight of the Belle Epoque, 2014), pg 337

[63] (McAuliffe, Twilight of the Belle Epoque, 64632014), pg 337

[64] (Giroud, 1986), pg 208

[65] (McAuliffe, Twilight of the Belle Epoque, 2014), pg 347

[66] (Curie E. , 1936), pg 304

[67] (Giroud, 1986), pg 204

[68] (Brian, 2005), pg 164

Chapter 11

[1] (Brian, 2005), pg 171

[2] (Curie E. , 1936), pg 373

[3] (Emling, 2012), pg 184

[4] (Emling, 2012), pg 32

[5] (Brian, 2005), pg 174

[6] (Curie M. , 1923), pg 4

[7] (Brian, 2005), pg 174

[8] (Curie M. , 1923), pg 4

[9] (Curie E. , 1936), pg 322

[10] (Curie E. , 1936), pg 323

[11] (Curie M. , 1923), pg 4

[12] (Curie M. , 1923), pg 9

[13] (Goldsmith, 2005), pg 192

[14] (Giroud, 1986), pg 230

[15] (Goldsmith, 2005), pg 192

[16] (Brian, 2005), pg 175

[17] (Curie M. , 1923), pg 9

[18] (Giroud, 1986), pg 231

[19] (Giroud, 1986), pg 233

[20] (Giroud, 1986), pg 234

[21] (Giroud, 1986), pg 234

[22] (Brian, 2005), pg 176

[23] (Brian, 2005), pg 178

[24] (Curie M. , 1923), pg 7

[25] (Brian, 2005), pg 179

[26] (Emling, 2012), pg xiii

[27] (Brian, 2005), pg 180

[28] (Emling, 2012), pg 107

[29] (Emling, 2012), pg 107

[30] (Brian, 2005), pg 183

[31] (Emling, 2012), pg xiv

[32] (Ogilvie, 2011), pg 139

[33] (Brian, 2005), pg 183

[34] (Giroud, 1986), pg 239

[35] (Brian, 2005), pg 185

[36] (Giroud, 1986), pg 241

[37] (Emling, 2012), pg xix

[38] (Emling, 2012), pg 62

[39] (Curie M. , 1923), pg 7-8

[40] (Curie M. , 1923), pg 9

[41] (Giroud, 1986), pg 243

[42] (Sheffield, 2004), pg xxvii

[43] (Giroud, 1986), pg 243

[44] (Giroud, 1986), pg 231

[45] (Goldsmith, 2005), pg 195-196

[46] (Goldsmith, 2005), pg 198

[47] (Emling, 2012), pg 184

[48] (Curie E. , 1936), pg xviii

[49] (Goldsmith, 2005), pg 151

[50] (Giroud, 1986), pg 279

[51] (Giroud, 1986), pg 280

[52] (Emling, 2012), pg 98

[53] (Emling, 2012), pg 207

[54] (Emling, 2012), pg 162

[55] (Emling, 2012), pg 168

[56] (Emling, 2012), pg 174

[57] (Emling, 2012), pg 184

[58] (Brian, 2005), pg 205

[59] (Emling, 2012), pg 85

[60] (Quinn, 1995), pg 417

[61] (Giroud, 1986), pg 255

Chapter 12

[1] (Giroud, 1986), pg 273

[2] (Ogilvie, 2011), pg 153

[3] (Giroud, 1986), pg 151

[4] (Quinn, 1995), pg 405

[5] (Giroud, 1986), pg 120

[6] (Brian, 2005), pg 192

[7] (Giroud, 1986), pg 260-261

[8] (Curie E. , 1936), pg 345

[9] (Brian, 2005), pg 192

[10] (Emling, 2012), pg 91

[11] (Emling, 2012), pg 92

[12] (Giroud, 1986), pg 280

[13] (Brian, 2005), pg 209

[14] (Giroud, 1986), pg 281

[15] (Goldsmith, 2005), pg 207

[16] (Emling, 2012), pg 98

[17] (Brian, 2005), pg 207

[18] (Brian, 2005), pg 207

[19] (Curie E. , 1936), pg 373

[20] (Giroud, 1986), pg 265

[21] (Emling, 2012), pg 107

[22] (Sheffield, 2004), pg xxix

[23] (Giroud, 1986), pg 268

[24] (Giroud, 1986), pg 268

[25] (Brian, 2005), pg 194

[26] (Emling, 2012), pg 120

[27] (Giroud, 1986), pg 268

[28] (Brian, 2005), pg 230

[29] (Quinn, 1995), pg 403

[30] (Brian, 2005), pg 197

[31] (Quinn, 1995), pg 422

[32] (Giroud, 1986), pg 273

[33] (Goldsmith, 2005), pg 212

[34] (Emling, 2012), pg 136

[35] (Emling, 2012), pg 188

[36] (Giroud, 1986), pg 284

[37] (Brian, 2005), pg 248

[38] (Brian, 2005), pg 249

[39] (Giroud, 1986), pg 285

[40] (Goldsmith, 2005), pg 214

[41] (Curie E. , 1936), pg 46

[42] (Curie E. , 1936), pg 383

[43] (Giroud, 1986), pg 286

[44] (Curie E. , 1936), pg 384

Epilogue

[1] (Curie E. , 1936), pg 384

[2] (Quinn, 1995), pg 433

[3] (Quinn, 1995), pg 433

[4] (Brian, 2005), pg 252

[5] (Brian, 2005), pg 252

[6] (Curie E. , 1936), pg 364

[7] (Emling, 2012), pg 145

[8] (Emling, 2012), pg 145

[9] (Emling, 2012), pg 152

[10] (Goldsmith, 2005), pg 231

[11] (Emling, 2012), pg 99

[12] (Goldsmith, 2005), pg 145-146

INDEX

Golda Meir ~ True Grit

Eleanor Roosevelt ~ Unleashed

Marie Curie ~ A Nobel Life

Paperback and ebook—available through
your favorite book dealer,
Amazon
or from the author at her website:
www.AnnAtkins.com

Contact Information:

Email: Ann@AnnAtkins.com
Facebook: Ann.Atkins.Author